PRACTICAL LAW FOR CORRECTIONAL PERSONNEL

a Resource Manual and
a Training Curriculum
by the National Street Law Institute

From The National Street Law Institute
and West Publishing Company

PRACTICAL LAW FOR CORRECTIONAL PERSONNEL

a Resource Manual and
a Training Curriculum
by the National Street Law Institute

Edward O'Brien, J.D.
Adjunct Professor of Law
Georgetown University Law Center

Margaret Fisher, J.D.
Adjunct Professor of Law
Georgetown University Law Center

David T. Austern, J.D.
Adjunct Professor of Law
Georgetown University Law Center

West Publishing Company
St. Paul   New York   Los Angeles   San Francisco

PHOTO CREDITS

Cover Photo — Bill Powers, Corrections Magazine

American Correctional Association Library, pp. 28, 90, 94; Bill Auth, pp. 3, 106; Corrections Magazine, pp. 46, 83, 88; Corrections Magazine, Tony O'Brien, pp. 26, 89; Corrections Magazine, Bill Powers, pp. 2, 34, 39, 41, 54, 74, 75, 85, 144; District of Columbia Police Department, p. 164; EKM Nepenthe, Bob Eckert, pp. 20, 121, 173; Magnum Photos, Marvin Dain, p. 158; National Conference of State Legislatures, p. 7; Bill Phillips, Orlando Sentinel Star, p. 163; Police Magazine, Tony O'Brien, pp. 32, 145; H. Armstrong Roberts, p. 169, Supreme Court Historical Society, p. 14; Bob Sullivan, pp. 122, 129, 147; U.S. Civil Rights Commission, p. 77, UPI, p. 177; Wide World Photos, pp. 57, 71.

Library of Congress Cataloging in Publication Data
National Street Law Institute.
  Practical law for correctional personnel.

  Bibliography: p.
  Includes index.
  1. Correctional law—United States. 2. Correctional personnel—Legal status, laws, etc.—United States.
I. O'Brien, Edward L. II. Fisher, Margaret E.
III. Austern, David. IV. Title.
KF9728.N37   344.73'035   80-23054
ISBN 0-8299-1034-4

2nd Reprint—1984

THE NATIONAL STREET LAW INSTITUTE

The National Street Law Institute is an outgrowth of a Washington, D.C. based practical law education program created in 1975 to provide increased opportunities for citizen education in law. The staff, listed on the next page, is made up of attorney-educators who conduct training program and courses for correctional personnel, high school students, teachers, and inmates in correctional institutions interested in establishing law for non-lawyer educational programs.

The Institute is under the direction of a National Advisory Committee composed of prominent individuals in the fields of law, education, and public affairs, which advises it concerning its past, present, and future activities.

NATIONAL ADVISORY COMMITTEE

Chairperson
Norma Holloway Johnson,
 Judge
Superior Court of the District
 of Columbia
Washington, D.C.

Vincent E. Reed, Superintendent
D.C. Public Schools
Washington, D.C.

v

CONTENTS

chapter six
Overview of the
Criminal Justice
Process 141

ASSISTANCE TO CORRECTIONAL TRAINERS AND OTHER INSTRUCTORS

The Institute has developed this text and its accompanying Instructor's Manual to form the basis of pre-service or in-service training in law for correctional personnel or for use in other courses in corrections law. The Institute has developed training programs in which its staff works with trainers (attorneys and/or non-lawyer professional trainers) who then conduct legal training programs for correctional personnel, or, in some instances, the staff conducts training or trains trainers for states and localities on a consulting basis.

The Institute has also published curriculum materials and general law courses designed for use by youths and adults either in institutions or outside of institutions in schools and community education settings. The books for these courses are *Street Law: A Course in Practical Law* (West Publishing Company) which covers Introduction to Law, Criminal, Consumer, Family, Housing and Individual Rights Law and *Street Law: A Course in the Law of Corrections* (West Publishing Company) which covers topics such as Sentencing, Parole, Probation, Prisoner Rights and Post

Conviction Relief. Both of those student texts have accompanying teacher's manuals.

For further information on the above training programs, courses and materials, contact: The National Street Law Institute, 4th Floor, 605 G Street, N.W., Washington, D.C. 20001. Telephone 202/624-8217.

ACKNOWLEDGEMENTS

We would like to thank the National Institute of Corrections (NIC) for funding a grant which assisted us in adapting previously developed materials for teaching law to non-lawyers into this present curriculum for correctional personnel. Grants from NIC also made it possible to field test the materials in the District of Columbia, Virginia, Louisiana and at NIC's National Jail Center in Boulder, Colorado. In particular, Allen Breed, Craig Dobson, Gary Bowker, Bill Wilkey, Paul Katsampes, and Alfredo Murphy, all of NIC, have been very helpful in this effort.

Many professionals in the field of corrections have given considerable guidance in the development of these materials. Most noteworthy assistance has come from Richard Crane, General Counsel, Louisiana Department of Corrections and a member of our Advisory Committee. Richard Crane recognized the strong need for this type of training and consequently has included a discussion of it in the American Correctional Association's conferences on corrections law which he conducted across the country. He also gave initial guidance on the overall format and later provided excellent detailed comments on drafts. Finally, he made it possible for the materials to be field-tested with personnel from the Louisiana Department of Corrections. Richard Crane's present successor at the Correctional Law Project, Jess Maghan, has also strongly supported our endeavors and has included a presentation on correctional training at five regional conferences in 1980.

Thanks should also go to the American Correctional Association's Committee on training and correctional law, in particular, Robert Martin, Cherry Scott, John Murphy, John Cocoras, Jess Maghan, Tommy Cave, Eugene Barkin and Anthony Travisano who gave direction to the general format. Valuable comments have also been received from William C. Collins and William Taylor of the American Correctional Association and Eugene Barkin of our Advisory Committee.

Our publisher, West Publishing Company, has also been very helpful, recognizing the need for these materials and providing excellent suggestions and assistance.

Much of Chapter 6 is an adaptation of the criminal and juvenile justice chapter of *Street Law: A Course in Practical Law*, Second Edition, by the National Street Law Institute, Lee Arbetman, Edward McMahon and Edward O'Brien, coauthors, published by West Publishing Company.

Ellen Cochrane developed the glossary and her efforts are greatly appreciated. Our entire support staff deserves the largest share of our gratitude for their efforts in the preparation of these materials, especially, Angela Brown, Annie Cole, Russell Keys, Hattie Johnson and Lori Moss. Nancy Bradley, our office administrator, and her successor, Fran Marie Kennedy, deserve a bow for their efforts in coordinating the administrative aspects of the project.

PRACTICAL LAW FOR CORRECTIONAL PERSONNEL

a Resource Manual and
a Training Curriculum
by the National Street Law Institute

one

INTRODUCTION

TO LAW

When may correctional personnel use force to break up a fight between inmates? What risks or *liabilities** are involved in using such force? What can be done if an inmate threatens an officer's family? Will the Department of Corrections always supply an attorney to represent personnel who are sued by an inmate? Suppose officers or administrators are sued by an inmate and the jury awards money *damages* against them; will the Department of Corrections pay the *judgment*, or must it come out of the employees' salaries?

The list is endless and we probably could pose hundreds of other questions about the rights and liabilities of correctional personnel. The point is obvious: correctional personnel have positions which require daily decisions about people and their rights; a knowledge of the law about such rights is necessary for performing the job effectively. Correctional

---

* The first time a legal term is introduced in this book it will appear in italics and be defined in Appendix A, the Glossary.

personnel are also a part of the criminal justice system, and some knowledge of criminal law, criminal procedure and post-conviction relief is essential.

Sometimes a knowledge of the law provides information that is both useful and important. For instance, do you know that under the Public Safety Officers' Act of 1976, depending on the circumstances, the family of an officer killed in the line of duty *may* be eligible for payment of $50,000? Correctional officers can enjoy other benefits without being killed or injured. Rights are protected by laws, and a knowledge of those laws is the best way to insure the full benefit of those rights.

In the past, correctional personnel generally have been given very superficial training in the law — perhaps as little as one or two hours of training. We believe more thorough training is essential. Most police officers, sheriffs, and other law enforcement personnel are given some legal training. Correctional personnel should also be trained in the law — indeed, it may be more essential for correctional officers and *jail* personnel to know the law than it is for other law enforcement officers.

Finally, although some areas of the law are not subject to frequent change, corrections law, perhaps more than any other area of the law, has changed remarkably in the past few years. It continues to change and develop in new and different directions; knowing what the law is and what it may become is important.

WHAT LAW IS

The answer to this question has troubled people for many years. In fact, an entire field of study, *jurisprudence*, is devoted to answering this question. Depending on one's point of view, there are many definitions of "the law," but for our purposes, law is best understood as that set of rules or regulations by which a particular group or community regulates the conduct of people within it.

Using this definition, many questions arise:

■ Where do laws come from? Who makes the law?

■ Do we need laws?

■ Are all laws written?

■ Can laws change? If so, how?

■ What is the difference between laws and morals?

■ Are all laws fair? Should we be permitted to ignore unfair laws?

Our legal system is influenced by traditional ideas of "right and wrong." Thus, most people would condemn murder, regardless of what the law said. On the other hand, everything that someone considers immoral is not illegal. For example, lying to a friend may be immoral, but would rarely be illegal. The point is that every society has recognized the need for some law. These laws may not have been written, but even primitive people had rules regulating group conduct. Without laws, there would be confusion, fear, and panic. This is not to say that all of our existing laws are "fair" or even good, but imagine how people might take advantage of one another without some set of rules.

Problem 1

Make a list of the things correctional personnel do during a normal shift in a correctional institution (e.g., sort mail, take count, feed the residents, clean up, etc.). Next to each item

in the list, indicate whether there are any laws affecting this activity. Are these federal, state, or other laws?

It is the application of laws to particular situations that concerns lawyers and the courts. Regardless of how simply stated or obvious the law in question — for instance, the *statute* involved in the next problem is only thirteen words long — applying the law is frequently difficult. As bizarre as it may seem, the facts described below are taken from an actual case.

The Case of the Shipwrecked Sailors

While working as sailors on an ocean-going oil tanker, three young men were cast adrift in a life raft after their ship floundered and sank in the Atlantic Ocean. The ship went down so suddenly that there was no time to send out an S.O.S. and as far as the three sailors knew, they were the only survivors. In the boat they had no food or water, and they had no fishing gear or other equipment for getting food from the ocean.

After recovering from the initial shock of the shipwreck, the three sailors began to discuss their situation. Dudley, who had been the navigator of the ship, determined that they were at least 1,000 miles from the nearest land and that the storm had blown them far off course from where any ships would normally pass. Stephens, who had been the ship's medical officer, indicated that without food they could not live more than 30 days. The only nourishment they could be assured of was from any rain that might fall from time to time. Stephens noted, however, that if one of the three died before the others, the other two could live awhile longer by eating the body of the third.

On the 25th day, the third sailor, Brooks, who by this time was extremely weak, suggested that the three of them draw lots and that the loser be killed and eaten by the other two. Both Dudley and Stephens agreed. The next day lots were drawn and Brooks lost. At this point, Brooks objected and refused to consent. Although Brooks refused to go along, Dudley and Stephens decided that Brooks would die soon anyway, so they might as well get it over with. Brooks was then killed and eaten.

Five days later, Dudley and Stephens were rescued by a passing vessel and brought to port where, after recovering from their ordeal, they were placed on trial for murder.

Problem 2

Assume that international law requires that the law of the home port be applied when a boat is at sea and the state in which they were tried had the following statute: "Any person who deliberately takes the life of another is guilty of murder."

a. Assume that they are tried for murder and you are on the jury, would you find them guilty or not guilty? Why?

b. If they are tried, convicted and you are the judge, what sentence would you impose?

c. Was the boat a separate society? Who made the law there? What similarities do you see between how law was made there and how law is made in a correctional institution?

The Constitution

The laws in our country — all of them — must be written and enacted with one law in mind because all other laws must meet its requirements to be valid: that "law" is the Constitution of the United States. It is a remarkable *instrument* in that it was written all at once, with comparatively few drafts, and although it has been added to by way of *amendment*, it has survived today in a society far more complicated and complex than the framers of the Constitution could ever have imagined. All laws, in their language, intent, and procedures, must fall within the limits of the Constitution as to what a law may permit or prohibit. For instance, the Constitution requires that laws be written in clear English, that they be unambiguous, and that they not restrict free speech.

As we will see throughout this text, when a law (e.g., a law which restricts free speech) comes into conflict with the Constitution, the highest law in the country, a court is often called on to decide if the law violates the Constitution. Or, for example, if an institution has a policy prohibiting visitors of any race different from that of the inmate, a court may be called upon to decide if this policy violates the Constitution.

Every state also has a constitution or charter that sets out the structure of state government and assigns powers and duties to the various parts of government. The state may also have its own bill of rights that repeats the rights set out

in the U.S. Constitution, or, sometimes, gives greater rights than those in the U.S. Constitution. If a conflict exists between the state constitution and the U.S. Constitution, the U.S. Constitution controls.

The Legislatures

Creation The most familiar lawmaker is the legislature. The U.S. Constitution created a Congress consisting of two branches, a House of Representatives and a Senate, and empowered it to pass federal laws. The subjects of these laws include federal crimes, federal taxation, federal courts, U.S. government programs, the national defense, and the national budget. Every U.S. citizen is subject to these federal laws. The constitution or charter of each state establishes the state governing body, which may be called a legislature or general assembly. State legislatures pass laws that apply only in the state. State laws passed by the legislature are called statutes.

Powers   The U.S. Constitution and state constitutions limit broad legislative power by specifically defining the powers of the legislature. Of importance to correctional personnel are state legislatures' powers to create state agencies, to spend state money, and to establish rights of state employees.

"Enabling statutes" passed by the legislature create the department of corrections and other state agencies in most states. The office of sheriff may also be created by the legislature in some states, or, it may be created by the state constitution or by county ordinance in others.

Increasing staff and upgrading physical plants and services, improvements which courts have ordered corrections departments to make, can, in the final analysis, only be done by the legislature through appropriation of funds and by laws authorizing and implementing these changes. Salaries, benefits and employee rights on the job are mandated by state statutes. State legislatures or their appointed commissions may also pass jail and prison rules and standards; frequently, in this way, the minimum standards for all jails and prisons are set.

Lobbying in the Legislature   Because state legislatures are extensively involved in corrections, it is important for jail and prison personnel to consider when, and in what way, they can bring their concerns to the legislature's attention. Sometimes the views of law enforcement personnel are not heard by lawmakers when legislation is being considered. However, since some states ban "lobbying" by government employees, correctional personnel should investigate what avenues of communication are open to them.

The Agencies

Many of the laws that affect corrections personnel are made by government agencies. For example, most state legislatures have passed enabling statutes that set up the state Department of Corrections (a state agency). This department then has the power to make rules governing prisoners and institutions. Disciplinary codes of inmate offenses are examples of agency rules that are usually created by either the Department of Corrections or the local government agency. All agency rules are the law and can only be successfully challenged if the rules go beyond the *scope of authority* given the agency, violate some constitutional rights, or are contrary to some other higher law that applies to that situation.

If the Department of Corrections passed a rule requiring the spouses of all inmates to be employed before being permitted visitor privileges, this rule would go beyond the scope of authority given to the agency by the state legislature. If the department enacted a rule that correctional employees could not belong to a political party, this would violate the U.S. Constitution and possibly the state constitution or state law. Or if the department *enacted* a rule that residents are not entitled to notice of disciplinary offenses before a hearing, this would be contrary to the rule set out by the Supreme Court requiring that inmates be given notice of the offense.

Federal government agencies administer and interpret laws passed by Congress. For example, Congress passed the Occupational Safety and Health Act (OSHA) requiring the maintenance of safe working conditions. To implement this law, Congress established the Occupational Safety and Health Review Commission and gave it the authority to develop specific regulations governing safety standards for places of employment. The regulations developed fill many volumes and cover such specific subjects as fire exits, or the height of guard rails in factories. These rules and regulations, as well as decisions by agencies interpreting and applying the rules, are all part of the law.

In drawing up regulations for a Department of Corrections or a local jail, administrators must be careful to conform to state laws and the U.S. and state constitutions as written and as they have been interpreted by courts. Failure to do this may result in rules later being held *invalid* in court.

The Courts

How Courts Make Law   Law is also made by courts. When individuals, businesses, states, associations, etc. have disputes they are unable to resolve, they seek a solution in the courts. The case is brought in a trial court where each party presents its side of the dispute. The jury decides the facts, unless there is no jury, in which case the judge decides the facts. The judge interprets and decides the law. This process of interpreting the law is also a process of making law because whatever the judge says the law is in that case is *binding* on all persons involved.

For example, an inmate sues the jail personnel because the sheriff has a policy that does not permit inmates awaiting trial to attend religious services. An inmate claims this rule has violated his constitutional rights under the First Amendment. The judge must interpret the U.S. Constitution to decide whether *due process* and freedom of religion mean that unconvicted inmates have a right to attend religious services, and whether the sheriff must allow ministers to come into the jail to hold services. If the judge finds that the Constitution requires this, the law as to this jail will be that inmates have a constitutional right to attend religious services.

Except in the most unusual cases, a party may not appeal a decision as to the facts— including the verdict — to an appellate court. Issues of fact are decided by trial courts and very rarely are changed by appellate courts. For example, if a trial court found that a jail had been uncomfortably cold during the winter (e.g., below 55 degrees for 30 days), an appeals court would usually not reverse this decision unless it was obvious from the court record that no evidence had been presented to support that *finding* of fact.

How Courts are Structured   There are two court systems in every state: state and federal. State courts hear *civil* and *criminal* cases based on state law. Persons charged with violations of state laws are tried in state courts and become state prisoners if convicted. Disputes between citizens of the same state about *contracts* or *injuries* are heard in the civil branch of state trial courts. Federal constitutional questions may also be heard in a state court, although *plaintiffs* — the people bringing the *suit* — generally choose to use federal courts to hear these cases.

There are also *appellate* courts (both state and federal) to which a losing party may *appeal* from the *verdict* or decision in a trial court. In an appellate court one party presents written and oral arguments asking the court to change the decision of the trial court, and the other party presents written and oral arguments supporting the decision of the trial court. It is important to remember that appellate courts only hear arguments and make decisions concerning the law involved in the particular case. When a judge makes a decision in a trial as to whether certain evidence may be heard by the jury, or when a judge instructs the jury, a mistake that may be made will probably be a "legal error." Such legal errors may form the basis of an appeal.

FIGURE 1   Federal and State Court Systems

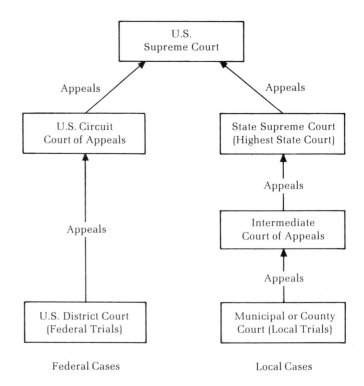

Federal courts hear cases where a federal law or the U.S. Constitution is involved, including civil rights and *habeas corpus* cases. Persons charged with violating federal laws (i.e., federal crimes) are tried in federal courts and become federal prisoners if convicted. Contract and injury cases may also be federal cases where the two parties are from different states and at least $10,000 in damages is claimed.

Throughout the country federal courts are divided into *circuits*; most circuits include the federal courts in several different states. The federal trial courts are called United States District Courts (there are 94) and the federal appellate courts are called United States Circuit Courts of Appeals (there are 11). Note the chart on pg. 12 to see what circuit your state is in. The decisions of your federal circuit court must be followed by all the U.S. District Courts in the states included in your circuit and therefore you should pay particular attention to new decisions involving corrections from your circuit court.

Courts hear both criminal and civil cases. Criminal cases are cases in which the government (the state or the United States), represented by the prosecutor, brings charges against the *defendant*, the person accused of committing the crime. If they represent the United States, prosecutors are called Assistant U.S. Attorneys and if they represent the state or local government, they may be called district attorneys, corporation counsel, commonwealth attorneys, county attorneys, assistant attorneys general, etc. Defense attorneys may be lawyers privately hired. If the defendant cannot afford an attorney, the court may appoint one.

A civil case is a case in which one party (called a plaintiff) sues another (called a defendant) either to collect an amount of money, or to force the defendant to do or not do something. There are several different types of civil cases, including actions based on such incidents as:

■ Joe is injured by Derek. He sues Derek to pay his medical bills and for pain and suffering incurred.

■ Mr. Garfield, a landlord, wants Gerry to leave his apartment. He sues Gerry for possession of the apartment (eviction).

■ Inmate Franklin falls down the steps at the jail on his way to lunch and breaks his leg. He claims another inmate

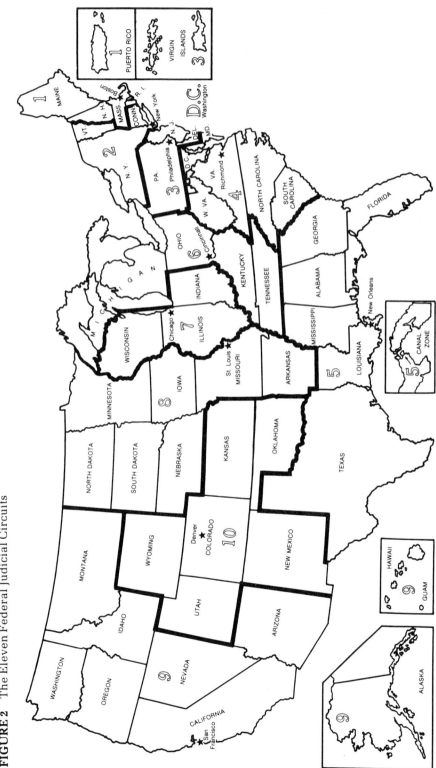

FIGURE 2 The Eleven Federal Judicial Circuits

pushed him and that the correctional officer saw it and made no effort to stop the other inmate or to assist Franklin once he had fallen. He sues the officer for damages.

■ Jones is fired from the corrections department. He claims discrimination, and files suit asking that the department be ordered to reinstate him and give him back pay.

Most of the problems discussed in this book will be civil cases. Typical examples will be situations where inmates are injured and file suit in a state or federal court for damages.

There are a number of specialized branches of trial courts, usually at the county or city level, which hear only certain types of cases. Examples of such courts are Small Claims Court (cases involving very small amounts of money), Landlord-Tenant Court (cases involving disputes between landlords and tenants), Family or Domestic Relations Court (cases involving divorce, separation, custody of children), and Civil Court (cases involving larger amounts of money).

As you can see on the court system chart on page 10, trials can be held in either the U.S. District Court (if it is a federal case) or the local state court (this may be called a county, district or circuit court). If you lose your case (trial) in the U.S. District Court, you can appeal to a U.S. Court of Appeals, and, if you lose again, to the U.S. Supreme Court. (Actually, the U.S. Supreme Court agrees to hear less than two percent of the cases appealed to it.) If you lose your case (trial) in your local trial court, you can usually appeal either directly to the State Supreme Court or first to an intermediate court of appeals if your state has one, and then to the state's highest court. Sometimes State Supreme Court decisions can be appealed to the U.S. Supreme Court.

Let us suppose that in a certain case the U.S. Court of Appeals decides 2 to 1 (majority rule) to reverse the decision of the trial court. Usually the Court of Appeals will issue a written opinion stating why it *ruled* as it did. This opinion is called a *precedent*, which means that in the future all judges in lower courts in the place (circuit) where the decision was made must follow the rule (or law) in the case. This is what we mean by courts making law. In the future, other courts may interpret the opinion of the U.S. Court of Appeals, and attempt to apply the general reasoning of the Court of Appeals in similar fact situations. You should note that a higher

court, or the same court if another case comes before it, can reverse this precedent and issue a new precedent. This might happen if judges die or retire and new judges come to the court, or if the judges change their minds. The most important precedents are set in cases heard and decided by the U.S. Supreme Court in Washington, D.C. (Nine judges hear each case and the majority determines the outcome). All courts in the United States must follow U.S. Supreme Court decisions.

Precedents are very important to our whole system of law. Not only must other courts follow the law announced in these cases, but the written decisions become part of law books in law libraries. Lawyers use these books in preparing written and oral arguments for their cases in court.

Sometimes the term "precedent" is used in a general sense to refer to the same or similar cases decided in other states or other federal circuits. Though no court is required to follow these kinds of "precedents," a court may choose to do so.

The Case of Johnson v. Avery

An inmate challenged a Tennessee State Penitentiary rule that prohibited inmates from assisting other inmates in preparing writs "or other legal matters." In fact, the inmate had been punished for violating the rule. A writ of habeas corpus was filed in the U.S. District Court where the penitentiary was located, and after a hearing, that court held that the regulation in question was void because it prevented prisoners who could not read or write from access to federal courts. The U.S. Court of Appeals (Sixth Circuit), which takes Tennessee appeals, reversed and ruled against the inmate, stating that the state had a legitimate interest in limiting the practice of law to licensed attorneys.

Such limitations had always been the "rule" as established by a number of prior cases in Tennessee and many other states — that is, the state could limit the practice of law to licensed attorneys, and could prohibit inmates from assisting other inmates in legal matters.

However, after an appeal to the U.S. Supreme Court, the rule, or "precedent", was changed. The Supreme Court held that unless the state provides reasonable alternatives to assist inmates in the preparation of petitions for post-conviction relief, the state must allow inmates to furnish legal assistance to other prisoners.

Thus, the precedent was changed; that is, whereas the state had previously been permitted to prevent one inmate from providing legal assistance to another inmate, the state would now have to either provide reasonable alternatives for such help or permit one inmate to assist another. Because this new precedent was set by the U.S. Supreme Court, it applied to every jail and prison in the United States.[1]

When court decisions establish precedents, they decide the issues in the case before them and also sometimes state a general rule that will have to be interpreted in future cases.

Appellate courts do not decide every issue that may later arise. Thus, after the *Johnson v. Avery* case, described above, future cases would have to decide what would be a "reasonable alternative" to allowing inmates to act as jailhouse lawyers, as well as other issues related to this, such as access to law libraries, the right to an appointed attorney, and the right to write letters to attorneys, courts and other legal organizations.

The Corporal Punishment Case History

In 1965, inmates in the Arkansas State Prison filed suit claiming that, because they broke prison rules, they had been whipped with a 5-foot-long, 4-inch-wide, quarter-inch-thick strap by assistant wardens and an inmate trusty. They claimed this "corporal punishment" violated the Eighth Amendment to the U.S. Constitution, which prohibits "cruel and unusual punishment."

The U.S. District Court ruled against the inmates, finding that corporal punishment was a method of enforcing discipline which had been used for many years in Arkansas and other states. The District Court also found that though the U.S. Supreme Court had not ruled on the issue, the Supreme Courts of Delaware and Florida had upheld the practice. The court did order that rules be developed listing what offenses could be punished and how much whipping could be received for each.[2]

In 1967 other inmates filed suit again claiming that corporal punishment and use of the strap were cruel and unusual punishment, but the court again denied the inmates' claims. The court relied on the 1965 decision and on the historical viewpoint that accepted corporal punishment and the strap as permissible forms of punishment.[3] This time the inmates appealed to the U.S. Court of Appeals (8th Circuit), which in 1968 reversed the District Court and ruled for the inmates, stating that use of a strap and corporal punishment offends concepts of decency and human dignity which have existed in the last third of the 20th century.[4] The Court of Appeals did not cite specific case precedents, but said that corporal punishment made inmates "hate" prison personnel, that it frustrated goals of corrections, and that public opinion was against it.

Problem 3

a. What were the three court decisions in the above case history?

b. What did the District Court base its decision in the 1965 case on? Was the 1965 decision binding on any prisons?

c. What did the District Court base its 1967 decision on? Did it have to rule as it did or could it have decided differently?

d. What did the Court of Appeals base its 1968 decision on? Didn't this court have to follow the other precedents mentioned in the case history? Explain.

e. Does the 1968 decision mean that correctional officers cannot use force against inmates under any circumstances?

f. The U.S. Supreme Court still has not ruled in a case involving corporal punishment in prisons. Therefore, could a state prison use a strap to punish inmates?

THE COURT'S ROLE IN CORRECTIONAL ADMINISTRATION

In recent years, the issues of how much power the courts have, should have or should extend over correctional institutions have frequently been raised. In discussing the problem below, refer back to the sections on the different branches of government and consider what is the designated role of each and what you believe that proper role should be.

Problem 4

The city of Ecalpon operates a jail that was constructed many years ago. After 51 years of continuous use, the jail facilities are in disrepair, the furnace does not adequately heat the building, the electrical system poses a potential fire hazard, and rotting and falling plaster and wood have resulted in many injuries to officers and inmates. All manner of rats, mice and some unrecognizable rodents and insects also inhabit the jail. The fire marshal has condemned the building, the Housing Department has issued thousands of citations against the jail, and the Health Department has ordered the facility closed. Of course nothing has been done because all of these departments, like the local jail itself, are part of the city of Ecalpon. The mayor has stated that the situation is deplorable, but there is nothing he can do because the City Council refuses to set aside funds to make the necessary repairs. Four inmates bring suit to require the city to repair its jail or, in the alternative, close the building.

a. Is the suit filed by the inmates a civil or criminal suit?

b. Would the inmates bring the suit in federal court or in state court?

c. List some laws or regulations involved in the case. Are they constitutional, federal, state, or local?

d. Do court precedents have any bearing on what the court does in this case?

e. List possible results in this case. If you were the judge, what would you do in this case?

f. Will agencies or legislatures be involved in this case after it is decided? Explain.

CORRECTIONAL STANDARDS

In recent years many organizations have undertaken the development of correctional and jail standards. The American Correctional Association has created a commission comprised of correctional and criminal justice administrators. The Commission has developed standards for both adult jails and prisons, and a system of accreditation whereby an institution may provide funds to pay for an inspection. Following inspection, if the institution is found to comply with a certain percentage of the standards, the institution receives a certificate of accreditation. Other organizations that have drafted correctional and jail standards include the American Bar Association, the U.S. Department of Justice, the United Nations, the National Sheriff's Association, the American Medical Association, and the American Public Health Association. (See Appendix D for a list of standards and how to obtain copies of each). Unfortunately, the standards adopted by different organizations differ, and much controversy exists over which standards should be followed.

The reasons why institutions or departments of corrections adopt standards or try to comply with certain standards include the following:

■ to prevent problems from occurring in the institutions that may result in *lawsuits*;

■ to use compliance with the standards as a basis for defense in a lawsuit;

■ in order to settle a lawsuit, some correctional officials agree to implement certain standards;

■ as the basis of a court order; and

■ to evaluate correctional programs and to use the results as the basis for financial requests from local, state and the federal government.

It should be noted that unless a governmental body formally adopts standards or a court orders them, compliance is voluntary. There is controversy over whether the federal government should adopt mandatory standards for either federal or state institutions. Many courts look at the different standards when deciding cases and may even select a particular standard as the basis for deciding whether rights of inmates have been violated.

Problem 5

a. Which of the following types of people should be involved in writing or passing standards? Why?

   1. inmates;

   2. lawyers;

   3. sheriffs;

   4. correctional administrators;

   5. correctional officers;

   6. state legislators;

   7. Congress;

   8. federal officials;

   9. judges; and/or

   10. citizens in the community.

b. Should there be mandatory or advisory standards issued by the federal government? Explain.

c. Should judges use standards in making decisions in corrections cases? Why?

Throughout this book, references or citations ("cites") are made to various laws relevant to corrections. This section is included to help you understand what these cites mean and how to find the law. Some readers will wish to better understand a case, law or regulation by reading it, while others may hear of a new law or case and decide to look it up to achieve a clearer understanding of its meaning.

    The law as it is written by judges in opinions, by agencies in rules, and by legislatures in statutes is contained in many volumes in law libraries. The ability to find the law on a particular subject in these volumes is a valuable and useful skill to acquire. Some corrections departments have set up law libraries for their employees so that correctional personnel may read the laws that set out their rights and duties. Other institutions have libraries started principally for inmates, but which also can be used by correctional personnel.

LEGAL RESEARCH

Statutes and Regulations

Laws made by legislatures are called statutes or codes. Laws passed by every state legislature are contained in state codes and those enacted by Congress are contained in the U.S. Code. Statutes passed in one state do not apply in other states, while statutes passed by Congress are binding on all citizens.

In order to find the statutes, you must first locate the proper code. For example, the Civil Rights Attorney Fees Award Act of 1976 is cited as 42 U.S.C. § 1988. The federal code is indicated by U.S.C., which stands for United States Code. "42" is the title number of the code and "1988" is the section. Therefore, you locate the volume of the U.S. Code with a "42" on the outside and then locate the page(s) with § 1988.

Regulations made by agencies are located in "registers" or "codes." For example, regulations made by federal agencies are printed in the *Code of Federal Regulations* and the *Federal Register.* The *Code of Federal Regulations* contains 50 titles representing broad areas subject to federal regulation. Each title contains chapters bearing the name of the federal agency issuing the regulation. Each chapter contains parts representing specific regulatory areas. This code has a subject index to help locate the regulations. To keep current on amendments and revisions to federal regulations, the *Federal Register*, published daily, provides lists of parts and sections changed and the changes themselves.

Case Law

Laws are made by judges who interpret statutes and decide cases that come before them. These judicial (or court) decisions are contained in "reports" or "reporters." Since there are state, federal and often local court systems, it is necessary to keep in mind which court decisions are binding upon which courts. A state's highest appeals court decisions will be precedent for all the state's future lower court (appellate and trial) decisions. In the federal court system, the higher court (that is, the U.S. Court of Appeals) will bind the lower courts (that is, the U.S. District Courts). U.S. Supreme Court decisions are precedent for all courts in the country.

References to cases first give the case name and then its cite and the date of the decision. Examples:

Bounds v. Smith, 430 U.S. 817 (1977)

| name of case | volume of reporter | name of reporter | page | year of decision |

The reporters are organized according to which court has issued the opinion. As new cases are decided by courts, the opinions are published in pamphlet form and are called advance sheets. Later these advance sheets are bound together in the proper reporter's most recent volume.

U.S. Supreme Court   Decisions of the U.S. Supreme Court, the highest federal court, are found in several reporters: "United States Reports", cited "U.S."; in "Supreme Court Reporter", cited "S.Ct."; and in "Lawyer's Edition", cited "L.Ed." Examples:

418 U.S. 539 (1974)

94 S.Ct. 2963 (1974)

57 L.Ed.2d 553 (1978)

The most recent Supreme Court opinions are found in weekly editions of the "United States Law Weekly" (U.S.L.W.), a multi-volume set of loose leafs. Example:

U.S. Court of Appeals   Decisions of these federal appeals courts from the 11 circuits (see chart on p. 12) are found in the "Federal Reporter", cited "F." for the first series containing older decisions and "F.2d" for the second series containing more recent decisions. Example:

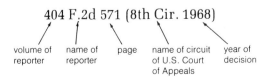

U.S. District Court   Decisions of the U.S. District Courts are found in the "Federal Supplement", cited "F.Supp." Examples:

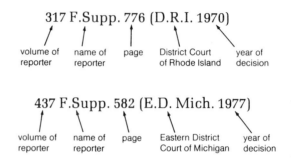

State Courts of Appeal   The states are organized into several regions. The highest court decisions are found in the regional reporter covering that particular state. These reporters include: "Pacific Reporter", cited "P."; "Atlantic Reporter", cited "A."; "South Western Reporter", cited "S.W."; "South Eastern Reporter", cited "S.E."; and "Southern Reporter", cited "So." More recent decisions are in the second series (2d) of the reporter. Examples:

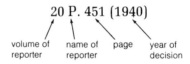

Many states have their own reporter systems that contain opinions issued by the state's courts. Example:

Shepardizing

Shepard's Citations is a publication that reports on the present status of all cases and statutes, that is, whether the law has been overruled, cited, followed in other states, etc. Before ever stating that a case is the latest on a particular topic, the case should be "Shepardized" to make sure that the law has not been changed.

Research Techniques

Since there is no way in this introductory chapter to teach legal research in any depth, reference is made to *West's Law Finder* published by West Publishing Co. for use in developing legal research skills.

References

1. Johnson v. Avery, 393 U.S. 483, 89 S.Ct. 747 (1969).
2. Talley v. Stephens, 247 F.Supp. 683, (E.D.Ark. 1965).
3. Jackson v. Bishop, 268 F.Supp. 804 (E.D.Ark. 1967).
4. Jackson v. Bishop, 404 F.2d 571 (8th Cir. 1968).

two
RIGHTS AND
LIABILITIES
OF
CORRECTIONAL
PERSONNEL

Generally, society does not allow one person to use force against another and, under some circumstances, even a verbal threat may constitute a crime. Use of force against another constitutes the crime of *assault* and may also result in a civil lawsuit whereby the person assaulted may sue the attacker for any damages caused. However, there are certain circumstances in which law enforcement officers may use force and when it is their duty or "right" to do so. In the circumstances where force is permitted, law enforcement officers may be guilty of criminal assault if excessive force is used, and may be liable for money damages from a civil lawsuit in which the arrested or assaulted person (or inmate) sues the officer.

In the following section, the law of the use of force will be discussed. However, be aware that the law in your state may be somewhat different from the general discussion stated here. The law in the state where the institution is located is the standard by which the courts will determine whether the exercise of force was proper. Generally, there are four circumstances in which a correctional officer has the right to use force:

1. self-defense;

2. defending or aiding another officer (or inmate);

3. enforcing institutional regulations; and

4. preventing commission of a crime, including escape.

It is difficult to state exactly how much force may be used in each of these situations, though the general rule is that the amount of force must be reasonable under the circumstances. Where an inmate believes that too much or an unreasonable amount of force has been used, a civil case may be filed, or a criminal complaint of assault may be made with the local *prosecutor's* office. The use of excessive force may constitute the crime of assault or may give an injured inmate the right to collect money damages in a civil suit against correctional employees. The use of too much force may also violate an inmate's constitutional right under the Eighth Amendment to be free from "cruel and unusual punishment." (See page 84). If such a case comes to court, a judge or the jury must look to the evidence in each particular case to determine if too much force was used.

Non-Deadly Force

The most common situation in which correctional personnel have a right to use force is when they are assaulted by an inmate or inmates. In general, personnel may use such reasonable force as may be, or reasonably appears to be, necessary to protect themselves, but should only use the amount of force required to subdue the inmate. This is called self-defense.

Correctional personnel also have a right to use force to help another correctional officer or an inmate under attack. Again, in these situations, the personnel may use such reasonable force as may be, or reasonably appears to be, necessary to protect the other officer or inmate, but should only use the amount of force required to subdue the attacker. If the officer continues to use force after stopping the attacker, the roles reverse and the defender becomes the attacker and the one committing the assault.

Here are some examples of recent cases that illustrate how the courts try to handle non-deadly force situations:

a. A riot was subdued in a state prison. Thereafter an attempt was made to segregate inmates who had participated in the riot. As one inmate was being taken to a maximum security cell, he was beaten with clubs by two prison guards. The court found this use of force to be unreasonable and awarded a $3,000 judgment against the two prison guards and the captain of the guard force.[1]

b. A fight occurred between five inmates and a number of officers. The inmates suffered severe cuts, broken bones and other injuries. One officer was hurt so badly he was taken to intensive care. After hearing the evidence, the court found that the inmates were resisting prison authority and that the force used to subdue them was reasonable and necessary.[2]

Traditionally, force also could be used to enforce institutional regulations, but this often resulted in what many people felt was unnecessary *corporal punishment.* Modern correctional philosophy calls for personnel to use force only as a last resort to enforce regulations, and even then to use only the minimum amount required. In describing its model rule on the use of force to enforce institutional regulations, the American Correctional Association Law Project states that: "While the model allows physical methods to enforce institutional regulations, it is hoped that the trend toward less physical control of inmates will be undertaken. Control and management of offenders should be by sound scientific methods, stressing moral values and organized persuasion, rather than primary dependence upon physical force".[3]

Therefore, to grab or strike an inmate who is talking out of turn or walking out of line could give rise to liability if the officer did not first attempt to correct the situation through a verbal reprimand. On the other hand, an inmate who is found writing on the wall in a jail dormitory and continues to do so after an officer tells him to stop, can be physically moved away from the wall. Again, the standard will be whether what the officer did under the circumstances was "reasonable."

Another difficult issue concerns the type of force correctional personnel may use. For example, when can correctional personnel use mechanical restraints, chemical agents, tear gas, etc.? Clearly, such devices can be an effective and necessary means of maintaining order, especially in particularly dangerous situations, such as riots or other types of prison disturbances. However, some believe that such devices should not be used unless absolutely necessary.

Mechanical restraints are most commonly used to prevent escape when transporting inmates, or to protect inmates whose past history and present behavior create the likelihood that they will injure themselves or others. Liability can result in situations where such restraints are used as punishment, or when they are applied about the head or neck of an inmate in a manner that causes undue physical discomfort, inflicts physical pain, or restricts the inmate's blood circulation or breathing.

Chemical agents should be used only by those trained to use them, and injuries resulting from improper use, especially by someone who is untrained, may result in liability for individual officers, their supervisors, the institution, or the department as a whole. Failure to follow institutional rules regarding the use of these agents, such as the requirement of first receiving the warden's permission, may also result in liability.

The evidence presented in a given case is extremely important. For example, in a recent case, an inmate claimed that officers beat him up, broke his nose, rammed his head into a grate, and sprayed him with mace for no reason. The court ruled against the inmate when he presented four witnesses, all of whom disagreed with one another and gave different accounts of what had happened.

A key question that judges or juries often ask themselves in deciding if excessive force was used is "were the officers using force because it was necessary to subdue the inmate, or were they using it for purposes of punishment?"

The courts have made it clear that corporal punishment may not be used against inmates and that correctional institutions must find other methods of disciplining prisoners. In addition, some states have laws (and most departments of corrections have rules) prohibiting such conduct. It should be remembered that when correctional employees violate the law or their own rules, this may form the basis of a civil lawsuit against them or subject them to disciplinary action within their agency.

CORRECTIONAL LAW PROJECT'S
[AMERICAN CORRECTIONAL ASSOCIATION]
MODEL CORRECTIONAL RULES AND REGULATIONS*

II. *Non-Deadly Force*

A. Non-deadly force is force which normally causes neither death nor serious bodily injury. It may be in the form of physical force or chemical agents.
1. Physical force or chemical agents may be used only in the following instances:
    a. Prior to the use of deadly force
        1. To prevent the commission of a *felony*, including escape.
        2. To prevent an act which could result in death or severe bodily harm to one's self or to another person.
    b. In defending one's self or others against any physical assault.
    c. To prevent commission of a *misdemeanor*.
    d. To prevent serious damage to property.
    e. To enforce institutional regulations.
    f. To prevent or *quell* a riot.
In every case, only the minimum force necessary shall be used.
2. Chemical Agents — Special Conditions
    a. Chemical agents may be used only by employees specifically trained in their use.
    b. Chemical agents shall not be used:
        1. Without approval of the warden or his representative, if approval is possible under the circumstances.
        2. Repeatedly against an inmate within a short period of time.
    c. In every case, individuals affected by the agents shall be permitted to wash their face, eyes or other exposed skin areas as soon as possible after the use of the agent.

---

* See Appendix D.

B. After the use of non-deadly force, the following steps shall be undertaken:
1. A notification of its use shall be given to the warden.
2. A report written by the officer who employed the non-deadly force shall be filed with the Director of the Department of Corrections. Such report shall include:
    a. An accounting of the events leading to the use of the non-deadly force.
    b. A precise description of the incident, and the reasons for employing the force.
    c. A description of the weapon used, if any, and the manner in which it was used.
    d. A description of the injuries suffered, if any, and the treatment given.
    e. A list of all participants and witnesses to the incident.
C. The use of any type of force for punishment or reprisal is strictly prohibited and is *grounds* for dismissal of the employee involved.

III. *Mechanical Restraints*

A. Mechanical restraints may be used only when reasonably necessary and only in the following instances:
1. In transporting an inmate from place to place.
2. When the past history and present behavior or apparent emotional state of the inmate creates the likelihood that bodily injury to any person or escape by the inmate will occur.
3. Under medical advice, to prevent the inmate from attempting suicide or inflicting serious physical injury upon himself.
B. Mechanical restraints shall never be used:
1. As a method of punishment.
2. About the head or neck of the inmate.
3. In a way that causes undue physical discomfort, inflicts physical pain or restricts the blood circulation or breathing of the inmate.

Problem 6

Using the Model Rules and Regulations set out on the preceding pages, determine in each case whether the correctional personnel had a right to use the force employed and, if not, what the officer should have done.

a. Officer Lewis is assigned to the jail intake unit. Three inmates are present and handcuffed. Lewis indicates in a somewhat abusive manner to Inmate Frank that he is to strip down for the customary intake search. He unhandcuffs Frank and in response to the instruction, Frank swings around and hits Lewis squarely on the jaw. Lewis, dazed, responds by slugging Frank, knocking him down, and then handcuffing him to restrain him.

b. Inmate Simmons refused to enter a punishment cell, having just received a negative decision from the Adjustment Board. Officer Jones, accompanying Simmons, tells him to go into the cell, whereupon Simmons responds by yelling "Shove it." Jones unlocks the cell and pushes Simmons into it with such force that the inmate smashes into the wall.

c. Officer Marshall discovers that Inmate Smith has violated institutional rules by sneaking food out of the dining room back to his cell. Smith yells an obscenity at Marshall. Marshall slaps Smith.

d. Inmate Green went on a rampage in his cell, setting mattresses on fire and wrecking it. He was transferred to an isolation cell where he requested medical and psychiatric care. He was told he would be required to wait. He again set his mattress on fire. A correctional officer tear-gassed him and left him alone in the cell for 11 hours.

e. Inmate Ferrari was continually yelling from his cell at officers and other inmates to rise up against the poor conditions in the jail. He was warned repeatedly to stop his disruptive behavior but continued to act in this way. Officer Moore and his supervisor, Captain Friendly, tear-gassed Ferrari's cell.

Deadly Force

The *general* rule is that deadly force can be used in only two instances:

1. To prevent a felony, sometimes including escape.

2. To prevent an act that could result in death or severe bodily injury.

It is well established that deadly force can be used only as a last resort. If used at any other time, such force may result in civil and/or criminal liability against the user. The general rules regarding self-defense also apply in that persons defending themselves or others may use only that amount of force reasonably necessary to subdue the attacker.

The question of whether deadly force should be used to stop a prison or jail escape is a difficult one. In most states, an escape is a felony and, therefore, many people argue that in those states deadly force always can be used to stop an escape. Others say that deadly force can only be used against a person known to be "dangerous." Others disagree and argue that fleeing convicted *felons* can be stopped through the use of deadly force. If this is the law, another problem may arise in an institution where both felons and misdemeanants are lodged. Is it the responsibility of the officer in the tower of a prison to determine if the escaping inmate is a felon or a misdemeanant before using deadly force? Should it make a difference if the inmate has been convicted or is being held before trial in a jail? These questions have not always been answered by the courts. To determine what should be done when a prisoner attempts an escape, the best you can do is to check carefully the law in each state by examining the state statutes, court cases, and regulations of the departments of corrections and/or correctional institutions.

Another potential area of liability if deadly force is used lies with supervisory personnel and the department as a whole, both for failing to provide adequate training in the use of firearms, and for failing to instruct when such force may be used. Some states have laws or rules requiring such training, and failure to provide required training may impose grounds for liability on additional persons.

Problem 7

Officer Burke, assigned to a guard tower about 100 feet from the gate, opens the gate to allow Officer Bradley to enter

CORRECTIONAL LAW PROJECT'S
[AMERICAN CORRECTIONAL ASSOCIATION]
MODEL CORRECTIONAL RULES AND REGULATIONS*

I.   *Deadly Force*

A.   Deadly force is force which will likely cause death or serious bodily injury.

B.   It may be used only as a last resort and then only in the following instances:

    1.   To prevent the commission of a felony, including escape.

    2.   To prevent an act which could result in death or severe bodily injury to one's self or to another person.

C.   When used, the following steps shall be undertaken:

    1.   An immediate notification of its use shall be given to the warden and to the proper law enforcement authorities.

    2.   A report written by the officer who used the deadly force shall be filed with the Director of the Department of Corrections, and the proper law enforcement authorities. Such report shall include:

        a.   An accounting of the events leading to the use of deadly force.

        b.   A precise description of the incident and the reasons for employing the deadly force.

        c.   A description of the weapon and the manner in which it was used.

        d.   A description of the injuries suffered, if any, and the treatment given.

        e.   A list of all participants and witnesses to the incident.

---

* See Appendix D.

along with an inmate returning from court. Burke observes the inmate, who is handcuffed, reach down to pull something out of his left shoe. Bradley's back is turned, he is 5 feet in front of the inmate and he is unarmed. Officer Burke has a .22-caliber rifle in the tower.

a. How much, if any, force is he allowed to use to protect Bradley from the possible attack by the inmate? What should Burke do?

b. What if Burke saw the inmate pull a shiny object out of his shoe? Place your opinion on the following scale regarding the statement, "Officer Burke should fire his weapon at the inmate."

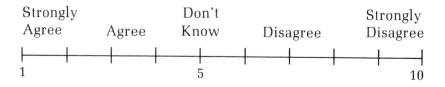

Strongly Agree   Agree   Don't Know   Disagree   Strongly Disagree

1   5   10

c. What if Burke is certain the shiny object was a knife? Does your opinion change?

Problem 8

Correctional Officer Murray works at a state prison where both felons and misdemeanants are housed. He observes an inmate climbing the wall from the recreation yard that leads to a wide space, and then to a 12-foot fence with barbed wire on the top. The officer has a shotgun. What should the officer do? In his state, escape by a felon is a felony and the state law only allows the use of deadly force against fleeing felons.

Problem 9

Inmates in a state prison have taken three officers hostage, and refuse to release them until a helicopter is provided for their escape. Prison officials refuse their demand. Can correctional officers use deadly force to try to secure the release of the officers?

Problem 10

Officer Wilson sees an inmate running for the wall of the jail yard. He fires but misses and hits another inmate who is watching but not trying to escape. Officer Wilson has never received training in the proper use of firearms. If the wounded inmate sues, who may be liable for damages?

SITUATIONS
INVOLVING
POSSIBLE
LIABILITY OF
CORRECTIONAL
PERSONNEL

Recently, an increased number of cases have been filed against correctional personnel by inmates who have been injured, by the families of inmates who have died while incarcerated, or by other persons who have been injured by inmates where some fault on the part of correctional personnel is claimed.

A civil suit against an officer may charge that the officer's conduct was *negligent*, grossly or wantonly negligent and/or intentional. Which degree of fault is *alleged* and proven against the officer makes important differences in the type of lawsuit that can be filed, the type of money damages that can be collected, the availability of various defenses that officers may use, and the availability of attorney fee awards against the correctional personnel.

Proof of negligence (simple negligence) requires showing that (1) a duty was owed to the person, (2) that duty was not fulfilled, and (3) the failure to fulfill the duty caused the injury and resulting damages. For example, a deputy is putting an inmate back in his cell. The deputy is thinking about something else and as he closes the cell door, he catches the inmate's hand in the cell door, breaking three fingers. The deputy was negligent because he had a duty to provide for the safety of the inmate. He failed to fulfill this duty when he let his mind wander, and this failure caused the inmate's injury and damages.

Gross or wanton negligence is like simple negligence except that it requires some intent on the part of the actor to create a situation where it is likely that some injury will occur. Going back to the cell door example, if the officer had a little game he played when putting inmates in their cells to see how close he could come to the inmate's heels as he closed the door, and he caught the inmate's hand in the door, his conduct would constitute gross negligence.

An intentional wrong requires that in addition to the elements of negligence, the actor intended to cause the injury. Therefore, if the deputy had a particular grudge against the inmate he was escorting back to the cell, and deliberately slammed the cell door on the inmate's hand, breaking the fingers, the officer could be charged with an intentional wrong.

Vicarious Liability

In each of these situations, the officer actually doing the act is liable for the injuries. It is possible and even probable that others will be liable as well — others who may not have even been physically present when the incident took place. This is called vicarious liability. When applied to the employer-employee relationship, it is called "respondeat superior," (which means "let the superior answer"). The result is that the employer may be responsible for the torts (wrongful acts) of employees, if the acts were committed while the employees were engaged in activity falling within the scope of their employment.

The underlying rationale for vicarious liability is to find a financially responsible defendant to pay for the injuries caused the plaintiff. Courts have stated that since an employer has control over the employees,—having selected, hired, assigned and supervised them,—he or she is also the proper person, in addition to the employees themselves, to hold liable for their acts. Who is held liable may go up the chain of command to the top officials and/or the unit of government involved. For example, when an escaped inmate raped four women, the city of the District of Columbia was held vicariously liable and ordered to pay $180,000.[4]

Supervisors of negligent employees may also be held liable for the actions of their officers on the theory of vicarious liability. For supervisors to be liable they must have failed to direct or train their officers or must have been negligent in hiring, supervising, assigning, or retaining them. The supervisors' failure or negligence must have contributed to the negligence of the officer.

For instance, if the warden fails to provide weapons training and an untrained officer in the tower shoots and harms an innocent inmate, the warden may be liable for the inmate's injuries.

The existence of a written manual of operating policies and procedures that actually is used as a guide and is kept up-to-date may be a valid defense to a claim that supervisors failed to direct. Supervisors should also train all personnel in departmental policies and procedures, and such training should be documented.

To prove negligence in hiring, supervising, assigning or retaining an officer, the injured person must show that the supervisor knew or should have known of the employee's past conduct or habits that were evidence of the employee's potential for negligent conduct.

Keep these distinctions in mind as you examine the various situations set out in the following pages.

Protection of Inmates

It is well accepted that both federal and state correctional institutions owe a duty of protection to inmates committed to their *custody*. This duty is sometimes stated in the following language (quoted from federal law): "The Federal Bureau of Prisons shall . . . (2) provide suitable quarters for and provide for the safekeeping, care and subsistence of all persons *charged* or convicted of offenses against the United States; (3) provide for the protection, instruction, and discipline of all persons charged with or convicted of offenses against the United States." This same duty may also be established by state law or court cases.

What constitutes "negligence" regarding the failure to protect in an institution is often a difficult question and depends upon the facts of each case. Liability frequently turns on the issue of whether the officer's conduct constituted a failure to fulfill the duty to protect. The test the courts use is one of "reasonableness": whether the judge or jury believes the correctional officer or official acted unreasonably.

NATIONAL COUNCIL ON CRIME AND DELINQUENCY'S
"A MODEL ACT FOR THE PROTECTION OF RIGHTS
OF PRISONERS"*

All persons imprisoned in accordance with law shall retain all rights of an ordinary citizen, except those expressly or
by necessary implication taken by law, which include . . . a
general healthful environment, . . . and protection against any
physical or psychological abuse or unnecessary indignity.

* See Appendix D.

Protecting Inmates from Other Inmates   The typical fail-
ure-to-protect case involves an inmate *claim* for damages
that resulted from an assault by another inmate. If the inmate claims an intentional wrong, the injured inmate may
file the claim in federal or state court, or, in some places,
with a claims commission. Intentional failure to protect has
occurred in cases in which an inmate was attacked, officers
were called for help, and the officers failed to respond. A
number of courts have found such intentional failure to protect to be cruel and unusual punishment that gives rise to a
constitutional claim. This constitutional claim is an alternative to the injury claims that usually can be filed in state
courts.

As most situations do not concern an intentional failure
to protect, many cases claim that the official, officer, and/or
institution was negligent or grossly negligent in failing to
protect the inmate. These claims can be filed in what are
called "tort" suits in a state court. It should be noted that in
some states the defense of *sovereign immunity* may be available to correctional personnel and may make it impossible
for an inmate to sue personnel for their negligence. Still, inmates can usually sue for gross negligence or intentional acts
in state court, or for violation of constitutional rights in federal or state courts. (See also pp. 116–120).

An example of the reasonableness test applied in one
case of alleged negligence is as follows:

*During an orientation period in the state's reformatory, Inmate
Hall made sexual advances to Inmate Barnard. At his request,
Barnard was moved to a new cell. Hall assaulted Barnard in his*

new cell with a razor blade issued by the prison, causing Barnard extensive injuries. Barnard sued the state for failing to protect him from Hall's attack.

The court said the state would be liable where it could be shown that it had unreasonably exposed inmates to risks. However, in this case, the court found no proof that the state had failed to take reasonable care for Barnard's safety, and found against the inmate.[5]

Crowded jail conditions may be a factor in determining negligence; for example, in a recent case:

An inmate was raped twice in one night, once by three inmates, and then by one of the three who returned and raped him. The court, noting the overcrowding in the jail, found against the local sheriff in the amount of $50,000.[6]

Some courts, however, are reluctant to find negligence unless officials knew or should have known of a dangerous situation. In one case, the court found no negligence because the officials did not know of any hostility, tension, or personal problem between the inmates prior to the attack. Some states also require a specific "danger signal" to come to the attention of employees who then fail to take adequate precautions. Other courts have said that if a correctional employee "should have known of the danger," this may be enough to establish liability.

Note that liability for failure to protect may arise not only from assaults by inmates, but from assaults by other law enforcement personnel. For example, in one case:

A jailer was held liable along with a police officer for $12,000 when it was proved that the jailer watched the police officer, who had brought his prisoner to the jail, attack the prisoner. The jailer denied the inmate's request for medical care and it was not until the jailer's shift ended 10 hours later that the inmate was released to his wife. The court ruled that the jailer had a duty to protect prisoners at the jail and had allowed the beating to take place.[7]

One federal court stated the following standard for determining when correctional supervisors may be liable — the court did not look for knowledge of the specific danger by the administrators but rather said it must decide: "(1) whether there is a pervasive risk of harm to inmates from other prisoners and, if so (2) whether the officials are exercising reasonable care to prevent prisoners from intentionally harming others or from creating an unreasonable risk of harm."[8] The question will usually be: Did the official (e.g., the sheriff or warden) act reasonably in attempting to correct the situation? Correctional officials will not be held liable if they did all they could or if what happened was totally outside their control.

Problem 11

An inmate in a jail was awaiting admission to a state mental hospital. After being found guilty by a group of inmates of being an informer, he was tied to his cell by other inmates, burned with cigarettes, and homosexually raped. He suffered a fractured skull, ribs, jaw, a broken nose and dozens of abrasions. Evidence indicated that patrols of the cellblock did not take place during the attack, prisoners were not segregated, and cell locks were broken. Should the county be liable for the inmate's injuries?

Problem 12

Inmate Gomez reached for a gun and then was shot to death by Inmate Warren. Gomez' estate sued the state for creating a situation where inmates could carry guns despite prison regulations prohibiting them. Should the state be liable?

Protecting Inmates from Themselves   In a number of recent cases, the claim has been made that institutions must protect inmates, especially ones under the influence of drugs or alcohol or who are suffering from mental problems, from inflicting wounds on themselves, or committing suicide. The courts have differed in their judgments in these cases. Some courts have stated that suicide or suicide attempts are intentional acts by inmates and that inmates should not profit from their own wrongdoing. Other courts have placed liability on the correctional personnel based on the fact that an institution's duty of care should be even greater for those under the influence of drugs or alcohol or who are mentally ill.

For example, in one case:

Walker was being held in a city's "drunk tank." Another intoxicated person, Smith, was placed in the same holding cell and almost immediately, without reason, punched and kicked Walker. Another inmate, fearing for his own safety, pounded on the window of the tank and yelled for help, but the jailers did not respond. Smith, an ex-professional prizefighter and escapee from a mental institution, dropped Walker on his head. Walker never recovered and can no longer talk or reason. Walker was discovered sometime

*later when the jailer admitted another drunk. The officers in-
volved and the city were held negligent and ordered to pay
$200,000 in damages. The jailer testified that fighting was to be ex-
pected among the drunks and that the jail rules required hourly
physical inspections as well as constant television and audio
monitoring. The state court held that the failure to conduct such inspections and not responding to the inmate's call constituted negligence. The court also noted that the jailer owed Walker a higher
degree of care because of his intoxicated state.[9]*

Where institutions have no written standards for handling special prisoners such as alcohol abusers or the mentally ill, some courts have applied standards to them. For example:

*Parsons, an inmate with a history of mental illness, was being held
in a local jail. He was examined by a psychiatrist who advised that
Parsons should be admitted immediately to a mental hospital to
protect himself or others. This advice was not immediately followed, but Parsons was segregated in a cell with a small window
through which officers could observe him. He was allowed to retain his matches and cigarettes.*

*Parsons "heard voices," and set his mattress and hair on fire
to scare them away. He suffered severe burns, and had to have
five fingers amputated.*

*Parsons sued and the court awarded him $117,000 because of
the jail employees' negligence. The jail had no written standards
for guiding its personnel in handling prisoners with mental problems, and the court accepted expert testimony that hospitals in the
area followed specific procedures with someone in Parsons' condition. These included continuous observations, stripping of personal effects, dressing in a hospital gown with no cord, and placing the
patient in a room with no overhanging pipes.[10]*

Problem 13

A 17-year-old boy tried to escape from a youth facility and
was caught and transferred to an isolation cell. He attempted to commit suicide, was found shortly thereafter, but
had already suffered irreparable brain damage. The facility
had a behavior modification program whereby it punished a
group of inmates for the antics of one of its members.
Evidence showed that this system of punishment had driven
the boy to a state of extreme depression, which the court

found was foreseeable on the part of the state. The court also ruled that the conditions in the isolation cell amounted to cruel and unusual punishment. Because of these findings, should the state be liable to the boy and his parents?

Protection and Classification A key issue in situations where inmates are attacked by others or harm themselves may be the classification process within the institution. For example, if classification officers and/or officials knew or should have known that an inmate would be in danger if placed in a certain cellblock but still placed him there and he was killed, they might be found liable in a later lawsuit. Likewise, if it was known that an inmate was a suicide risk and was still classified and placed in an area where there was little observation or separation from dangerous instruments and the inmate stabbed himself, it is possible that a lawsuit and liability might result.

The following are standards developed by the American Correctional Association for Classification in Adult Local Detention Facilities but most would also be applicable to prisons as well:

CLASSIFICATION STANDARDS*

5335.   There is a written plan for classifying inmates in terms of level of custody required, housing assignment and participation in correctional programs.

5336.   The written plan for inmate classification specifies criteria and procedures for determining and changing the status of an inmate, including custody, transfers and major changes in programs.

5337.   The facility provides for the separate management of the following categories of inmates:
    Unsentenced females;
    Sentenced females;
    Unsentenced males;
    Sentenced males;
    Other classes of detainees, e.g., witnesses, civil prisoners;
    Community custody inmates, e.g., work releasees, weekenders, trustees;

---

* *Manual of Standards for Adult Local Detention Facilities*, Commission on Accreditation for Corrections, (1977), pp. 70-71.

Inmates with special problems, e.g., alcoholics, narcotics addicts, mentally disturbed persons, physically handicapped persons, persons with communicable diseases;
Inmates requiring disciplinary detention;
Inmates requiring administrative segregation;
and Juveniles.

5338.   Juveniles in custody are provided living quarters separate from adult inmates, although these may be in the same structure. (Detention — Essential, Holding — Essential)

5339.   Female inmates are provided living quarters separate from male inmates, although these may be in the same structure.

5340   Written policy and procedure specify an appeals process for classification decisions.

5341.   Written policy and procedure prohibit segregation of inmates by race, color, creed or national origin.

5342.   Male and female inmates have equal access to all programs and activities.

Problem 14 Classification Roleplay*

Assume that your institution has minimum security (dormitories), medium (cell blocks holding 4 persons each), maximum (single-person cells) and lockup (no interaction with other inmates), and that the following 4 people are sitting on a classification committee for new inmates:

■ Deputy Warden/Security

■ Deputy Warden/Treatment Programs

■ Institutional Nurse

■ Industrial Shopkeeper

One person should play each of the above persons at a classification committee meeting for a new inmate, George Beam, who may be present at the entire meeting or called for part of it by the committee. Each participant should represent the typical viewpoint of a person in his or her position and then come to a decision on Beam's classification.

---

* Adapted with permission from a roleplay developed by William Gimignani and Samuel Coleman, Trainers from the New Haven, Connecticut Corrections Center.

CASE HISTORY

Inmate Name	—George Beam #77805 Age 31
Sentenced	—2 years
Charge	—Carnal knowledge of female minor (has prior cases of this type)
Education	—Has I.Q. of 110. Two years of college, five years of Machine Shop experience. Has excellent employment record. (Inmates in maximum or lockup may not work in the vocational programs)
Social	—Reports state that Beam is a loner. His outward appearance is poor. During Beam's presentence status, he was harassed by peer inmates and at one point "snitched" on a fellow inmate. This snitching resulted in several inmates in this institution (they are in medium security) receiving strong disciplinary sentences.
Medical	—Beam has a medical history of epilepsy. He is on stabilization medication. He has made several suicide attempts. On his last attempt 3 months ago, first aid was necessary to revive him. Beam still shows signs of depression.

Escapes

In some instances, escapes occur due to negligence on the part of correctional employees. The inmate who escapes may commit a crime, and the victim of the crime may have a right to claim damages against the correctional employees who allowed the escape. For example:

An inmate who had escaped from a local jail fired a rifle through a window, injuring a woman inside. The female victim filed suit, and the court stated that the jail employees' negligence in not providing proper security in the institution could make them liable to compensate the woman for her damages. The principal issue in a situation like this is whether the injury occurring in the street was "a probable and foreseeable consequence" of the escape.[11]

Problem 15

A jail's rules require that all visitors be searched before entering the institution. Correctional Officer Willard, who is

working the gate, fails to search a visitor. It is later shown that a gun was brought into the institution by the visitor and given to an inmate who then was able to escape. During the escape, an innocent bystander was shot. Could Officer Willard be held liable for this act? What if Willard's supervisor or the jail manager knew Willard often neglected to search and they did nothing about it?

Fires

When a fire occurs in a correctional institution and inmates are injured or killed, it is likely that lawsuits will result. The usual claim in these cases is that negligence on the part of correctional employees was the reasonable and foreseeable cause *(proximate cause)* of the fire. This means it must be proven that what the correctional employees did or failed to do was the direct cause of the fire and the resulting injuries. In some cases, the local fire department may also be named a defendant. Common types of claims have been that the fire or injuries occurred because of:

■ poor conditions in the institution, such as improper ventilation or unsatisfactory means of exit from rooms of confinement;

■ careless storage of dangerous liquids;

■ improper training of correctional officers in fire fighting;

■ failure to make regular checks on prisoners;

■ incorrect stationing of officers; or

■ incomplete searches of inmates.

In fire cases, courts have not always decided against corrections employees. In many cases, it has been shown that the fire was caused by the negligence of an inmate, and was not the result of actions by corrections employees. In such cases, the employees have not been held liable.

Although a fire may never occur, it is best to prevent fires by examining the present conditions in a jail or prison.

CHECKLIST OF FIRE HAZARDS IN INSTITUTIONS*

1. Are the cells "fireproof" in design and construction?

2. Will the ventilation system vacate smoke, noxious gases and flames, or will it spread them?

3. Are mattresses and clothing which are provided fully fireproof, or only flame resistant? At what sustained temperature will they burn on their own? What tests have been conducted by the manufacturer or independent laboratories? Are mattresses promptly replaced when the covers are torn?

4. Are fire, smoke and gas sensors installed? Ionization chamber sensors are the first to respond, but cannot be used in furnace rooms and some laundry areas, where photoelectric eye smoke detectors must be used. Thermal (heat sensitive) detectors should be used in the facility's kitchen and lounge areas where smoking is allowed.

5. Is the alarm system independent of the institution's electrical system? Are there sufficient bells or horns in the institution and lights in the communications room?

6. Is there a master system for unlocking cellblocks in times of disaster? Are there sufficient extra keys for manual op-

---

* Adapted from *AELE Jail Administration Law Bulletin*, with permission. Sample issues may be obtained from AELE, 960 State National Bank Plaza, Evanston, Ill. 60201.

eration of cell doors for a mass exodus if the master system fails?

7. Are there sufficient escape routes? Are they well marked and compartmentalized or protected by sprinklers? Is there a battery-operated emergency lighting system in all corridors?

8. Are there enough standpipes, fire hoses and extinguishers? Are there several smoke masks or facial air packs? Does every correctional officer have a set of keys to fire suppression equipment cabinets?

9. Are officers taught fire suppression techniques? Have they rehearsed evacuations in regularly scheduled drills?

10. Is there a sufficient number of officers on duty to prevent or quickly detect fires? If not, have remote-controlled closed circuit televisions been installed?

11. Are frequent inspections made to insure that all equipment is properly functioning, that torn mattresses are not accessible to inmates, and that other problems are prevented?

Problem 16

A fire broke out in a cellblock injuring a number of inmates. A case was filed and at the trial it was shown that the correctional officer with the key to the main door of the cellblock was located in another building, 300 yards away. Who could be held liable for the injuries incurred?

False Imprisonment

Under the law in most states, and pursuant to the Federal Civil Rights Act, a person who is either falsely arrested or imprisoned has the right to file a suit for damages against the person or persons—or in some places, the government agency—that caused the false imprisonment. In many states, government officials, employees, and the state as a whole have been held *immune* from such lawsuits (i.e., not liable), but the trend in recent years, especially in federal cases, has been to do away with immunity and to hold corrections employees liable.

To win a false imprisonment suit against corrections employees, negligence or intentional action that resulted in the unfair imprisonment must be shown. Therefore, if it can be shown that a jailer mixed up the records of one inmate with another and that, consequently, an inmate was held for a longer period than legally permitted, the jailer may be held liable for damages. It should be noted that usually the present law allows corrections employees to raise the defense of "good faith," which means that if it can be demonstrated that the employee was acting reasonably and that the error took place outside his or her area of responsibility, then the employee will not be liable.

Problem 17

County Sheriff Brown received notice from the District Attorney's office that one *indictment* against Inmate Caulfield had been dismissed, but that another indictment against Caulfield was still in effect. The second notice was in error and Caulfield was improperly held for 36 days in the county jail. Who could be held liable for this error?

Medical Treatment

Under local, state, and federal law, correctional facilities are required to provide adequate medical treatment to inmates in their custody. Treatment must be provided for medical needs inmates had when they entered the institution or developed after they were there. The duty also includes care provided after an operation.[12]

Failure to provide treatment in accordance with general medical practices may constitute negligence and give rise to a case in a state court against the doctor, the correctional employees involved, and/or the institution or other governmental unit. Inmates may also be able to file a suit in federal court claiming a violation of a constitutional right, but the U.S. Supreme Court has ruled that more than negligence must be proved to establish that medical treatment supports a "cruel and unusual punishment" constitutional claim. The court has held that inmates may sue in federal court only if there was deliberate indifference to (their) serious medical needs." (See pp. 89–92)

A typical health care delivery system* includes an initial medical intake interview upon admittance, a physical by a doctor within a few days, sick call several days per week, weekly visits by a dentist, a psychiatrist and psy-

---

*See Appendix E.

chologist, transportation services to take immediate medical problems to the closest emergency room, and procedures to deal with mental, drug, and alcohol problems.

Some courts have held that if two doctors disagree as to appropriate medical care, and the warden follows the advice of one in providing a specific type of medical care, this action will be viewed as a medical difference of opinion, and the warden will not be held liable. However, this does not mean that the doctor could not be held liable if his or her advice was found to constitute "medical *malpractice*," and under certain conditions, the county or state government can also be held liable for a doctor's negligent action.

Many complaints from inmates concern the quality of health care, including such problems as long lines and waiting periods, foreign staff who can't understand and speak English very well, staff whose attitudes indicate a disrespect for inmates, inappropriate treatment, insufficient use of diagnostic tests and lack of feedback on tests. These problems are usually not serious enough to constitute "cruel and unusual punishment" or medical malpractice, especially if no specific harm can be shown, but some courts have begun to look more closely at quality-of-care issues and sometimes issue broad orders to improve medical practices.

May an inmate refuse medical treatment? May an inmate be forced to submit to a medical examination upon admission to an institution? The general rule for inmates is the same as that for persons on the outside: a doctor may not treat a competent adult until the treatment, its risks, alternatives and success rates have been explained to the patient and the patient's consent has been given. This rule is primarily based on the constitutional right to privacy.[13]

This general rule has some exceptions: (1) where the state can show some compelling state interest in administering the treatment; (2) where the adult is not competent; or (3) emergency situations where consent can be implied.

The state has a valid interest in stopping the spread of communicable diseases and for that reason could justify giving shots for contagious diseases despite a person's refusal.[14] The institution's duty to provide for the safety of its inmates could justify the requirement that all submit to physical examinations by a doctor upon admission.

As stated earlier in this chapter, the state has a duty to protect inmates from themselves. Correctional personnel, when confronted with an attempted suicide victim, do not have to allow the inmate to die if he or she refuses medical treatment. In some cases, the courts have permitted institutions to give forced treatment on the grounds that the refusing victim is not mentally competent and/or the giving of medical treatment in such a case is sufficiently related to the security needs of the institution.[15] Also, in emergency situations, such as when an inmate is unconscious, treatment may be given.[16]

Problem 18

An inmate's glasses were broken during a scuffle at which he was an innocent bystander. Despite repeated requests, including a letter to the warden, the inmate was not examined for three months, at which time the physician found the inmate's vision to have been permanently impaired. Who could be held liable for this injury?

Problem 19

Some people have argued that because inmates are in the custody of the government, when they are hurt by anyone, whether it be another inmate or a correctional officer, they should receive compensation to make up for this loss. This is similar to workers' compensation plans for employees, and might be paid with insurance carried by the jail or prison.

a. What would be the arguments against this?

b. Would this be better than the present system of compensating injuries? Explain.

c. If this system awarded an inmate a set amount of money, e.g., $5,000 in a medical malpractice case, could inmates argue they were being treated unfairly and discriminated against?

INJURIES AND LOSSES TO CORRECTIONAL PERSONNEL

As an employee of a governmental unit, the correctional employee is likely to be the *beneficiary* of certain types of insurance policies covering medical costs and paying benefits upon the employee's death (life insurance). In addition to these benefits, employees may also be the beneficiaries of certain other types of insurance.

Life Insurance

Under regulations implemented by the U. S. Department of Justice in accord with the Public Safety Officers' Act of 1976, an officer's family may be eligible to receive $50,000 if he or she is killed in the line of duty, if the death is the direct result of an injury sustained while working, and if the deceased was a "law enforcement officer" as that phrase is defined in state statutes or the applicable job description.

a. *"Line of Duty."* The Justice Department defines "line of duty" as follows: "Any action which an officer is obligated or authorized by rule, regulation, condition of employment or service or law to perform, including those social, ceremonial or athletic functions to which he is assigned, or for which he is compensated, by the public agency he serves." Note that this definition does include females and does *not* require that employees be engaged in hazardous duty nor does it require that they be engaged directly in crime control.

b. *"Cause of Death."* As noted above, for coverage under the act, the death must have been the result of an injury sustained on the job. An "injury" is defined as: "A traumatic event, caused by extensive force, including injuries inflicted by bullets, explosives, sharp instruments, blunt objects or other physical blows, chemicals, electricity, climatic conditions, infectious disease and bacteria, but not those caused by stress and strain." Note that coverage is in effect even if the injury was deliberately inflicted on the officer by a third person.

c. *"Law Enforcement Officer."* A "law enforcement officer" is defined as any person who is "involved in crime and deliquency control or reduction, or enforcement of the criminal laws." The dead person need *not* have had the authority to enforce all criminal laws.

Workers' Compensation

As employees, correctional personnel may be covered under a workers' compensation policy. As a general rule, workers' compensation statutes have the following effect: If employees are injured (not killed) on the job, there is a duty to pay a prescribed amount of money. Payments are usually made under an insurance policy purchased by the employer. The favorable part of such a system is that employees are paid compensation for the injury whether or not the employer was at fault. In other words, negligence by the employer need not be proven. If an employee is injured while working and the employee is covered under workers' compensation, a certain amount of money will be paid.

On the other hand, in most jurisdictions the existence of workers' compensation makes it impossible to sue the employer. In other words, if the employee is injured on the job, the employee may apply only for workers' compensation even if the prescribed payments are far less than what the employee might recover from the court if he or she sued the employer. Some states give greater protection, covering occupational diseases or death that result from activities in the course of employment.

Compensation for Property Losses

Assume an inmate assaults a correctional employee and breaks her glasses. Will the state pay for a new pair of glasses? States have different answers to this question. Many times there is a commission or board that has the authority to pay money to replace such items up to a certain dollar amount. Some states cover this type of loss in their workers' compensation policy. Other institutions may just pay for the item out of supplies or petty cash. The employee may also be able to sue the inmate in a small claims type court. Other states have a policy that the job assumes certain risks and that there is no *remedy* for such losses.

RIGHT TO BE FREE FROM JOB DISCRIMINATION

Under federal law, employers of 15 or more persons (with certain exceptions) are prohibited from discriminating on the basis of race, color, religion, sex, or national origin. Discrimination is banned in hiring, firing, paying, classifying, training, apprenticing, referring for employment and in union membership.

An "employer" includes state and local governments and governmental agencies (except in the District of Columbia). Since the state Department of Corrections is a state agency, it is an employer that may not discriminate under the federal law. Likewise, a local jail will be subject to this law if it has 15 or more employees.

If a correctional officer believes that his or her employer has discriminated on any of the grounds listed above, the officer must file a charge with the Equal Employment Opportunity Commission. A suit in federal court cannot be brought until the charge has been filed and the EEOC has acted or has issued a "letter to sue."

However, most states also have their own fair employment practices agencies to protect their citizens from discrimination. Generally, a discrimination charge must first be filed with the state agency and then with the EEOC. There are strict time limits for filing that must be met.

The state statute may prohibit discrimination in employment for reasons in addition to race, color, sex, religion and national origin. For example, a state law may also prohibit discrimination on the basis of age, marital status, political affiliation, sexual orientation, physical handicap, etc.

Why are some regulations or acts by employers permitted under the law even though they clearly treat persons differently based on factors prohibited by the law? Why, for instance, did the Supreme Court in 1976 say that the Alabama Department of Corrections could make a rule keeping female correctional officers out of "contact positions" with male inmates?[17]

The answer is that certain acts which ordinarily constitute discrimination fall within the *exceptions* to the law. The main exceptions to the federal law are (1) *bona fide occupational qualification* or BFOQ, (2) national security, and (3) results of a professionally developed ability test.

The BFOQ applies only to discrimination based on sex, religion and national origin (not to race and color) where the discrimination is reasonably necessary for the normal operation of that business. For instance, if a Kosher meat processor had a practice of hiring only Jews to kill the livestock, this would appear to be employment discrimination based on religion. The employer might admit only that Jews were being hired, but would argue that being Jewish was a BFOQ for a Kosher meat processor and was reasonably necessary to the normal operation of the business.

GEE!!
SURE WISH I WERE
A GUY*

I BECOME
A PRISON
GUARD

BE A MAN WHO LIKES TO GUARD PEOPLE
VISIT YOUR **STATE CORRECTIONAL FACILITY**
RECRUITING STATION
*AND WOMAN, TOO

The Alabama example mentioned above was a unique situation in which the court found that being a male was a BFOQ for contact positions in this maximum security prison. The court found that male sex offenders were distributed throughout the population and that women officers were likely to be raped, thus creating an even worse atmosphere.

The *national security exception* permits an employer to refuse to employ a person who is unable to obtain a security clearance if the clearance is required in the "interest of the national security of the U.S."

Another exception permits an employer to refuse to hire a person based on the results of a professionally developed ability test, so long as the test is not designed to discriminate.

The requirement that employers not discriminate on the basis of sex has come into conflict in some cases with the inmates' right to privacy. Usually this involves situations where correctional officers of one sex are working in areas where they observe inmates of the opposite sex undressing, using the toilets or being strip searched. Inmates have claimed that such exposure is humiliating and degrading and in violation of their right to privacy.

What can the Department of Corrections or employer do — should it refuse to hire females for male institutions and males for female institutions? Although the Supreme Court has not yet made a ruling, lower courts have ruled on this question in several institutions. The courts have attempted to balance the inmates' right to privacy with the equal employment rights of the officers, and most decisions on this issue have granted inmates their right to privacy without completely denying employment to officers of the opposite sex.[18] The courts have done this by ordering selective work assignments for officers of the opposite sex so they are not in areas during times that the inmates' privacy might be invaded.

A few courts have upheld the decision not to hire persons of the opposite sex.

The Case of the Male Who Applied to be a Female Officer

Robert Carey applied for the female position of correctional officer because it had a higher age limit for applicants than the comparable male position, and he had already passed that limit. After he was not selected, he filed a sex discrimination suit. The female position required observing and guarding female prisoners, conducting body searches, and being present at baths or showers and medical examinations.

The court, after looking at the interest of the institution in maintaining security and the inmates' need for privacy in the intimate aspects of their lives, upheld the decision not to hire the male officer.[19]

How do people prove that illegal discrimination has been practiced against them? For example, a correctional officer believes he did not get a promotion to lieutenant because he is black. It is almost impossible to get those who made the promotion to admit that their decision was due to discrimination. Therefore, the courts permit the use of statistics to prove that discrimination has occurred. The black officer, or his attorney, may be able to obtain statistics from the officer's performance evaluation to determine whether whites with worse records were being promoted or whether black and white officers as groups receive different rates of promotion based on their performance evaluations.

If the court finds discrimination, what remedies are available? The federal court may do any of several things. It may *enjoin*, that is, order the employer to stop doing certain acts, or to take some action such as reinstating or upgrading the employee, or providing retroactive pay increases. The court may also award damages and/or grant attorney fees to the winning party.

In a recent case, the judge awarded attorney fees to the government, thus requiring the employee who was not successful in proving discrimination to pay the government for the costs of defending the case. The court decided that the employee's claim was not made in good faith, finding that her lawsuit was "the culmination of a long series of intentionally vindictive and abusive actions taken to harass her supervisors."

Problem 20

a. Diane Rawlinson is refused employment as a correctional officer because she fails to meet the 120-pound weight and 5-foot-2-inch height requirements. Do you think Diane would win if she argued that she was discriminated against on the basis of her sex? What proof would be helpful to show the court in order to get a decision in her favor?

b. In a state correctional institution, the Department of Corrections adopted a regulation that any correctional officer who wanted to be promoted to lieutenant had to pass a certain personality test. An Hispanic correctional officer is denied a promotion because he has not been able to pass such a test. If he is able to show that 3 percent of all Hispanic people pass this personality test while 40 percent of all non-minorities pass, does he have a valid discrimination claim? What additional factor might your answer depend on?

c. The administrator of a jail for male inmates has hired male and female officers. In an attempt to provide for the inmates' right to privacy, the administrator has made selective work assignments so that females only work the guard tower and monitor the video screens at the control center. A male officer believes that the women have the easy jobs and that the men have to do all the difficult jobs. Does he have a valid claim of job discrimination?

EMPLOYEE UNIONS

Under the Constitution's freedom of association clause, employees in both the public and private sectors have the right to join or to refrain from joining unions. This right extends to law enforcement personnel and correctional officers, even if the organization advocates illegal strikes.[20]

Collective bargaining is a form of negotiation giving employees the opportunity to meet and set wages and other conditions of employment with their employer. For it to be effective, both parties must deal with each other in an open and fair manner with the goal of achieving a workable agreement. Some collective bargaining agreements call for outside *mediators* or *arbitrators*. In some cases, if both sides can't agree, an arbitrator will make a binding decision. Others do not allow binding agreements but rather have "meet and confer" arrangements. Though non-governmental employees have a right to bargain collectively under the National Labor Relations Act, public employees must look to their state laws to determine if collective bargaining is permitted. About one-half of the states allow government employees to do this but only about one-third of state correctional agencies have signed collective bargaining agreements with one type of employee organization or another.

Unions and collective bargaining among correctional personnel are controversial issues, especially since corrections traditionally has been organized more on the military than the industrial model. Therefore, some believe unionization can undermine the necessary order, discipline and control required for work in corrections. Others believe that correctional personnel should be able to bargain for higher wages, employee safety, benefits and even a voice in decisions regarding inmate programs and prison policy. This last request by some corrections unions may raise particular problems because it may diminish the power of corrections administrators or even the state legislature to make policy decisions for corrections.

Unless a state requires collective bargaining with unions or unless there is a collective bargaining agreement, correctional administrators and state officials are not required to recognize or deal with unions.

Correctional employees cannot be required to be full members of unions, but if the state recognizes a union as the only bargaining agent for employees, the employees can be required to pay union dues. Some corrections unions allow administrators and supervisors to join local unions along with correctional officers while others do not. The courts are split as to whether restricting union membership in this way is legal. Therefore, state law will have to be checked on this issue. However, if higher ranking officers are not allowed to join, they can form their own union.

A controversial issue involving unions is whether there should be a right to strike. In most states, public employees do not have this right and can be arrested for such action; law enforcement personnel are almost always specifically forbidden to strike.

Problem 21

Place your opinion on the scale following the statement: "Every state should have a law allowing correctional employee unions and collective bargaining."

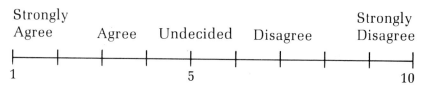

Strongly
Agree   Agree   Undecided   Disagree   Strongly
Disagree

1   5   10

a. What are the reasons for your opinion?

b. If correctional officers do unionize, can the union help them with the following complaints or problems? If so, how?

     1. Assaults on officers;

     2. Officer coverage during inmate transfers;

     3. Wages;

     4. Life insurance;

     5. The number of positions to be filled by females;

     6. The number of civilian and non-civilian positions;

     7. Training programs and college benefits;

   8. Overtime pay;

   9. Uniform allowances;

   10. Grievance procedures; or

   11. Inmate educational programs.

c. Do you think a correctional officer union should share in decision-making in the areas listed above? Explain.

References

1. Davidson v. Dixon, 386 F.Supp. 482 (D.Del. 1974).

2. Green v. Hawkins, U.S.Dist.Ct. (D.Md. 1977).

3. ACA Correctional Law Project. See Appendix D.

4. Anonymous v. District of Columbia, D.C. Sup. Ct. (1977).

5. Barnard v. State, 265 N.W.2d 620 (Iowa 1978).

6. Anonymous v. Swinson, U.S.Dist.Ct. (W.D.Va.1976).

7. Harris v. Chanclor, 537 F.2d 203 (5th Cir. 1976).

8. Woodhous v. Virginia, 487 F.2d 889 (4th Cir. 1973).

9. Daniels v. Andersen, 195 Neb. 95, 237 N.W.2d 397 (1975).

10. Porter v. County of Cook, 42 Ill.App.3d 287, 355 N.E.2d 561 (1976).

11. Walker v. Interstate Fire and Casualty, 334 So.2d 714 (La.App.1976).

12. West v. Keve, 571 F.2d 158 (3rd Cir. 1978).

13. Robert Ellis Smith, *Privacy*, (New York: Anchor Press/Doubleday, 1979).

14. Jacobson v. Mass., 197 U.S. 11, 25 S.Ct. 358 (1905), State ex rel. Holcolm v. Armstrong, 39 Wash.2d 860, 239 P.2d 545 (1952).

15. William Paul Isele, "Jail Inmate's Right to Refuse Medical Treatment," *Americans for Effective Law Enforcement*, Vol. 78-9:14.

16. Owens v. Alldridge, 311 F.Supp. 667 (W.D.Okl.1970).

17. Dothard v. Rawlinson, 433 U.S. 321, 97 S.Ct. 2720 (1977).

18. Susan L. Reisner, "Balancing Inmates' Right to Privacy with Equal Employment for Prison Guards," *Women's Rights Law Reporter*, 4, No. 4 (1978), p. 227.

19. Carey v. N.Y. State H.R. Appeal Bd., 402 N.Y.S.2d 207 (A.D.1978). See also, City of Philadelphia v. Pennsylvania H.R. Comm., 300 A.2d 97 (1973).

20. Police Officers Guild, National Association of Police Officers v. Washington, 369 F.Supp. 543 (D.D.C.1973).

three
PRISONERS' RIGHTS

Problem 22

The Constitution gives certain fundamental rights to each citizen. These include freedom of speech, freedom from unreasonable searches and seizures, privacy, and freedom of association. When a person enters a jail or prison, these rights are limited by the needs and nature of the institution.

a. Give your reasons for and against limiting these rights in a correctional institution.

In the past, courts were reluctant to interfere with the day-to-day operation of correctional institutions. Early federal court decisions frequently expressed the general policy of leaving prison administration solely to correctional officials. In more recent years, many courts changed their "hands off" policy and began to listen to cases brought by inmates who claimed their constitutional rights had been violated. However, this trend of courts being active in the corrections area may be changing. For example, note the words of Justice William Rehnquist in the recent Supreme Court case of *Bell v. Wolfish:*[1]

> The deplorable conditions and draconian restrictions of some of our Nation's prisons are too well known to require recounting here, and the federal courts rightly have condemned these sordid aspects of our prison systems. But many of these same courts have, in the name of the Constitution, become increasingly enmeshed in the minutiae of prison operations. Judges, after all, are human. They, no less than others in our society, have a natural tendency to believe that their individual solutions to often intractable problems are better and more workable than those of the persons who are actually charged with and trained in the running of the particular institution under examination.[2]

In discussing "rights" of prisoners in this chapter, we are generally referring to rights which come from the U.S. Constitution. How the Constitution applies to jails and prisons has been determined principally by the Supreme Court and other federal courts. However, it should be remembered that state and local laws, cases from state courts, and regulations of each individual Department of Corrections, prison and/or jail also define such "rights." In some cases, local and state regulations have provided inmates with greater rights than the courts or the Constitution guarantee. Always check these regulations, because violations of rules or regulations can also form grounds for a lawsuit.

Generally, constitutional rights are more restricted in institutions than on the outside, but it is inaccurate to state that rights do not exist when a person is *incarcerated.* As now Supreme Court Justice Harry Blackmun said in one of his Circuit Court opinions: "Fundamental rights follow the prisoner through the walls which incarcerate him, but always with appropriate limitations."

In deciding how much a right should be limited, the courts often use what is called "the *balancing test.*" This means that the court balances the importance of protecting the individual's rights against the importance of restricting them. For example, in a free speech case the courts look at the need for allowing an inmate to say something and weigh it against the danger to security in the institution if the speech is made. The courts will grant prison and jail administrators a great deal of latitude in deciding what limits are properly placed on inmates' rights. However, the courts will act to protect constitutional rights when the institutions have failed to provide the constitutional guarantees. Courts look for the following when an inmate complains of constitutional rights' violations:

■ whether or not the activity is actually protected by the Constitution;

■ what danger(s) is (are) involved in the institutions (specific dangers which are backed up by specific explanations of the connection between the alleged danger and the activity);

■ what governmental interest is at stake; and

■ whether the governmental interest at stake is a proper one for the particular institution involved.

The court will then balance the right of the inmate with the government's interest.

RIGHTS OF PRETRIAL DETAINEES

A further and more recent development in inmate rights is the issue of whether those who are in jail awaiting trial but have not yet been *convicted* (called "*pretrial detainees*") should be provided greater rights than those who have already been convicted.

Why should pretrial detainees have greater rights? The answer sometimes given is that these inmates are still presumed innocent and are in jail only to ensure their appearance in court, not to be punished or rehabilitated. The courts have acknowledged that making sure the defendant appears at trial requires that jails be secure and orderly managed. Most pretrial detainees are in jail solely because they could not produce the money *bond* placed on them. If they had the money, most pretrial detainees would be on the street, enjoying the much fuller protection of the Constitution accorded to ordinary citizens.

In the past, the constitutional rights of prisoners have been restricted due to the prison's interest in security, order, rehabilitation and punishment. Until recently, most prisoners' rights cases have been applied to jails and prisons without drawing a distinction between them. This practice has been justifiable to the extent that most jails house a mix of both categories of inmates.

In *Bell v. Wolfish*, the U.S. Supreme Court decided that restrictions on the rights of pretrial detainees will be judged for their constitutionality under a "punishment" test.[3] The court ruled that the due process clause of the Fifth Amendment to the Constitution prohibits restrictions on pretrial detainees that amount to punishment. "A sentenced inmate, on the other hand, may be punished, although that punishment may not be 'cruel and unusual' under the Eighth Amendment."[4]

This case changes the law as established by several federal courts, which had decided that restrictions on the right of pretrial detainees could only be justified by a "compelling necessity standard."[5] This was clearly a difficult justification for correctional officials to make. For example, the federal district court and the Second Circuit Court of Appeals in the *Wolfish* case had found that double-bunking of inmates in cells designed for one person failed to meet the compelling necessity test and was therefore unconstitutional.[6] The Supreme Court reversed this finding because it did not believe double-bunking was "punishment" for pretrial inmates who stayed in the jail for less than 60 days.[7] Instead, the court found it was merely a proper response by correctional officials to overcrowding.

How jail personnel are to decide what amounts to punishment for pretrial detainees is a very difficult problem. The Supreme Court listed the following factors as guideposts in determining whether actions by officials are punishment of pretrial detainees:[8]

■ Whether the action involves an affirmative disability or restraint;

■ Whether historically the action was regarded as punishment;

■ Whether the action comes into play only on a finding of knowledge;

■ Whether the action will promote the traditional aims of punishment—retribution and deterrence;

■ Whether there is another rational purpose for the action besides punishment; or

■ Whether this other purpose for the restriction is excessive.

In summary, the Supreme Court said that actions will constitute punishment: (1) if there is an expressed intent on the part of correctional officials to punish; (2) if there is no rational connection between the rule or restriction and the purpose for the rule other than punishment (e.g., security reasons); or (3) where that other purpose is excessive in relation to the nonpunitive reason given for the rule.

It will take many court cases to hammer out what specific rules and policies constitute punishment. The best that can be said now is that future court decisions will have to be guided by this new Supreme Court standard, which appears to give correctional officials greater leeway than before in restricting the freedoms of pretrial detainees. However, it should be noted that the *Wolfish* case specifically dealt with a new correctional institution where inmates usually were released within 60 days. Therefore, some correctional law experts believe that when courts are faced with older type jails in future cases, they may reach very different results.

The Supreme Court did not specifically spell out whether pretrial detainees must be provided greater rights than convicted inmates but it did say that detainees had "at least the same rights as those who had been convicted."[9] Future cases will have to determine when or if such rights are ever different. However it should be noted that several lower federal courts citing the *Wolfish* case, have already granted pretrial detainees greater constitutional protections than convicted prisoners.

Problem 23

Should pretrial detainees be provided different rights than convicted inmates? Why or why not?

The First Amendment: *"Congress shall make no law respecting an establishment of religion, or prohibiting the free exercise thereof; or abridging the freedom of speech, or of the press; or the right of the people peaceably to assemble, and to petition the Government for a redress of grievances."*

RIGHTS TO FREEDOM OF SPEECH, RELIGION ASSOCIATION AND THE PRESS

Freedom of Speech

Speech can be defined as the communication of thoughts and ideas. This may include an inmate talking to another inmate, writing a letter to a friend, publishing a newsletter, or wearing an armband as a symbolic act.

Identify what dangers to and interests of correctional institutions are involved in limiting the various activities protected by the First Amendment. For example:

Activity	Danger	Government Interest in Limiting Activity
Talking to another inmate	Make escape plans, plan other crimes, create riot or disturbance	Security, order, rehabilitation
Sending outgoing mail to friend	Escape plan, contact with bad types, unauthorized entry by others	Security, rehabilitation
Receiving mail from persons with attorney address	Imposter sending escape plans, *contraband*, too much mail	Security, rehabilitation, administrative convenience

In trying to determine when free speech under the First Amendment can be restricted, the U.S. Supreme Court has used a number of different tests. One of the oldest tests is called the *clear and present danger* test. In this test, the court looks at the circumstances under which the words were used and decides whether the speech would create a "clear and present danger" of causing harm to another person or society.

Another test in free speech cases is the balancing test in which the court looks at the circumstances involved and attempts to balance the interests of society against the interests of the individual in expressing his or her ideas.

There are also certain types of speech that are not protected by the First Amendment. For example, a person's speech may not be expressed in a manner that will incite others to riot or violence. The speech cannot be obscene, nor can it be "abusive, threatening" or what the court has called "fighting words." Moreover, the speech cannot be slanderous (speaking false statements that damage another's reputation).

The Case of Procunier v. Martinez

In a 1974 U.S. Supreme Court case, inmates complained that California prison rules on mail violated their First Amendment rights. These rules prohibited sending letters that "unduly complain" or "magnify grievances", express "inflammatory political, racial or religious or other views", or "pertain to criminal activity; are lewd, obscene, or defamatory; contain foreign matter, or are otherwise inappropriate."

Correctional officials claimed that censorship of inmate mail that "magnified grievances or unduly complained" was a precaution against the danger of riots and furthered inmate rehabilitation. However, correctional officials could not explain how outgoing mail containing such statements could lead to riots or could harm inmate rehabilitation. The court went on to find that these rules did not further legitimate institutional interests of security, rehabilitation or the preservation of internal order and discipline, but were overbroad and vague and had as their sole purpose the suppression of expression and were, therefore, invalid.[10]

Courts also consider to whom the mail is being sent in determining the kinds of restrictions that will be enforced. Courts agree that mail to and from lawyers and courts should not be censored. The Sixth Amendment right of access to counsel and the courts, as well as the First Amendment right of free speech, apply to this category of mail.

In *Wolff v. McDonnell*, a 1974 Supreme Court case, the court said that mail to convicted inmates, even from an attorney, could be opened to inspect for contraband. The court went on to say that attorney mail should only be opened in the inmates' presence because officials would then be less likely to read the mail.[11]

Other than the general standard stated in *Procunier* that "the regulation must further an important or substantial government issue unrelated to suppression of free speech," the U.S. Supreme Court has not dealt with such issues as with whom, other than attorneys and courts, inmates have a right to correspond. However, lower courts have examined specific mail regulations and the institution's reasons for them, and sometimes ruled they violated the First Amendment. For example, in one case, little or no restriction was allowed regarding mail to the news media. The court ruled such mail to be similar to attorney mail. A court has struck down rules that required officials to approve names on an inmate's mailing list and restricted the number of persons on the list and the overall number of letters sent. This same court required that postage be provided an indigent inmate for letters to attorneys and the media and five others per week.[12]

Another question regarding free speech is the censorship of publications that can be received by or distributed to inmates. One district court allowed the distribution of *Fortune News*, which is published by the Fortune Society "to create public awareness of the prison systems." The court said the prison officials needed to show a "compelling state interest" to justify banning the newsletter or a "clear and present danger to prison discipline or security." Other courts, however, have only required officials to show that the censored material would have a detrimental effect on a legitimate government interest.[13]

In *Bell v. Wolfish*, the U.S. Supreme Court also upheld a "publisher only" rule for pretrial detainees who spent a maximum of 60 days in jail. This rule allowed correctional officials, who were concerned about serious security and administrative problems, to require that hardcover books be received by inmates only when they were mailed directly from bookstores, publishers, and book clubs.[14]

Problem 24

Does your First Amendment right to free speech protect you if:

a.   You call your friend on the telephone and say you think the President is a bum? Can you be convicted of a crime for this? What if you stand on a park bench and do this? What if you block an intersection and do it?

b.   You keep a diary at home and write that the city government is racist and should be overthrown. What if you said the same things to a crowd on a street corner, or on television? Can you be arrested?

c.   You wear a black arm band to school signifying your protest of a war and arguments take place. Can you be suspended or expelled?

d.   You receive a communist publication at home which calls for the overthrow of all capitalist countries. Can the government stop this or arrest you?

Problem 25 - Freedom of Speech Roleplay

Martin Sostre, while an inmate in Green Haven Prison in New York, violated prison rules and was placed in solitary confinement. Shortly after his release, he was deprived of the use of the prison exercise yard and the privilege of attending movies because he had "inflammatory racial literature" in his cell. The literature consisted of articles written by Sostre on paper properly in his possession. Most of the articles were extracts from magazines and newsletters Sostre was permitted to have in his cell. The literature included quotations from Mao Tse Tung; poetry of another inmate; the names of officers, party program and rules of conduct of the Black Panther Party; officers and the oath of allegiance of the Republic of New Africa; a "program" for Black Student Unions; the poem "If We Must Die" by Claude McKay, and a self-written article "Revolutionary Thoughts."

a.   Was the punishment imposed on Sostre for putting his thoughts on paper a violation of his First Amendment rights?

b.   Should he have been able to keep his writings?

c.   Can Sostre hand them out to other inmates?

Sostre had initially filed a Section 1983 Civil Rights claim alleging that the warden's actions in punishing him for his writings violated his First Amendment rights. This situation should be role-played as a *mock* hearing of legal arguments at a trial. Those playing attorneys should base their arguments on the facts above and law described in this section. Both sides agree to these facts.

    A panel of three judges is needed to hear the arguments, to question the attorneys, and to decide (majority wins) which position is correct on each of the three questions. Two attorneys will represent and argue the state's position on each of the above three questions, and two attorneys will argue the inmate's position.

Problem 26

Discuss whether an inmate's First Amendment rights are violated in the following situations:

a.   Can an inmate be stopped from verbally criticizing the way a jail is run? Does it make a difference if he actively seeks out other inmates to discuss his views?

b.   A prison has a rule forbidding the possession of obscene materials. An inmate has a copy of what Officer Dean considers to be an obscene homosexually oriented magazine. Can the officer take it away? Can the officer take *Playboy* or *Hustler* away?

c.   A convicted inmate is reading a letter from the outside. Can correctional personnel in the institution take it and read it, or censor it before the inmate receives it?

Freedom of Religion

The First Amendment prevents the government from either establishing religion or restricting its free exercise. Therefore, the state cannot tell people what church to go to (this would be "establishment") or tell them they cannot go to church at all (this would be "restricting free exercise"). As the Supreme Court has said, there is supposed to be a "wall of separation between church and state" in our country.

Freedom of religion may sometimes be restricted outside correctional institutions, as when it conflicts with a serious governmental interest. For example, the Mormon religion allowed men to have more than one wife and state law made this a crime. The U.S. Supreme Court ruled such marriages could be outlawed because the government's interest in preserving the American family was more important than this religious practice.

Religious belief or thought cannot be restricted in a correctional institution but religious practice may be curtailed when it affects security within the institution or is too much of a burden on the prison administration.

During the 1960s, many cases were brought by Black Muslims concerning their right to practice religion in prison. Recent decisions have held that Black Muslims should be permitted to have congregational services, a minister, and religious literature. The courts have generally said that prison officials should create rules and regulations that, as much as possible, permit religious groups what they want, provided prison security is protected.

An interesting case arose in a federal prison where a group of inmates organized their own religion and called it "The Church of the New Song." A court held that prison of-

ficials must allow this if it was really a religious group and not a cover-up for some other purpose.[15] In deciding whether a religion is truly a religion, courts have used such standards as looking at its history, age, whether it has characteristics similar to other religions and how sincere the followers appear to be.

This "Church of the New Song" has subsequently spread to other prisons. A federal district court in Texas found that despite a belief in a supreme being, the political and non-religious tone of its services showed that the church was not a religion but rather a masquerade designed to obtain First Amendment protection for acts that would otherwise be unlawful in prison. The court said that even if it were a religion, prison officials would have the right to deny an inmate's demand to have all the rights of a prison chaplain. This "chaplain" inmate was classified as an escape artist and dangerous felon. The right to exercise of religion can be restricted by a compelling state interest—here, the maintenance of prison discipline.[16]

Courts differ on how much religious practice may be restricted. In one case, the court said that it was permissible to forbid dangerous prisoners from attending religious services. However, the trend in recent cases has been toward allowing greater exercise of religious freedom unless it places an unreasonable burden on the institution's administration.

One area of contention has been religious diets. Some courts have held that a prison need not provide special religious dietary foods, particularly where prison policies provide inmates with nutritionally adequate diets by substituting more of one menu item for the prohibited food.[17]

However, similar cases brought by jail inmates have found the courts more obliging to requests for religious diets. One court required reduced use of pork in meal preparation at a jail to allow a Black Muslim a pork-free diet. In *Miller v. Carson*, a federal court of appeals found that restrictions on the religious activities of pretrial detainees in a Florida jail violated the freedom of religion clause. Inmates were not provided any special dietary considerations, and, because the sheriff raised hogs, pork was served or used as a seasoning in all meals.[18]

In a Michigan jail, pretrial detainees with bonds of $5,000 or more were not allowed to attend chapel while those with less than $5,000 bonds were allowed to attend. The federal district court found this restriction to be arbitrary and a denial of the right of free exercise of religion.[19]

Another freedom of religion issue occurs when inmates are transferred as a penalty for their religious beliefs. A California court held this a violation of the First Amendment.[20]

Problem 27

Are a person's First Amendment rights violated in the following situations:

a. Can you be forced to salute the U.S. flag in school if your religion forbids this?

b. Can a state pass a law forbidding you to read Black Muslim religious writing because it is considered racist?

c. A Buddhist inmate wants to use the chapel and write a letter to his religious advisor. Can he be prevented from doing so? If an institution pays for Catholic and Protestant chaplains, must it also hire a Buddhist one?

d. A prison has a rule against wearing medals of any kind. Can a Muslim inmate wear a religious medal?

e. An inmate who has been placed in segregation wants to go to the chapel. Can he be prevented from doing so?

Problem 28

Are there any benefits to the institution or society if inmates are allowed to practice their religion in an institution? If yes, list them.

Problem 29

Five inmates get together and declare themselves to be the Church of the New Faith. They say prayers to their God and establish ten pages of rules they must practice. Decide if each of the following items they request must be provided:

a. their own paid chaplain because the institution pays for a Catholic and a Protestant chaplain;

b. pizza to have as communion in their services;

c. the right to use the chapel for a service on Sunday just as other religions do;

d. a special service for the entire prison population of 500 in the yard;

e. the right to circulate their rules to members; or

f. complete privacy from staff during their services.

Freedom of Association: Visitation and Prisoner Unions

Visitation Restrictions on inmate visitation are discussed in the context of the First Amendment's freedom of association or under the prohibition of cruel and unusual punishment.[21] Whether visitation by family and friends is a right or a privilege has not yet been decided by the Supreme Court.

Several federal courts have found that visitation for pretrial detainees is a right. A few courts have gone so far as to require contact visits as a matter of right to the pretrial detainee.[22]

A Michigan federal court ordered that pretrial detainees be allowed to visit with whomever they pleased, especially with family members, for a substantial period each week. This court also held that the right to contact visits could be denied only to those inmates identified as security

risks.[23] What effect the recent Supreme Court case on pre-trial detainees will have on this issue remains to be seen.[24]

Although it is not exactly clear how much visitation must be provided to inmates or pretrial detainees, the following rules have been struck down as too restrictive:

1. A regulation permitting a pretrial detainee one visit with family members for no more than 15 minutes a week.[25]

2. A regulation allowing inmates one visit during the week with two of five persons on the inmate's approved list.[26]

Lawsuits demanding *conjugal visits* as a right have not been successful and very few institutions allow this.

Privacy during visitation has been raised in a number of cases but the courts have always ruled that inmates have no absolute right to privacy. The one instance where inmates appear to have the right not to be monitored by correctional personnel is when the visits are by attorneys.

Monitoring inmates' phone calls by use of an extension phone or other device may violate federal and/or state law. In one recent case, the federal law protecting people against willful interception of telephone calls (Title III of the Omnibus Crime Control and Safe Streets Act of 1968, § § 2510–2520.) was applied to correctional officials' eavesdropping on an inmate's phone call. The inmates had not been notified that calls were monitored and no departmental regulations permitted it. The usual procedure for monitoring calls in this prison was for an officer to be stationed near enough to the phone to hear the conversation. A single incident of eavesdropping through a phone extension was not justifiable within the usual course of business exception and, therefore, correctional officials were required to pay damages of $100 a day or $1,000, whichever was greater, punitive damages, and reasonable attorney's fees. *Campiti v. Walonis*, 611 F. 2d 387 (1st Cir. 1979).

Due process requires that regulations limiting visitation be clear and not applied in an arbitrary way. Additionally, the *equal protection* clause forbids prison officials from differentiating between inmates on the basis of race, religion or some other unlawful criteria.

Problem 30 - Legal Hearing Roleplay on Changing the Visitation Rules

Assume that the rule in your institution is that each inmate who is not in disciplinary segregation has the right to have two visitors per week. These visits are each 20 minutes long and take place on a telephone and through a window.

An inmate files a lawsuit in federal court stating that the rule violates the Constitution. Roleplay a legal argument before a three-judge court in which two attorneys for the inmate and two attorneys for the institution argue this case. The three judges should then discuss this case out loud and give their decision.

a. How would you rule in this case? Why?

b. If you were the head of this institution, would you change the rule or fight the issue in court? Why? If you would change it, how? Explain.

Prisoners' Unions   Can a prison legally enact rules to prohibit inmates from soliciting other inmates to join a union, to *bar* all union meetings, and to refuse to deliver packets of union publications that had been mailed to several inmates for distribution to other inmates? The following facts are from a recent Supreme Court case:

The Case of Jones v. North Carolina Prisoners' Labor Union

Inmates in a state prison, claiming that the First and Fourteenth Amendment rights of the union and of its members were being violated, filed a Section 1983 lawsuit (see p. 116). The state's position was that while it allowed inmates to be members of the union, for reasons of security and the orderly functioning of the institution, it did not allow solicitation (asking inmates to become new members), union meetings (although other groups were allowed to meet, e.g., Alcoholics Anonymous and the Jaycees), or bulk mailings to inmates. The Supreme Court upheld the prison limits on these union activities, leaving it up to correctional officials to determine the dangers involved.

The court found that solicitation of members involved more than the simple expression of views but was an invitation to engage collectively in an activity that could be prohibited. The court found that freedom of association could be restricted in view of reasonable considerations of penal management. In regard to the argument that other groups were allowed to solicit members and make mailings, the court required that the corrections department show only a rational basis for distinguishing between its treatment of groups like Alcoholics Anonymous and the Jaycees, and the inmate union. The rational basis accepted by the court was that the former groups, which were allowed to meet, worked in harmony

with the institution while the union posed a threat to security.
Likewise, a restriction on bulk mailings did not violate freedom of
speech, since other means of providing outside information were
available to the union.[27]

Problem 31

A state prison inmate claimed he had a right to wear a button
showing a picture of a barred window or door, with the
words "Prison Union." The state Department of Corrections
did not permit unions to solicit or have meetings in the prison.

a. Does wearing the union button constitute "speech" protected by the Constitution?

b. Can the prison legitimately prohibit wearing the button?
Why or why not?

Freedom of the Press

Two issues regarding freedom of the press are: (1) an inmate's right to publish a newsletter or a manuscript, and (2)
the press' right to interview inmates.

Many institutions have rules stating that inmates may
not publish materials without the approval of correctional

officials. Institutions have justified these rules for reasons of security, e.g., that obscene materials are harmful, that criminal histories promote crime, or for reasons of justice, e.g., that criminals should not profit from their wrongdoing. Though only a few cases have challenged such rules, they usually have not been ruled unconstitutional.[28] However, many institutions allow inmates to write or publish freely and some states have even passed laws guaranteeing inmates the right to own their own writings. In a state that had such a law, a prison rule requiring inmates to pay 25 percent of any income received from publishing to the institution was ruled invalid.[29]

In regard to the right to be interviewed by the press, the U.S. Supreme Court has ruled that no such right exists and that prisons may restrict access to the press.[30] Because the press through other regulations had access to prisons, could inspect all conditions, and conduct brief interviews with inmates and interview recently released inmates, the court upheld regulations giving newspersons the same restricted right to the prison as the general public. The general rule was that only inmates' families, attorneys, and religious counsel had a right to visit inmates.

In another case:

A local television station reported on a suicide in a California jail and included a statement by the institution's psychiatrist that the conditions of the facility were responsible for his patient-prisoner's suicide as well as a statement by the sheriff denying that this was the case. The station then requested permission from the sheriff to inspect and take pictures of the jail. After permission was denied, the station filed a Section 1983 lawsuit to gain access at reasonable times, to use cameras and recorders, and to interview inmates. The station based its claim on the First Amendment right of freedom of the press. While the suit was pending, the sheriff established a program of regular monthly tours but the tours did not include the facility where the suicide had taken place. Although pictures of some areas were provided, no cameras or tape recorders were permitted on the tour. No interviews of inmates were allowed and inmates were generally out of sight.

The station claimed that under the press' constitutional right to gather news and information, it had an implied special right of access to government controlled information. Access to penal institutions was argued as necessary to prevent officials from concealing conditions from the voters and impairing the public's right to discuss and criticize the correctional system and administration.

The sheriff said his reasons for limiting access by the press were that: (1) unregulated access by the media would infringe on inmate privacy; (2) interviews tend to create "jail celebrities," who in turn often generate internal problems and undermine jail security; and (3) unscheduled tours could disrupt jail operations.

The sheriff outlined the alternatives by which jail information could reach the public: mail, visits by news reporters to inmates whom they personally knew, and phone contact by social service workers to help inmates with problems.

The U.S. Supreme Court agreed with the sheriff's finding that the First Amendment did not give the news media the right of access to government information or sources of information beyond that available to the public generally.[31]

Problem 32

In the following situations, what, if any, First Amendment rights are involved:

a. You believe the police are unduly harassing citizens who drive cars at night in your neighborhood. Can you publish a newsletter criticizing the police and distribute it to all your neighbors? Can you call up the local newspaper and talk to a reporter about it?

b. Inmates wish to publish a newspaper criticizing prison policies, and list officials by name. Can the prison forbid such a publication?

c. An inmate writes a letter to a newspaper and tells about jail conditions. Can the paper interview him?

The Fourth Amendment: *"The right of the people to be secure in their persons, houses, papers, and effects, against unreasonable searches and seizures, shall not be violated, and no warrants shall issue, but upon probable cause, supported by oath or affirmation, and particularly describing the place to be searched, and the persons or things to be seized."*

SEARCHES AND PRIVACY ISSUES

This amendment established the right to be free from unreasonable searches and seizures. Though this right applies in correctional institutions, it is very limited. For the most part, courts have given correctional officials broad rights to search inmates and their personal belongings, and no search warrant has been required. Some recent cases, however, have pointed out that inmates have the right to be free from arbitrary, harassing or unnecessary searches.

What governmental interests are involved in conducting searches of inmates? The courts have accepted the following reasons given by correctional personnel: to prevent riots, the flow of contraband and escapes, and to protect guards and other inmates. Whether specific types of searches are allowed may depend on the particular security classifications of inmates. For instance, a requirement that rectal searches of all maximum security inmates be conducted by a paramedic before they are released to the custody of the U.S. Marshal has been upheld,[32] and strip searches of pretrial detainees in administrative segregation have been permitted.[33]

The Supreme Court recently clarified the rule regarding body cavity searches of pretrial detainees following contact visits with persons from outside the institution. Correctional personnel justified such a rule on the basis of security—the need to discover contraband and to deter people from smuggling in weapons, drugs and other contraband. In balancing the need for these searches against the invasion of personal rights, the court found that these searches were reasonable and that no probable cause to search must be shown. The court also noted "that on occasion a security guard may conduct the search in an obscene fashion. Such abuse cannot be condoned. The searches must be conducted in a reasonable manner."[34]

As on the street, the reasonableness of searches in institutions determines whether or not evidence seized may be admitted in court. In one case, because an institution had no published rule regarding random body cavity searches, drugs found on an inmate returning from school could not be used against her in a trial.[35]

Related to searches is the issue of whether inmates have a right to return of confiscated items. Clearly there is no right to the return of illegal items such as weapons or drugs. However, courts have held that a receipt should be issued for legitimate items the inmate owns (e.g. books, clothes, jewelry) and these items should be returned when the inmate leaves the institution. Inmates have won money damages for lost items.

The right to privacy has also been raised in other circumstances involving correctional institutions. Cutting inmates' hair has been allowed by some courts for purposes of discipline, rehabilitation, security (in being able to identify inmates), and health reasons. Some recent cases, however, have restricted this practice. For example:

The Baltimore city jail, which has no standards for hair style or length, cut the hair of several inmates. The officials stated that long hair invited "deviate sexual advances and created hygienic problems." In finding that there were no health care or identification problems within the jail with regard to the style or length of inmates' hair, the court said that the jail should have a definite and reasonable policy if it finds it necessary to cut long hair. The court also distinguished between pretrial and post-trial detainees, finding that it was constitutional to require convicted prisoners to conform to definite and reasonable hair regulations. But, the court noted, the right to cut hair is less insofar as pretrial detainees are concerned.[36]

Rules that forbid beards and long hair, though generally upheld by courts, have in some cases been ruled unconstitutional on religious grounds. For example, in one case a Native American was allowed to have long hair as his religion required.[37] It should also be noted that in 1978 Congress passed the American Indian Religion Act, which makes it an express federal policy to protect the religious freedom of Native American people. This act should make it more difficult to restrict Indian religious practices, at least within federal prisons.

Some courts have also found it improper to cut an inmate's hair as punishment, and damages have even been awarded in some such cases. In recent years, many institutions have liberalized rules regulating hair length and facial hair.

Another area of privacy that is beginning to be recognized by courts is the claim that the assignment of male correctional officers to duties in the housing and hospital units of a women's facility may violate the women's right to privacy. In one recent case, a preliminary *injunction* was granted to keep men from these assignments. The court concluded that the conflict between an individual's right to work without regard to his or her sex and the inmate's right to privacy can be resolved by selective work assignments among correctional officers. On appeal, this case was reversed and *remanded* for a hearing to determine whether involuntary exposure had taken place.[38]

Problem 33

Bobby Seale and Ericka Huggins filed a case in federal court claiming their right to privacy had been violated. While he was being held in a Connecticut prison awaiting trial, Seale was put in segregation because he refused to shave off his one-fourth inch beard and goatee, which were in violation of a prison rule. Huggins claimed a rule that allowed her to have only a watch, one pair of small earrings, a ring, and a necklace while she was in a women's prison awaiting trial, violated her right to privacy.

The prison administration argued that Seale's beard was a health hazard (possible lice problem) and Huggins' jewelry could present theft problems and harm the decorum of the institution.

a.   How should the court rule?

b.   Should it rule differently if Seale and Huggins had already been convicted?

Problem 34

a.   When can police on the street conduct a search? Why is their right to do this restricted?

b.   List five examples of instances where a correctional officer should conduct a search.

c.   If you suspect inmates are planning an escape, can you search them anytime you want? Can you search them every hour for three days straight?

d.   A prison's rule calls for inmates in solitary confinement to submit to a body cavity search before and after going to the recreation yard. Only inmates from solitary are allowed in the recreation yard at that time. Is this rule legal?

ACCESS TO THE COURTS

This right involves inmates' ability to communicate with a lawyer or a court, to receive legal assistance from others, and to obtain legal materials to work on their cases by themselves. (See the Free Speech section of this chapter (p. 67) for a more extensive discussion of inmates' rights to mail letters to attorneys and courts.)

In one of the early "access to the court" cases decided by the Supreme Court, it was held improper for prison officials to prohibit the mailing of a writ because it was improperly drawn.[39] In a later case, prison officials in Tennessee limited the use of "jailhouse lawyers" in the prison, and the Supreme Court in *Johnson v. Avery* held that this could not be done unless a reasonable alternative for access to the courts was provided. Many questions have arisen in subsequent cases as to what this "reasonable alternative" is.[40]

The traditional rule in federal courts has been that indigent inmates are not entitled automatically to court-appointed counsel for federal *habeas corpus* proceedings, although the judge may appoint one if she or he desires. However, the American Bar Association recommends appointment in all *pro se* actions for post-conviction relief.

Appointment of counsel in a Civil Rights Act §1983 action is left to the discretion of the court. Since these cases are civil, not criminal, in nature, there is no right to an appointed attorney.

In 1971, the U.S. Supreme Court decided its first case on law libraries, *Younger v. Gilmore*, where it upheld a court decision from California that had ordered law libraries for inmates. However, the court did not spell out in detail exactly what was required.

The 1977 Supreme Court case of *Bounds v. Smith* gave more detail on the high court's thinking when it held that prison authorities must assist inmates to prepare meaningful legal papers by providing an adequate law library or assistance from persons trained in the law. This case upheld a lower court decision approving a plan for seven law libraries across the state of North Carolina. The plan included a system of periodic transporting of inmates from other facilities to and from libraries, and training certain inmates as research assistants and typists.[41] Based on this decision, federal district courts are being called on to decide whether a local jail or prison is providing either access to an adequate law library or adequate assistance from those trained in the law.

Problem 35

a. An armed robbery victim identifies you as the person who committed the crime, and you are arrested by the police and released pending trial. You are told to work each day and be home at night. Make a list of the things you might do before trial to help your case.

b. Assume you are the same person in the above problem, but instead of being released before trial, a bail of $5,000 is set and you can't pay it. Make a list of what you would do while awaiting trial in jail.

c. Look at the two above lists. Could a police officer on the street stop you from doing anything on the list in number one? Can jail authorities stop you from doing any of the things on your list in number two?

d. Inmate Brown was in a jail that had an adequate law library. He was allowed access to the library for 45 minutes at a time, three times a week, but no research assistance was provided. Does this library program provide reasonable access to the courts?

e. Inmate Williams was confined in a maximum security prison where prisoners were not allowed into the law library. Instead, they were taken to a library cell where guards brought law books requested by the inmates. The state also had funded programs of legal assistance. Does this procedure provide adequate access?

FREEDOM FROM CRUEL AND UNUSUAL PUNISHMENT

"Excessive bail shall not be required, nor excessive fines imposed, nor cruel and unusual punishment inflicted."

Under the Eighth Amendment, an institution has the obligation to furnish prisoners with adequate food, clothing, shelter, sanitation, medical care, and personal safety. These duties were discussed on p. 35 in the context of providing a basis for civil cases: either tort suits for negligence or Section 1983 suits for constitutional violations.

There is no agreement among courts as to what exactly constitutes "cruel and unusual punishment." Some courts have required inmates to prove that acts or conditions are "shocking" or "barbarous" before they will order a change, while other courts have used lesser standards. Situations where the punishment is deemed much more severe than the act may also be violations of the Eighth Amendment.

More and more courts are looking to accepted professional standards, such as the ACA Standards (see the Standards Section on p. 17), when deciding whether the Eighth Amendment has been violated.

The Eighth Amendment ban on cruel and unusual punishment does not apply to pretrial detainees because they cannot be punished at all.[42] However, the due process clause

of the Fifth Amendment, which governs actions taken in regard to pretrial detainees, requires conditions that satisfy either the Eighth Amendment or even higher standards.

Totality of Conditions of Confinement

Holt v. Sarver is one of the leading federal district court cases discussing when conditions and practices within the institution and the entire penal system are such that confinement amounts to cruel and unusual punishment. In that case, the court ordered the prison system in Arkansas to phase out the trustee system where trustees had "life and death" power over other inmates; ordered changes in barracks so that inmates would not be subject to homosexual attack; ordered improved medical and dental facilities; and ordered an end to racial segregation.[43]

This case was one of the first to challenge not just one or more problems, but rather the "totality of conditions," and though the judge issued orders, he did not provide specific timetables for implementation or set up any mechanism to oversee the order. Therefore, numerous subsequent court hearings and appeals occurred, and in 1974 the U.S. Court of Appeals again found that the Arkansas prison system was unconstitutional.[44]

The following case history illustrates the changing role of many courts in recent years and the problem courts have in attempting to improve conditions in jails and prisons:[45]

A Case History: Challenging Conditions

In 1974, inmates in a state prison that housed pretrial and convicted inmates filed a major "conditions of confinement" case. After a number of hearings and submissions of evidence, the U.S. District Court judge in 1977 issued an opinion that included the following:

1. all pretrial and convicted inmates to be separated within 90 days;

2. new classification procedures to be implemented within 9 months to reduce the population in maximum, with maximum to be shut down within a year;

3. each building to be brought into compliance with the minimum standards of the U.S. Public Health Service, the American Public Health Association and the State Department of Health;

4. hot and cold running water to be provided in every cell;

5. each inmate to be provided a working toilet that flushes from inside the cell, and a clean mattress;

6. each cell to contain at least 60 square feet; and

7. new vocational programs to be provided as well as mental health professionals and a drug treatment program.

Problem 36

The following questions refer to the above case history:

a. What problems, if any, would you anticipate might occur in carrying out the judge's orders?

b. If you were the judge, which of the items mentioned, if they were not complied with, do you believe would be "cruel and unusual punishment?" Would you be more likely to declare the prison to be cruel and unusual if some, all, or just one of these items were not provided?

c. Who is going to make sure the orders in the 1977 case are carried out? Assume you are the judge and you are convinced that the head of the institution is not going to carry out the orders. What would you do? Would you order him fired? Would you appoint a committee or some outside person (e.g., a master) to oversee implementation of the orders?

Specific Conditions

Personal Safety   When does the failure of correctional personnel to provide for the safety of inmates amount to cruel and unusual punishment? As discussed in Chapter 2, intentional failure to protect (for instance, when an inmate under attack calls for help and the officers fail to respond) has resulted in a finding of cruel and unusual punishment in a number of cases.

Another situation is described in this case:

> An inmate claimed he had been sexually assaulted many times in the jail. The inmate claimed the sheriff was intentionally indifferent to the safety of inmates because for the past two years he had allowed conditions to exist that resulted in inmates being constantly attacked by other inmates. The inmate sued the sheriff for damages for violating the inmate's right to be free of cruel and unusual punishment. The court said that if the inmate could prove his claim, he would have established a case of cruel and unusual punishment.[46]

Another basis for a possible suit would be a fire that resulted from a serious fire danger officials knew or should have known about.

Shelter   Conditions of housing facilities for convicted inmates may constitute an Eighth Amendment violation, or, for pretrial detainees, may be considered "punishment" in violation of the due process clause. Exactly how much space an inmate has a right to has not been clearly decided by the courts. The U.S. Supreme Court has said there is no absolute "one man, one cell" requirement under the constitution.[47] However, each court must still look at the amount of space provided and, after considering other factors such as the type of space and the number of hours and days an inmate spends there, decide if it violates the constitution.

Confinement for long periods without an opportunity for regular exercise has been held a violation as well.[48]

Where overcrowding has forced prisoners to sleep in garages, barber shops, libraries, and stairwells, and where they are placed in dormitories without shower and toilet facilities, courts have held that the Eighth Amendment was violated.[49] A general lockup of all inmates in a maximum security facility for five months amounted to an Eighth Amendment violation.[50] But the Supreme Court recently ruled that double-bunking of pretrial inmates for less than 60 days in cells designed for one person in a new jail was not punishment in violation of due process.[51]

A number of federal courts have held that certain conditions of solitary confinement constitute cruel and unusual punishment. However, most courts rule that solitary confinement is not in itself an unconstitutional form of punishment where it is used: (1) to protect the general inmate population or personnel or individual prisoners; (2) to punish a prisoner for disobeying orders; or (3) to prevent escapes.[52]

Sanitation   An infestation of rats and vermin in the correctional institution may give rise to an Eighth Amendment claim.[53] Sanitation and health problems that included, among other things, an accumulation of sewage under the main kitchen and a serious rodent problem, constituted a violation in one prison system.[54]

However, in another case, a court found that unsanitary conditions which existed for about 2-1/2 weeks in one prison

were created by the inmates themselves during a prison riot. While the stench and filth would have constituted an Eighth Amendment violation if imposed by correctional personnel, the inmates' case was dismissed since the inmates had created the conditions.[55]

Food Inmates are entitled to a balanced diet. This has been measured in terms such as calories, nutrition, etc. Many times food quality is challenged in an overall "totality of conditions" suit.

Clothing Inmates are also entitled to clothing that adequately covers them and is suitable to the climate. However, according to one case, inmates do not have the right to wear their own clothes instead of assigned jail garb.[56]

Medical Care Inmates are entitled to adequate medical care at the same level of treatment a person on the outside would get. Negligence by doctors gives rise to possible medical malpractice actions in state courts.

Although courts generally agree an inmate is entitled to treatment prescribed by a qualified doctor, most courts have not interfered with the general quality of medical care unless it is very inadequate. However, some courts have ordered institutions to improve medical services as well as other conditions.

CORRECTIONAL LAW PROJECT'S
(AMERICAN CORRECTIONAL ASSOCIATION)
MODEL CORRECTIONAL RULES AND REGULATIONS*

II. ATTIRE

A. Clothing
1. Inmates shall be permitted to wear any personal clothing they wish unless it can be shown that such clothing may constitute a security problem.
2. If an inmate is not allowed to wear personal clothing, he shall be provided with a sufficient supply of clothing suitable for the climate and adequate to keep him in good health.
3. No clothing issued to an inmate shall be degrading or humiliating.
4. All clothing shall be laundered on a regular basis.

* See Appendix D.

A 1976 Supreme Court case, *Estelle v. Gamble*, established the standard courts are to apply to determine if inadequate medical care constitutes cruel and unusual punishment. The court said that to state a claim of a constitutional violation, the inmate must show that the failure to provide adequate care was the result of "deliberate indifference."[57] This makes it difficult to win a Section 1983 federal action for the usual case of improper treatment, but inmates may also file suit under state law for medical malpractice.

Although no Supreme Court case has said prisoners with special problems such as alcoholism or drug addiction have a constitutional right to treatment, some cases have suggested the right may exist. Many questions still exist about the use of inmates in medical experimentation. Of course, the participation must be voluntary, and Eighth Amendment problems are raised if there is any pressure on the inmate to participate. Many question whether "voluntary" experimentation is ever possible, because the inmate makes this decision while incarcerated and cooperation may reflect favorably on his or her prison record.

Problem 37

In the following situations, consider whether Eighth Amendment rights were violated (in prison cases) or whether the due process clause was violated (in a jail situation). If not, consider whether a suit could be filed on other grounds:

a. A potentially dangerous x-ray machine was used on inmates after officials were warned of its danger.

b. The institution had a sick wing where it was extremely difficult for the patients to signal the staff and there was inadequate patient observation.

c. Inmates were disciplined by being placed in segregation and being handcuffed to bars and cells, and tear-gassed. They were provided only bread and water.

d. A group of inmates gang raped another inmate while a correctional officer looked on from a hall but, because of fear, did not act to stop it.

e. A correctional officer saw Inmate Smith tampering with the lock on Inmate Bourgeois' cell and told Smith to move on. Later Smith threw a Molotov cocktail into Bourgeois' cell that burned over 30 percent of Bourgeois' body.

Problem 38

a. An inmate complains of chest pains and asks to see a doctor. You think he may be faking. What should you do?

b. An inmate was injured when a 600-pound bale of cotton fell on him while unloading a truck. He continued to work, but after four hours became stiff and was granted a hospital pass. He was checked for a hernia by a medical assistant and sent to his cell. Within two hours the pain was so intense he returned to the hospital, where he was seen by a nurse who prescribed pain pills, and he was then seen by a doctor.

The next day a second doctor saw him, gave him pain pills and a muscle relaxant, and relieved him from work. A week later the doctor continued the treatment program and the following week extended the treatment again.

At this point, despite the inmate's statement that his back hurt as much as it did the first day, he was certified for light work and given pain pills by the doctor. The inmate refused to work and was ordered to administrative segregation. A prison disciplinary committee sent him to a new doctor, who performed tests and prescribed a blood pressure drug and pain relievers.

A month later the inmate, still in administrative segregation, still refused to work and requested to go on sick call. A medical assistant prescribed pain pills and high blood pressure medicine for 30 days. The inmate was again brought before the disciplinary committee, which ordered him to solitary confinement after the medical assistant testified the inmate was in "first-class medical condition."

Four days later, the inmate asked to see a doctor because of chest pains and blackouts. He was seen by a medical assistant, who ordered the inmate hospitalized. A new doctor ordered an electrocardiogram and began treatment for an irregular cardiac rhythm. The inmate was moved to administrative segregation. Three days later he experienced pain and asked to see the doctor. The guards refused. The next day they again refused his request. The third day he saw the doctor and filed a Section 1983 action claiming cruel and unusual punishment. Has the inmate been a victim of cruel and unusual punishment? Does he have grounds for any kind of lawsuit?

EQUAL PROTECTION OF THE LAWS

The Fourteenth Amendment: "*All persons born or naturalized in the United States and subject to the jurisdiction thereof, are citizens of the United States and of the State wherein they reside. No State shall make or enforce any law which shall abridge the privileges or immunities of citizens of the United States; nor shall any State deprive any person of life, liberty, or property, without due process of law; nor deny to any person within its jurisdiction the equal protection of the laws."*

Equal protection requires that people who are in the same circumstances be treated alike under the law. Persons in similar circumstances who are convicted of the same crime, for instance, should be subject to the same sentencing laws. For example, a law that makes it possible for women to get longer sentences than men for the same offense would violate the equal protection clause of the Fourteenth Amendment.[58]

In one case, prison officials committed an inmate whom they believed to be mentally insane to the state mental institution. This was done on the certification of one doctor (not even a psychiatrist) without a hearing or judicial review of any kind. However, civilians were committed only after an examination by two qualified examiners, notice of the commitment proceedings, a hearing before a judge on the question of sanity with the right to call and confront witnesses, etc., and a court order of commitment. The court could find no reasonable basis for classifying inmates and civilians differently with regard to commitment procedures, and therefore held that committed inmates' rights to equal protection had been violated.[59]

Though not all courts have ruled this way, federal courts in at least two states have found there was no rational basis for permitting pretrial detainees to be held in conditions worse than convicted persons.[60] Note that in this situation there was no law that set up different conditions for pretrial and convicted groups. However, the state *practice* of allowing such conditions to exist was sufficient to violate the equal protection clause.

When classifications set out by the law involve what the court has called "suspect classes"—such as race, alienage or nationality—or a "fundamental right"—such as the right to travel, to privacy or to vote—the state must show a compelling state interest to justify different treatment. This means that it will be much more difficult for the state to treat people differently because of race, alienage or nationality.

For example, racial segregation in institutions is unconstitutional because inmates, regardless of race, must be treated similarly. If the state were able to show a compelling state interest for segregation, such as a recent race riot, the

court might find that a temporary period of racial segrega-tion until the danger is past is constitutionally permissible.[61]

Laws or practices that require different treatment of persons because of sex or illegitimacy require a strong justi-fication by the state that the treatment furthers some partic-ular legislative goal. In some states, women have won cases against state departments of corrections for their failure to provide them with services and programs available in male institutions. However, some courts get around these dif-ferences in treatment by finding there is no right to re-habilitation or educational services in the institution for anyone, male or female.

Equal protection issues also arise where programs or services are established and particular individuals are arbi-trarily denied use of them. For example, if a visitation schedule is established at a correctional institution and In-mate Smith, for no specific reason, is not allowed visitors, her rights to equal protection have been violated. However, if she were denied visits because she is being properly pun-ished for abuse of visitation or because of her security sta-tus, there would be no violation of equal protection.

Problem 39

A female inmate was not provided with a work release pro-gram, although male inmates had such a program. Has this woman's right to equal protection been violated? If so, what remedies could the court order?

Fill in the chart below, indicating whether you think correctional personnel may limit each of the listed constitutional rights either "greatly" (G), "some" (S), "a little" (AL) or "not at all" (NA).

Rights	How Much Can Each Be Limited?	Rights	How Much Can Each Be Limited?
Free Speech:		Access to Courts	————
Thinking	————	Freedom from	
Speaking	————	Unreasonable	
Writing	————	Searches	————
Distributing &		Due Process:	
Writing	————	In Disciplinary	
Mail to Attorneys		Hearings	————
& Courts	————	In Transfer	
Mail to Others	————	Hearings	————
Union Organizing	————	In Classification	————
Union Member-		Freedom from	
ship	————	Cruel & Unusual	
Religion:		Punishment	————
Belief	————		
Reading	————	Freedom from	
Speaking	————	Discrimination	————
Religious Diets	————		
Religious Dress		Freedom of	
Starting New		Movement:	
Religions	————	Inside the	
		Institution	————
Free Association:		Outside the	
Visitation	————	Institution	————
Unions	————		
Free Press	————		

References

1. 441 U.S. 520, 99 S.Ct. 1861 (1979).

2. Id., at 1886.

3. Id.

4. Id. at 1872, ftn. 16

5. U.S. ex rel. Wolfish v. Levi, 439 F.Supp. 114 (S.D.N.Y. 1977) and Wolfish v. Levi, 573 F.2d 118 (2d Cir. 1978).

6. Wolfish v. Levi, 573 F.2d 118 (2d Cir. 1978).

7. Bell v. Wolfish, Supra.

8. Kennedy v. Mendoza-Martinez, 372 U.S. 144, 83 S.Ct. 554 (1963).

9. Bell v. Wolfish, Supra.

10. Procunier v. Martinez, 416 U.S. 396, 94 S.Ct. 1800, (1974).

11. 418 U.S. 539, 94 S.Ct. 2963 (1974).

12. Guajardo v. Estelle, 580 F.2d 748 (5th Cir. 1978).

13. O'Bryan v. Saginaw County, Michigan, 437 F.Supp. 582 (E.D.Mich.1977).

14. Bell v. Wolfish, Supra.

15. Theriault v. Carlson, 495 F.2d 390 (5th Cir. 1974).

16. Theriault v. Silber, 453 F.Supp. 254 (W.D.Tex.1978).

17. Cochran v. Sielaff, 405 F.Supp. 1126 (S.D.Ill.1976); Walker v. Blackwell, 411 F.2d 23 (5th Cir. 1969); Adams v. Carlson, 352 F.Supp. 882 (E.D.Ill.1973) cause remanded 488 F.2d 619, on remand, 368 F.Supp. 1050 (E.D.Ill.1973).

18. 563 F.2d 741 (5th Cir. 1977).

19. O'Bryan v. Saginaw County, Michigan, Supra.

20. Fajeriak v. McGinnis, 493 F.2d 468 (9th Cir. 1974).

21. Mabra v. Schmidt, 356 F.Supp. 620 (W.D.Wisc.1973); Almond v. Kent, 459 F.2d 200 (4th Cir. 1972).

22. Miller v. Carson, Supra.; Wolfish v. Levi, Supra.

23. O'Bryan v. Saginaw County, Michigan, Supra.

24. Bell v. Wolfish, Supra.

25. Brenneman v. Madigan, 343 F.Supp. 128 (N.D.Cal.1972).

26. Tate v. Kassulke, 409 F.Supp. 651 (W.D.Ky.1976).

27. Jones v. North Carolina Prisoners' Labor Union, Inc., 433 U.S. 119, 97 S.Ct. 2532 (1977).

28. Stroud v. Swope, 187 F.2d 850 (9th Cir. 1951); Berrigan v. Norton, 322 F.Supp. 46 (D.Conn.1971), aff'd 451 F.2d 790 (2nd Cir. 1971); Maas v. U.S., 371 F.2d 348 (D.C.Cir.1966).

29. In re Van Geldern, 5 Cal.3d 832, 97 Cal. Rptr. 698, 489 P.2d 578 (1971).

30. Pell v. Procunier, 417 U.S. 817, 94 S.Ct. 2800 (1974) and Saxbe v. Washington Post Co., 417 U.S. 843, 94 S.Ct. 2811 (1974).

31. Houchins v. KQED, Inc., 438 U.S. 1, 98 S.Ct. 2588 (1978).

32. Daughtery v. Harris, 476 F.2d 292 (10th Cir. 1973), cert. denied 414 U.S. 872, 94 S.Ct. 112, (1973).

33. Giampetruzzi v. Malcolm, 406 F.Supp. 836 (S.D.N.Y.1975).

34. Bell v. Wolfish, Supra.

35. U.S. v. Lilly, 576 F.2d 1240 (5th Cir. 1978).

36. Collins v. Schoonfield, 344 F.Supp. 257 (D.Md.1972) supp'd 363 F.Supp. 1152 (D.Md.1972).

37. Teterud v. Burns, 522 F.2d 357 (8th Cir. 1975).

38. Forts v. Ward, 434 F.Supp. 946 (S.D.N.Y. 1977) on appeal 566 F.2d 849 (2nd Cir. 1977).

39. Ex parte Hull, 312 U.S. 546, 61 S.Ct. 640 (1946).

40. 393 U.S. 483, 89 S.Ct. 747 (1969).

41. 430 U.S. 817, 97 S.Ct. 1491 (1977).

42. Bell v. Wolfish, Supra.

43. 309 F.Supp. 362 (E.D.Ark.1970), aff'd 442 F.2d 304 (8th Cir. 1971).

44. Finney v. Arkansas Board of Corrections, 505 F.2d 194 (8th Cir. 1974).

45. The information in this exercise is largely adapted from "PRISON RE-FORM: THE JUDICIAL PROCESS" a BNA Special Report in the Criminal Law Reporter (August 2, 1978).

46. Stevens v. County of Dutchess, N.Y., 445 F.Supp. 89 (S.D.N.Y.1977).

47. Bell v. Wolfish, Supra.

48. O'Bryan v. Saginaw County, Michigan, Supra.

49. Battle v. Anderson, 447 F.Supp. 516 (D.C. Okla.1977).

50. Jefferson v. Southworth, 447 F.Supp. 179 (D.R.I.1978).

51. Bell v. Wolfish, Supra.

52. Krist v. Smith, 309 F.Supp. 497 (S.D.Ga.1970) aff'd per curiam, 439 F.2d 146 (5th Cir. 1971). Hardwick v. Ault, 447 F.Supp. 116 (M.D.Ga.1978).

53. McIntosh v. Haynes, 545 S.W.2d 647 (Mo.1977).

54. Williams v. Edwards, 547 F.2d 1206 (5th Cir. 1977).

55. Carlo v. Gunter, 392 F.Supp. 871 (D.Mass.1975).

56. Wolfish v. Levi, Supra.

57. 429 U.S. 97, 97 S.Ct. 285 (1976).

58. U.S. ex rel Robinson v. York, 281 F.Supp. 8 (D. Conn. 1978).

59. U.S. ex rel Schuster v. Herold, 410 F.2d 1071 (2d Cir. 1969).

60. Hamilton v. Love, 328 F.Supp. 1182 (L.D. Ark. 1971); Inmates of Suffolk County Jail v. Eisenstadt, 360 F.Supp. 676 (D. Mass. 1973).

61. Washington v. Lee, 263 F.Supp. 327 (M.D. Ala. 1960) aff'd sub. nom. Lee v. Washington, 390 U.S. 333, 88 S.Ct. 994 (1968).

four

DUE PROCESS
RIGHTS OF
EMPLOYEES
AND INMATES

The Fifth Amendment to the U.S. Constitution guarantees that *"No person shall be . . . deprived of life, liberty or property, without due process of law."* This amendment requires the federal government to provide "due process" to persons facing the loss of rights or property. The same requirement of "due process" applies to states through the Fourteenth Amendment.

The concept of "due process" is intended to ensure that people do not lose their rights or property through unfair procedures. When people are threatened with being punished and losing their liberty in criminal cases, it is well established that they must be provided due process, which includes the right to written notice, and opportunity to present witnesses and other evidence, to confront and cross-examine their accusers, to be heard by an impartial judge and to appeal a decision against them. However, in other situations where a person may lose property or some other liberty interest, it is not clear as to exactly how much due process must be provided.

In some cases, only partial due process applies. For example, when a student is being suspended from school, the courts have held that only a very informal hearing is needed and that no lawyer need take part. Reasons for not giving full due process rights in certain situations include high costs and the difficulty and complexity of following strict legal rules.

DUE PROCESS RIGHTS OF EMPLOYEES

Problem 40

Assume you are a correctional employee. One morning you arrive at work and are told to report to the superintendent's or warden's office. There you are told that the administration has evidence that you have been bringing drugs into the institution and have been distributing them to inmates. You are told that you are fired.

a.   What would you do in this situation?

b.   List all rights you believe have been violated.

The U.S. Supreme Court has not established an absolute right to a hearing for public employees when they are fired, suspended or demoted. However, a great many correctional employees come under state, local or federal civil service laws that provide such rights. These laws usually include the right to notice of charges, an adequate amount of time to present a defense, an opportunity to present evidence and to cross-examine the opposing witnesses, the help of a lawyer (if the employee pays for one), an unbiased decision maker, and a written decision including the reasons for the decision.

In states with no civil service laws or other rules that require due process for employees, there are still three general situations where courts have required due process hearings: (1) When an employee is fired for exercising his or her constitutional rights, (2) When the firing takes away an employee's property rights, or (3) When the firing takes away the employee's "liberty."

The first occurs when an employee is fired for exercising a constitutional right. For example, assume that a correctional officer felt that conditions in an institution were dangerous, wrote a letter to the warden pointing this out, and was then fired for doing so. A court would probably hold that a hearing was required to determine if the employee was being fired because he or she had exercised the constitutional right under the First Amendment to petition for grievances. A claim that the action against the employee was motivated by or constituted discrimination would also require a hearing.

The second situation requiring hearings is when an employee's "property rights" are violated. Exactly what is meant by "property rights" is not clear. The best definition the U.S. Supreme Court has stated to date is that employees must show they have a "legitimate claim of right" to the job.[1] This situation arises when an employee has earned what is called "tenure." A probationary employee is unlikely to have this right, and in one case the courts held that although a police officer was classified as "permanent," he still held his job "at the will and the pleasure of the city" and therefore had no right to a hearing before dismissal.[2] This issue, however, has not been clearly decided, since courts have ruled differently and some have required hearings in similar situations. It should also be noted that higher level employees do not have greater rights in this regard. Because such employees often are political appointees or work directly for an elected official, as long as they are policy-making," confidential employees, they may be fired with even less due process than lower ranking employees. However, the U.S. Supreme Court has ruled that employees, including a deputy sheriff in one case, cannot be fired solely because they are not members of one particular political party.[3]

A third situation requiring hearings is when the "liberty" of the employee is violated. Examples given by the Supreme Court include: (1) if the action seriously damages the employee's standing and associations in the community, or (2) imposes a stigma or other disability that forecloses the employee's freedom to take advantage of other employment opportunities.[4] For example, in one case:

Mr. Faulkner, a correctional employee, was fired for holding a second job and using a department car for personal purposes. A supervisor was interviewed by the press and he said Mr. Faulkner "had not been completely honest with his supervisor and that a federal investigation was underway to determine if he had defrauded the government." The court held that Faulkner should be given a hearing because the statements made to the press hampered his ability to find another job and thus involved a "liberty" issue.

Most states, departments of corrections, and local jails have laws and/or rules that specify under what circumstances an employee can be fired. These may include a general standard such as "for just cause" or "the good of the public service will be served thereby." Courts have upheld these standards as long as rules specify what constitutes "just cause" and as long as the dismissal is not arbitrary or unreasonable. In addition, courts will sometimes interfere in dismissals when the punishment seems very severe compared to the seriousness of the offense.

The procedures that must be provided to protect rights of an employee who is suspended, demoted or laterally transferred have not been clearly decided by the courts, but as has been noted, in many localities laws and rules exist that provide hearings and other due process protections.

Problem 41

a. Wilkins, a correctional officer, has just been appointed the union representative in his institution. He receives notice that the budget has been cut and his job has been terminated. Neither the state nor his institution has rules that require a hearing. Must he be given a hearing? Should he be reinstated in his job?

b. A prison had a rule that an employee could be fired for "cause." The prison doctor did not stay on duty for the entire sick call and was fired. Was this proper?

c. A correctional officer, during a period of unusual tension in an institution, left his post without permission and got into an argument with a deputy warden, threatening him. The officer was fired. Before this, he had a clean disciplinary record for 12 years. He filed suit in court protesting the firing. How should the court rule?

DUE PROCESS RIGHTS OF INMATES

Disciplinary Actions

Where an inmate faces the possibility of losing good time or being put in solitary confinement, the Supreme Court decided, in *Wolff v. McDonnell*, that due process requires inmates be given the following notice and opportunity to be heard:

1. written notice at least 24 hours before the hearing;

2. a written statement of the evidence and reasons for proposed discipline; and

3. at the hearing, the right to call witnesses and present other evidence as long as this does not endanger institutional safety.[5]

One exception to the requirement of a hearing before confinement in segregation is in emergency situations. An attempted escape plus an assault on a guard justified temporary segregation without a hearing in one case;[6] segregating 40 inmates without an immediate hearing pending completion of an investigation into a series of serious assaults was permitted in another case because of the emergency nature of the situation and the large number of inmates involved.[7]

The Supreme Court has said that for disciplinary hearings there is no constitutional right to counsel, nor to cross-examine and confront the witnesses testifying against the inmate. However, if inmates are illiterate or the issues are complex, either a lawyer, another inmate or a staff member must be appointed to provide adequate representation.[8]

In another U.S. Supreme Court decision, *Baxter v. Palmigiano*, the Court reaffirmed its earlier decision in *Wolff* that an inmate does not have a right to retained or appointed counsel at the hearing.[9] The Court also emphasized that the right to call, confront, and cross-examine witnesses lies in the sound discretion of the prison officials and that the officials need not give inmates written reasons for denying this right. The Court refused to discuss the issue of whether due process rights would be different if a prisoner faced a denial of privileges rather than loss of good time, though it seems to imply that in that case due process might be less.

The Fifth Amendment also states that people cannot be forced to be a witness against themselves. This has application at: (1) a criminal trial where the defendant has the choice to testify or to remain silent, and (2) other proceedings, criminal or civil, where a person may choose to remain silent as to matters that may be *incriminating*.

Inmates have the right to remain silent at disciplinary hearings in cases where the conduct they are charged with also constitutes a crime. However, prison officials are allowed to draw a negative inference from an inmate's silence at a hearing, although they are not permitted to find the inmate guilty solely on the basis of the inmate's silence. In other words, evidence other than the inmate's silence must be introduced to establish the inmate's guilt.

Prison officials, like prosecutors, have the option of granting *use immunity* to the accused. This means that the individual must testify, but that nothing the individual says may be used in a subsequent criminal prosecution. Note that this does not mean the individual will not be tried for the criminal conduct; the immunity only limits the evidence that can be used to prove guilt. In one case:

An inmate was charged with possession of drugs. At a disciplinary hearing two days later, assisted by a resident advisor, he pled guilty. He was not informed before his plea that he had the right to remain silent, that he was entitled to counsel other than a resident advisor who was provided for him, or that anything he said at the disciplinary hearing could be used against him at a subsequent prosecution. He later sued, claiming he was forced to plead guilty because he was not given his Miranda warnings. The court held that the inmate need not be given Miranda warnings when disciplinary hearings are begun.[10]

However, this court and the Supreme Court in *Baxter* said that if inmates are forced to give testimony against themselves, this testimony may not be used against them in subsequent criminal proceedings stemming from the same set of facts that gave rise to the disciplinary hearing. In another case:

An inmate was charged with two disciplinary offenses: possession of a hypodermic needle and syringe, and assault and use of abusive language on a correctional officer. He was also charged by state police with criminal violations regarding the incident. Nine days after pleading "not guilty" at his criminal court arraignment, he appeared before the institution's disciplinary board and requested legal counsel and immunity regarding testimony he might give on the violations for which he was also facing state charges. Both requests were denied and he refused to testify. The board found him guilty and the inmate filed suit claiming constitutional violations for being denied counsel and being denied immunity. The court held that the inmate's rights had not been violated since he had not been automatically found guilty of an infraction by electing to remain silent. Thus, he was not being directly compelled to give testimony that might incriminate him in a later criminal proceeding.[11]

It should be noted that some state constitutions, corrections departments or local institutions provide greater due process rights than the Supreme Court has required. In addition, courts in some states and federal circuits have provided greater due process rights than the U.S. Supreme Court. In such a case, the institution must follow its own rules unless those rules are legally changed.

Problem 42 - Disciplinary Hearing Roleplay

DISCIPLINARY REPORT

Inmate:	Roger Gray #821-417
Date of Report:	June 5, 1979 8:15 P.M.
Charge:	Violation of Rule 65 from Rules and Regulations: Assault Possible Penalty: 30 days in segregation; loss of good time for period in segregation; or referral for prosecution

Facts:

On June 5, 1979, at approximately 5:15 P.M., I was sitting at my desk in the visitor's area where I had just finished signing out the last visitor for the day. I heard shouting coming from two inmates, Roger Gray #821-417 and Rodney Miller #657-277, both of whom had been in the visiting area for the last hour or so.

As I looked up, I saw Roger Gray with a knife, trying to stab Inmate Miller. At that point I yelled out, "What's going on here?" The knife fell to the floor and I went over, picked the knife up and placed Inmate Gray in custody.

This Gray had been a troublemaker for a long time and this time he'd gone too far. The only other person besides Gray and Miller in the room at the time was another inmate who will back me up on this.

/s/Lt. William Jones

I have been given a copy of this report.

Roger Gray
Inmate
7:45 A.M., June 6, 1979

Hearing to be held: June 6, 1979
10:00 A.M.

Mock Disciplinary Hearing

ADJUSTMENT BOARD

Associate Superintendent Smith, Chairperson
Major Carter
Psychologist Brown

Steps to follow during the hearing:

1.   Chairperson Smith should call the hearing to order.
Hearing should begin by reading the charges aloud and the
possible penalties. Then Smith should read the disciplinary
report aloud.

2.   Chairperson should ask Inmate Gray to relate his version of the story. First, Gray will request a postponement
and the board should deny this. Next, Gray will request legal
counsel and the board should deny this, stating that the law
student who usually comes to the hearings is ill, and besides,
since Gray is one of the jailhouse lawyers, he can articulate
his story and defend his position adequately without counsel.

3.   After Gray gives his version, the board may question him
about his story.

4. Gray will ask to call and question Officer Jones and the board should decide whether this will be allowed.

5. Gray will ask to call Inmate Miller, but the board will inform Gray that Miller is no longer housed in the jail, having been transferred early that morning to another detention facility.

6. Gray will then request the presence of ten witnesses from his cell block who will testify that Officer Jones has been hassling him for weeks. The board should deny this request.

7. Then Smith should ask Gray to step out of the room because the board wants to question a person in private who claims to have seen the incident. The board does not tell Gray the name of this person. Gray will argue that he has the right to be present and question this person, and the board must decide whether to allow this.

8. The inmate (Reynolds) will then be called to testify.

9. The board will then consider whether Gray committed the assault. If the board finds Gray guilty, it must then decide what punishment it will give him. Board members should discuss this out loud among themselves as if they were in private. Chairperson Smith should state the decision to Gray.

Testimony of Roger Gray, Inmate

Look, I've had hassles before with Jones. He's always trying to frame me. What really happened was that I was writing a letter to my lawyer about my case. I told her I was willing to turn state's evidence against Miller, who is the co-defendant in my case. Anyway, Miller must have snuck up behind me and read the letter, because all of a sudden, he snatched it out of my hands and pulled a knife on me.

I just tried to defend myself in fighting him off. I grabbed the knife from Miller and dropped it on the ground. That's when Jones came over and took me into custody, trying to say it was me who had the knife. I asked him to get the letter back from Miller, but he didn't do anything about it.

Steps for Gray to follow during the hearing:

1. After the board reads the report aloud, you will be asked to give your version.

First, you should request a postponement since you didn't see the report until 7:45, only two hours earlier, and you need more time to put together your side of the story. The board will deny this request.

Second, you should request a lawyer to defend you, especially since law students usually represent people at hearings. The board will deny this.

2. You should then give your testimony. (Tell the board your side of the story; look at your testimony above).

3. After the board has asked you questions, you should ask to call and question Officer Jones. The board will decide whether or not to allow this request.

4. You should then request to call Inmate Miller, but the board will tell you that the inmate was transferred out of the jail earlier that morning.

5. You should then ask whether you may call ten other men from your cell block as witnesses. You should claim that all ten will be able to tell how Officer Jones is always hassling you and trying to get you into trouble. You should demand to have all ten testify, not just one. The board will deny this request.

6. The board will then ask you to leave the room since it wants to call the witness (an inmate) referred to in the disciplinary report who saw the whole incident. You should say you want to be present and question this man, that you think it's Reynolds, and Reynolds is someone you don't get along with who will say anything to hurt you.

The board will decide to deny or grant your request to remain, hear Reynolds' testimony, and question him.

7. Inmate Reynolds will testify.

8. You will then be told the board's decision. If the board doesn't give reasons for the decision, you should request them.

Testimony of John Reynolds, Inmate

It was right around 5:15 last night and I had just finished talking to my lawyer in the visitors' room. I saw Gray and Miller arguing with each other. Gray is a natural born troublemaker. Why, just last week he was hassling me, accusing me of ripping off a carton of his cigarettes. He's just a bully, lots of trouble for most of the guys.

Anyway, I saw him with a knife trying to cut Miller. Miller tried to stop him and knocked the knife out of his hand. Then Jones came over and got Gray.

I know Officer Jones also thinks Gray is a troublemaker. I've heard him say he thinks Gray should spend more time in solitary.

And Miller's a good man. He and I have been buddies on the street since we were seven or eight years old. I know he wouldn't try to hurt anybody.

Transfers and Security Classifications

The Case of Montanye v. Haymes

After being sent to Clinton Correctional Facility, Inmate Haymes found himself several hundred miles from his home and family in Buffalo, New York. Not only was he effectively separated from his only contact with the world outside the prison, but he was also removed from the friends he had made among the inmates at Attica and he was forced to adjust to a new environment where he may well have been regarded as a troublemaker. Contacts with counsel would necessarily be more difficult. A transferee suffers other consequences as well: the inmate is frequently put in administrative segregation upon arrival at a new facility; personal belongings are often lost; he may be deprived of facilities and medications for psychiatric and medical treatment; and educational and rehabilitative programs can be interrupted. Moreover, the fact of transfer, and perhaps the reasons alleged therefor, will be put on the record reviewed by the parole board, and the prisoner may have difficulty rebutting, long after the fact, the adverse inferences to be drawn therefrom.

Haymes had been an inmate at Attica who worked as a law clerk. Because he allegedly violated prison rules by helping other inmates prepare their legal papers without first getting the warden's permission, he lost his position in the library. He circulated a letter addressed to a judge among the inmates, requesting signatures attesting that they were deprived of legal assistance due to Haymes' removal as law clerk. This letter, signed by 82 inmates, was seized and Haymes was transferred to another institution.[12]

Does due process require that Haymes be given a hearing with notice, the right to present witnesses, to confront his accusers, etc? The Supreme Court in 1976 said no, that there is no due process liberty interest of convicted inmates when transferred with or without a hearing, unless there is a right or justifiable expectation from state law that an inmate will not be transferred except for misbehavior or in certain specified events.

In explaining its decision, the court said that as long as the conditions or degree of confinement are within the sentence imposed on the inmate, and otherwise do not violate the Constitution, the courts have no basis for reviewing prison officials' decisions.[13] It should be noted that at least one state has interpreted the due process clause of its state constitution as requiring due process rights for transfers.[14]

One situation that "otherwise violates the Constitution" is where the decision to transfer is an attempt to penalize the inmate for religious beliefs.[15] The Equal Protection clause has also been held to be violated when inmates are transferred to mental institutions without a hearing.[16] The U.S. Supreme Court has also recently held that before inmates are transferred involuntarily to a mental hospital, they must be afforded full due process rights. The state created an expectation that inmates would not be transferred without a finding of mental illness for which no adequate treatment existed in the correctional facility. Also, the court found that transfers to mental hospitals stigmatize inmates and subject them to forced behavior modification treatment which involves a liberty interest protected by due process.

The court required written notice, a hearing to inform the prisoner of the evidence relied on for the transfer, an opportunity to be heard and present evidence, a chance to present witnesses and to confront and cross-examine state witnesses, unless good cause exists to deny these rights; an independent decision maker, a written statement as to the evidence relied upon, qualified and independent assistance (not necessarily a lawyer), and effective and timely notice of all of the above rights.[17]

The Supreme Court's ruling on transfers applied to classification transfers as well; for example, in the following case:

Inmates suspected of arson were given security classification hearings with some due process rights. After they were transferred from a medium security facility to a maximum security facility where conditions were less favorable, they sued arguing that their due process rights had been violated by the fact that they were not given a hearing with the same rights provided at a dis-

ciplinary hearing. The Supreme Court said that due process rights were not available to inmates in classification transfers since the state had not granted prisoners a right to remain in the same prison to which they were originally assigned.[18]

Although the Supreme Court has not ruled on this issue, some federal courts have required certain due process rights when individual inmates are given particular security classifications that restrict their freedoms within the institutions. For instance:

An inmate in a federal prison was classified as a "Special Offender" for being a member of organized crime. This finding was based on information in his presentence report indicating a probable link to organized crime. The decision to label him a "Special Offender" was made without notice, a hearing, or a written decision. The inmate claimed that the designation resulted in denial of social furloughs, parole, transfers to community treatment centers, and long delays in decisions on various of his applications. This was because decisions on "Special Offender" cases had to go through the central office of the Bureau of Prisons in Washington, D.C.

Despite the bureau's argument that this classification was an internal management tool, the court found that because the inmate's classification as a "Special Offender" had adverse consequences on his status in prison, the inmate was entitled to due process. The court then determined the following:

1. There must be ten days' notice that a "Special Offender" classification is being considered, giving the reasons for the designation and a brief statement of the underlying evidence relied upon.

2. The inmate must be allowed a personal appearance at a hearing before a disinterested decision-maker, with the right to call witnesses and to present documentary evidence, subject to the right of the hearing officer to keep the hearing within reasonable limits.

3. Except in unusual instances, confrontation and cross-examination of witnesses is not required.

4. Counsel need not be provided.

5. No transcript is required.

6. Written findings are required if "Special Offender" classification is found warranted.

7. A recommendation for "Special Offender" classification is subject to review by the chief C & P officer, the warden, and the Bureau of Prisons.[19]

In another case, this procedure was *affirmed* on appeal.[20] However, in another circuit, the Court of Appeals found the same "Special Offender" classification system required due process, but would not require a hearing until it determined how a new Bureau of Prisons policy worked. That policy would provide the inmates with notice, a statement of reasons for the classification and an opportunity to oppose such classification with oral or written evidence.[21]

Another issue in this area is what due process is required before an inmate is transferred from the general population into the maximum security section of an institution. The courts are split on this issue. Some have held that inmate transfers are not subject to due process requirements.[22] However, a federal court in California has ruled that the due process protections of *Wolff v. McDonnell* are required before such an internal transfer. This includes written notice, a fair hearing, representation by counsel in a complex case or if the inmate is illiterate, an opportunity to present witnesses and evidence (unless unduly hazardous to safety), and a written decision.[23] This decision was upheld by the U.S. Supreme Court, which did not issue a written opinion stating the reasons for its decision.[24]

Are the rules different for transfers of pretrial detainees? In one case, an inmate awaiting trial on certain criminal charges was indicted for the additional charge of murder. As a result of the new indictment, he was transferred to isolation. Although the District Court denied his claim that he was entitled to a hearing before being transferred to more restrictive confinement, the Court of Appeals reversed and ordered the trial court to consider whether *Meachum* and *Montanye* (cited above) apply to pretrial detainees.[25]

Problem 43

The Georgia prison system used a disciplinary cellblock to confine prisoners found guilty of serious disciplinary offenses. Inmates from all state prisons were sent to the "H-House," a behavior modification unit, and confined for an indefinite period, many times for periods of years. There was no due process hearing before the transfer. Do you think prisoners should be entitled to a due process hearing before a transfer to H-House? Why?

References

1. Perry v. Sindermann, 408 U.S. 593, 92 S.Ct. 2694, (1972).

2. Board of Regents of State Colleges v. Roth, 408 U.S. 564, 92 S.Ct. 2701 (1972).

3. Branti v. Finkel,   U.S.   , 100 S.Ct. 1287 (1980) and Elrod v. Burns, 427 U.S. 347, 96 S.Ct. 2673, (1976).

4. Bishop v. Wood, 426 U.S. 341, 96 S.Ct. 2074 (1976).

5. 418 U.S. 539, 94 S.Ct. 2963 (1974).

6. Mathis v. DiGiacinto, 430 F.Supp. 457 (E.D. Pa. 1977).

7. Gilliard v. Oswald, 552 F.2d 456 (2nd Cir. 1977).

8. 418 U.S. 539, 94 S.Ct. 2963 (1974).

9. 425 U.S. 308, 96 S.Ct. 1551 (1976).

10. Tinch v. Henderson, 430 F.Supp. 965 (M.D. Tenn. 1977).

11. Roberts v. Taylor, 540 F.2d 540 (1st Cir. 1976).

12. Montanye v. Haymes, 427 U.S. 236, 96 S.Ct. 2543 (1976).

13. Meachum v. Fano, 427 U.S. 215, 96 S.Ct. 2532 (1976).

14. Montanye v. Haymes, 427 U.S. 236, 96 S.Ct. 2543 (1976). Watson v. Whyte, 23 Cr.L.Rptr. 2411 (W.Va. 1978).

15. Fajeriak v. McGinnis, 493 F.2d 468 (9th Cir. 1974).

16. United States ex rel Schuster v. Herold, 410 F.2d 1071 (2d Cir. 1969).

17. Vitek v. Jones,   U.S.   , 100 S.Ct. 1254 (1980).

18. Meachum v. Fano, 427 U.S. 215, 96 S.Ct. 2532 (1976).

19. Catalano v. United States, 383 F.Supp. 346 (D.Conn. 1974).

20. Cardaropoli v. Norton, 523 F.2d 990 (2d Cir. 1975).

21. Polizzi v. Sigler, 564 F.2d 792 (8th Cir. 1977).

22. Hodges v. Klein, 562 F.2d 276 (3d Cir. 1977).

23. Wright v. Enomoto, (U.S.D.C. ND.Ca. 1976).

24. Enomoto v. Wright, 434 U.S. 1052, 98 S.Ct. 1223 (1978).

25. Maldonado v. Garza, 579 F.2d 338 (5th Cir. 1978).

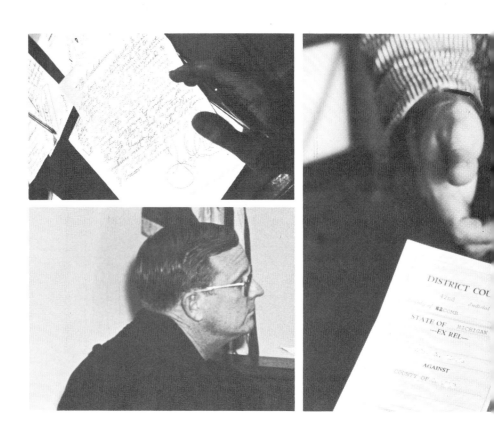

five

THE ROLE OF CORRECTIONAL PERSONNEL IN A TYPICAL CIVIL LAWSUIT

As has been seen in earlier chapters, courts in recent years have become more willing to review occurrences in jails and prisons. It is important, therefore, for every employee to remember that what he or she does may ultimately be examined at some future time by a court or other agency.

While it is initially upsetting to be named as a defendant in a lawsuit, an understanding of the civil process and the protections afforded employees may lessen the anxiety brought about by being sued.

Of the various types of lawsuits occurring in a prison or jail setting, a correctional officer is involved in either:

TYPES OF CIVIL CASES

1. Lawsuits challenging the conditions of confinement or the policies of correctional administrators (e.g., a claim that the jail's heat is inadequate or that mail censorship violates an inmate's constitutional rights); or

2. Lawsuits challenging the conduct of the correctional staff (e.g., a claim that an officer's failure to protect an inmate resulted in a serious injury).

In the first case above, the correctional officer *may* be a witness, but it is more likely that other corrections officials will serve as witnesses for the government. However, in the second case above, the correctional officer is almost certain to be a witness and, indeed, the most important witness. It is important, therefore, for correctional officers to understand the types of legal actions that can be brought by inmates challenging the officer's conduct. All these cases are civil cases.

State Tort Suits

A common form of action is a tort case, which is filed when the plaintiff (an inmate) claims that a wrong has been committed by the defendant (the correctional employee). The plaintiff usually requests money damages for the wrong done. The inmate will have to show negligence, gross or wanton negligence, or intentional wrong. In some places, a city or state will have agreed to have it or its employees, or both, sued for acts of negligence. This is because of the doctrine of "sovereign immunity." Essentially, this states that a unit of government cannot be sued for a tort or for a negligent act without its consent. But sovereign immunity is not a defense to gross negligence or intentional torts, and many jurisdictions have now passed statutes or have had recent court cases that have done away with the idea of sovereign immunity.

Civil Rights Act: Section 1983 Actions

This act has provided the basis for most claims by inmates that their constitutional rights have been violated, and these cases have usually been filed in federal district courts. However, the act applies in state courts, and some recent Section 1983 cases have been decided by state judges. Section 1983 provides that:

> Every person who, under color of any statute, ordinance, regulation, custom or usage, of any State or Territory, subjects, or causes to be subjected, any citizen of the United States or other person within the jurisdiction thereof to the deprivation of

any rights, privileges or immunities secured by the Constitution and laws, shall be liable to the party injured in an action
at law, suit in equity, or other proper proceeding for redress.[1]

Parties to the Action   "Persons" who can be sued as defendants in a Section 1983 suit include state and local governmental employees. In the past, state and municipal governments had not been considered "persons" under the act
and therefore only individuals could be sued. However, a
recent U.S. Supreme Court case allows municipalities and
local government units to be sued when they violate a person's constitutional rights through their "policy or custom."[2]
Most courts still do not allow state governments to be sued
under the act, although this may be changing. A recent case
allowed a state to be sued because its stated policy violated
constitutional rights.[3]

Liability and Defenses   In order to determine liability on
the part of the official or local government agency, the officer has to be acting with authority of the state. Employees
may be held liable in situations where they had authority to
act for the state, but went beyond the scope of that authority
(e.g., where correctional officers use too much force against
an inmate). Employers, municipalities and/or local governments may also be liable where the law or policy is in violation of the Constitution.

Employers (the local government unit or sheriff, for example) will not be liable where the only connection between
the employer and violation of the inmate's rights by the employee was that the employer hired the employee.[4] The employer must have taken some further action or failed to perform some duty in order to be liable. For example, an employer who failed to train employees properly in some facet
of correctional work (for example, firearms training) could
be held liable for rights violations by the employees resulting from this failure.

Not every type of injury to an inmate can be remedied
under Section 1983. An injury due to negligence on the part
of the officer will not be a proper basis for a Section 1983 action. (See Chapter 3 for a discussion of the rights of inmates
under the Constitution.)

Many situations discussed in Chapters 2 and 3—such as
the use of too much force by correctional officers, failure to
protect inmates from themselves or others, deliberate indifference to inmates' medical needs, or a violation of an in-

mate's established constitutional rights to free speech, religion, etc.—may form the basis for a Section 1983 suit in federal court. Remember that just because a suit is filed does not mean the claim is valid or that the correctional employee or agency lacks a defense that will be accepted by the court.

Although the "sovereign immunity" defense for actions in state court discussed on p. 116 does not apply in federal court in defense of a claim that constitutional rights were violated, the U.S. Supreme Court has recognized that in certain circumstances correctional personnel may have "limited immunity." The court has held that if correctional officials take action "in good faith fulfillment of their responsibilities and within the bounds of reason," they may be shielded from liability (i.e., immune). However, the court went on to say that this limited immunity will not protect officials where they "knew or reasonably should have known" that their acts were taken with the "malicious intention to cause a deprivation of constitutional rights."[5]

An example of a case where a federal court did find correctional administrators liable for violating a constitutional right was as follows:

An inmate was accused of violating the prison's disciplinary code. He was given a disciplinary hearing, but was only allowed to admit or deny the charges. He was not given the opportunity to present evidence as required by Supreme Court decisions relating to due process. The inmate filed suit and was awarded $765 (or $25.50 per day for each of the 30 days he was in segregation) to be paid by the correctional administrators who were present at his hearing.[6]

Another recent U.S. Supreme Court case that gives some guidance as to when correctional employees may be held liable in Section 1983 suits is *Carey v. Piphus* where:

An inmate sued prison officials on the grounds that they failed to mail various letters, including letters to legal assistance groups, news media, inmates of other prisons and friends. This occurred in 1971 and 1972, at a time when there was no established First Amendment right protecting the mail privileges of inmates.[7] (As was seen on p. 67, it was not until 1974 that the U.S. Supreme Court in Procunier v. Martinez *firmly established some mail rights for inmates.[8])*

In Carey, the Supreme Court ruled that corrections employ-
ees will not be held liable for violations of constitutional rights un-
less they knew, or should have known, that their conduct violated
the prisoner's rights. The Court held that since the incident in
question took place before it had been established that inmates
have the right to mail letters to attorneys and others, corrections
employees could not be held to know that their actions violated the
inmate's rights.[9] *Municipalities, however, are not entitled to this*
qualified immunity from damages liability in Section 1983 actions,
even if the unconstitutional conduct was undertaken in good
faith.[10]

Remedies   If successful in a Section 1983 lawsuit, the inmate can request and receive money damages and injunctive or *declaratory relief.* The Supreme Court will only
sustain a nominal money damages award (such as a symbolic award of one dollar) unless the inmate can prove actual
damages. The court will not presume that damage occurred
to the inmate on the mere showing of a constitutional violation.[11]

Inmates can claim both compensatory damages (to compensate the inmates for their losses) and punitive damages
(to punish the wrongdoers). Injunctions are court orders
directing defendants to do or to refrain from doing a particular thing. For instance, the court could issue an injunction ordering the jail official to stop censoring inmate mail. Declaratory relief means that the court will announce the rights
and liabilities of the parties without ordering anyone to do
anything. For instance, jail officials decide to implement a
new set of mail rules forbidding *Playboy* Magazine and the
inmates believe them to be unconstitutional. The inmates
might request a declaratory judgment that the court decide
whether or not the pending rules meet constitutional standards.

Problem 44

If inmates have the choice of filing cases claiming violations
of constitutional rights in either state or federal courts under
Section 1983 of the Civil Rights Act:

a.   Why do you think most are filed in federal courts?

b.   For inmates, why might a federal civil rights action have
advantages over a state tort claim?

Problem 45

Inmate Williams believed he was unjustly convicted and wished to file a habeas corpus suit in federal court. He did not have an attorney but had learned how to use a law library a few years before in another prison. Though the prison had a law library, he was in segregation for his own protection, and in May 1977 was refused access to the library until a new library was set up in the segregation unit in May 1978. Williams then used the new library and filed suit, winning his release in December 1978. His release was granted because of legal points he had researched in the law library and included in his court case.

a.   Could Williams win a damage suit for violation of his constitutional rights? Why or why not?

b.   What damages could Williams claim he had suffered?

Civil Rights of Institutionalized Persons Act

On May 23, 1980 Congress passed the "Civil Rights of Institutionalized Persons Act." This law gives the federal government the authority to bring civil suits for equitable relief (injunctions), not damages, against a state, its subdivision, official, employee or agent. To bring a suit the Attorney General must have reasonable cause to believe that the defendant is subjecting persons confined in jails, prisons, pretrial detention facilities or other correctional facilities to "egregious or flagrant conditions" in violation of federal law or the Constitution, causing them to suffer grievous harm. The deprivation must also be pursuant to a pattern or practice of resistance to the full enjoyment of those rights. Before a suit is brought in federal district court, however, the Attorney General must certify to the court that he has taken certain steps to notify and attempt a voluntary resolution of the conditions and that the need for the suit still exists.

This law also gives the federal government the authority to join in any similar civil action by institutionalized persons already filed in any court. Again, the Attorney General must certify to the court that specific steps were taken to notify and remedy the conditions before joining in the suit.

Also of importance in this act is the section on administrative remedies. The federal government will promulgate standards for the development and implementation of a grievance mechanism for adult correctional institutions. The standards at a minimum will allow for:

■ an advisory role for employees and inmates in developing and operating a grievance system;

■ specific time limits for written replies to grievances;

■ priority processing of emergency grievances;

■ safeguards to avoid reprisals; and

■ an independent review of the resolution.

The law allows for judges to suspend Section 1983 lawsuits for 90 days for administrative processing when a grievance procedure meeting these standards exists within the institution. (Public Law 96-247, 96th Congress, 1980)

Habeas Corpus

Habeas corpus in Latin means "you have the body." Today, the term refers to a writ of habeas corpus, which directs a sheriff or a warden to produce an inmate under his or her control in a particular court at a particular place and time.

The procedure requires the inmate to file an "application", "petition", or "*motion*" for a writ of habeas corpus. The court may then issue an order to the sheriff or warden with custody of the inmate to show cause why the writ of habeas corpus should not be issued.

On the basis of the sheriff's or warden's response, the court may choose to dismiss the application, to issue the writ of habeas corpus, or to hold a hearing to obtain more facts and arguments before deciding on the merits of the application.

Habeas corpus can be used to attack the legality of the *conditions* of confinement. If a court agrees that the conditions are illegal, it will order the inmate released from those conditions. For example, an inmate in isolation who believes that the lack of access to legal materials, visitors, daily showers, and religious services in the chapel are illegal conditions, may petition a court to issue a writ of habeas corpus ordering his release from isolation. If the court finds the conditions violate his constitutional rights, it can order his release, or at least order the conditions improved.

Habeas corpus is also used as a form of post-conviction relief to challenge the legality of an inmate's conviction after the ordinary appeal process is completed. (See Chapter 6)

State Habeas Corpus   Many states have habeas corpus statutes. Under these, inmates file the application on their own behalf and the action is brought against the person having legal custody of the inmates.

One problem for inmates is that this kind of action is civil, not criminal, so that many rights they would have had in criminal cases do not exist. For example, most states will not pay for legal counsel, and inmates usually do not have a right to be present at the hearing on the motion. Many states do not even require a hearing on the motion.

State prisoners are not entitled to raise the same issues again and again in their applications. Many states have specific restrictions on whether an issue can be raised again.

Federal Habeas Corpus   Federal habeas corpus is available to state prisoners under 28 U.S.C. §2241(c) (3) only after they have exhausted all other state remedies. In addition, the motion must claim that the conditions of confinement violate an applicable federal law or a constitutional right.

As in the state system, there is a limit to the number of habeas corpus applications that can be filed for any particular issue.

PREPARATION OF REPORTS

Correctional officers are frequently witnesses or parties to an incident out of which a lawsuit will arise. Whenever an officer encounters an unusual incident, the officer should write up an incident report. Years later, it is possible that a

lawsuit may be filed based on the incident. If the report was done well, this will be very helpful in the case. In addition to their importance in anticipating future lawsuits, reports help the institution perform its daily functions.

Lawsuits are started by the mere filing of a complaint. Since the truth of the claim is not investigated before filing and since there is generally a period of years within which to file a complaint, correctional officers often encounter lawsuits involving incidents about which they have little or no recollection. Unless the officer documented the facts in a report at the time of the incident, there is little hope for a good defense. Additionally, if correctional personnel keep good reports and records and these are submitted to the court as part of the official answer, the case may be dismissed at an early stage.

The American Correctional Association's Correctional Law Project has the following to say:

> Clear, concise, factual reporting of incidents as they occur is important to the administration and the courts. The correctional officer is not only the first official involved in the resolution of important issues dealing with correctional institutions and offenders, but he may well determine the outcome. Reports filed at the time of an event are a valuable means of making an accurate record of an event while memory is fresh. This can be used later to refresh one's recollection and to permit superiors to review the officer's action without taking his time away from the job. Contemporaneous records can also be introduced in court proceedings under certain circumstances. The correctional officer's job is eased considerably by accurate "after-action" reports. None of these purposes can be served, obviously, by a record which does not exist.[12]

One Department of Corrections advises its employees to keep in mind these seven essentials and four requirements when preparing reports:[13]

THE SEVEN ESSENTIALS

■ *WHAT:* What happened? What occurred that made a written report necessary?

■ *WHEN:* When did it happen? Indicate by stating the exact time, day, the date.

■ *WHERE:* Where did it happen? Give the location as exact as the situation requires.

■ *HOW:* How did it happen? This is the greater part of the report. It should be a word description of what happened in chronological order.

■ *WHO:* Who was involved? All persons affecting and witnessing the incident must be indicated. What did each person say that was important to the incident?

■ *WHY:* Why did it happen? State only the facts. Don't guess or include something someone else told you unless you state who told you.

■ *ACTION:* What action did you take? What was done with the evidence, and with the inmate or inmates involved?

THE FOUR REQUIREMENTS

■ *COMPLETE:* All essential facts are to be included so as not to require additional information.

■ *CLEAR:* Stick to the facts and use simple descriptive words. Keep your report in chronological order. Avoid using conclusions instead of facts. For example, "I used that amount of force necessary to maintain custody and control of the inmate", is a conclusion.

■ *CORRECT:* Record only the actual facts. Make certain your words are spelled correctly and that you have used correct grammar. Keep your report neat in appearance.

■ *COURTEOUS:* Be cooperative and not hostile; be objective and fair.

A good report is a permanent record and it reflects your training and personality. The report should be typewritten, if possible. If you can't type, then use ink or ballpoint pen. If your handwriting is difficult for others to read, you should print your report carefully. Occasionally, additional copies of your report are requested by the administrators charged with making a decision, so be prepared to furnish the requested copies.

■ *PROFANITY:* When profanity is to be quoted, each profane word should be spelled out. Since these utterances are recorded on a legal document, it is proper to give each word in full.

■ *AUTHENTICITY:* When you are certain the report is correct and complete, your signature at its end indicates the report is authentic.

■ *CHECK IT OVER:* Before submitting a report *read it over twice* and correct all poor grammar, spelling, etc., and add any facts, names, or missing information. Hand it in only when you are sure it is clear and complete.

If some physical item connected with an incident is needed as evidence, the following procedures are outlined as advice to correctional personnel:[14]

EVIDENCE

Preservation of Evidence

Evidence should be picked up by the person who found it and not passed from person to person. If the evidence may later be used in a criminal trial, use a plastic glove or tongs to avoid adding your fingerprints to the item.

The evidence should be properly marked for identification (for instance, with the officer's initials and the date) and placed in some type of plastic container. The evidence should be turned over to the person responsible for storing things, normally with no more than two persons handling it before it is taken to court.

An item cannot be admitted into evidence unless you can show it was the same item found on the scene. One way this can be done is to prove exactly who had possession of the item at all times between when it was found and the day of trial. Therefore, each person who takes possession should mark his or her initials and the date on a tag attached to the evidence. (This is called chain of custody.)

The evidence should be tagged with a memo stating when and where it was found and a physical description of the item so that the person who picked it up can identify it later on the witness stand.

Photographs

Photographs can be admitted in court as evidence under certain circumstances. At least two photos should be taken of the area where the incident occurred and of each item. Vary the angle at which the photo is taken, while trying to get as much background in the photo as possible.

Put the location, date, time and signature of the photographer on the back of the photo, but no other remarks. Photos may be declared inadmissible if, for instance, you write on the back of the photo of an empty room: "The room where Jones assaulted Officer Duke."

If the incident was an assault, you should take photos of the victim's wounds and also full-face and profile shots of the victim. If the incident involves a *homicide*, take both close-up and distance shots of the body. In most cases, close-up shots of very gory scenes will not be admitted into evidence because these photos may prejudice the jury.

If the incident constitutes a possible crime, you will want to get photos of the crime scene. If the scene where the crime occurred is indoors, photograph all possible entrances and exits, including the outside of the building and walkways leading to and from the area.

If the scene is outdoors, be sure to get a building or permanent object in the background of the picture to establish relative distance, location and what possible witnesses may have seen.

The Crime Scene

Certain special procedures should be followed if the incident may be prosecuted as a crime. If at all possible, seal off the area and identify as many witnesses as you can. (As soon as possible, write down the names of all witnesses.) If the area is a room or building, lock it up.

Post staff to guard the area. This staff member should keep a record of who enters and leaves the area and should seal off the area until the investigation is completed. No staff should be allowed to handle any evidence until each item has been photographed, unless, of course, the security of the institution is endangered.

Make a diagram of the area with measurements and make detailed notes of the findings. All staff who were near the crime scene should write a memo describing their movements and observations. These memos should be specific and state exactly what each staff member saw, (see earlier section on writing reports).

The general steps taken in the civil process are as follows:

1. Complaint filed by plaintiff—Papers filed in court by the plaintiff or the plaintiff's attorney, claiming a civil wrong done by the defendant. The complaint sets out factual and legal *allegations* in support of the claim.

2. Answer by defendant—Papers filed by defendant (or defendant's attorney) that admit or deny the factual allegations made by the plaintiff and state the defense in the case.

3. Pre-trial proceedings—Requests are filed for *discovery*, that is, an exchange of information between the parties.

4. Trial—Presentation of evidence by plaintiff and defendant.

5. Decision—Verdict by trier of fact, who may be jury or judge.

6. Judgment—Pronounced by the judge in favor of plaintiff or defendant.

7. Enforcement of judgment—Court forces the person against whom a judgment was decided to pay or do something.

Complaint and Answer and Attorney Representation

Civil suits formally begin with the filing of a *summons* and complaint. In most states and in the federal system, a summons and complaint must be served at the same time; in other states a summons is served in advance of the complaint. Basically, a summons is a document that brings the civil defendant — the person against whom damages or some other form of relief is sought—to the court. The person bringing the action is called the plaintiff. (In some states and with some kinds of legal cases, the plaintiff is called the petitioner and the defendant is called the respondent). A complaint spells out for the court and the defendant what civil wrong the plaintiff claims to have suffered. (See sample complaint on following page.)

The next step in the process is for the defendant, through counsel, to file an answer to the complaint. Because all courts have strict time limits within which complaints must be answered, it is important for correctional officers to notify their superiors and legal representatives immediately

STATE COURT OF THE STATE OF MARYLAND
CIVIL DIVISION

John Newman
Maximum Security Facility
Baltimore, Maryland 19234
    Plaintiff

   v.   CA NO. 42-78

Correctional Officer David Austern
Henderson Youth Facility
Baltimore, Maryland 19767
    Defendant

Correctional Officer James Morgan
Maximum Security Facility
Baltimore, Maryland 19878
    Defendant

Joann Gill, Director
Maximum Security Facility
Baltimore, Maryland 19878
    Defendant

COMPLAINT

Plaintiff comes before this court and represents that:

1. The jurisdiction of this court is based on 82 Maryland Statutes 581.

2. Plaintiff is a resident of Maryland, presently residing in the Maximum Security Facility, Baltimore, Maryland. Defendant Austern is a Maryland resident presently employed by the Maryland Department of Corrections at the Henderson Youth Facility. Defendants James Morgan and Joann Gill are presently employed by the Maryland Department of Corrections at the Maximum Security Facility in Baltimore, Maryland.

3. On or about the night of August 29, 1977, Plaintiff Newman was housed in A wing, Tier 1 of the Maximum Security Facility in Baltimore, Maryland. Correctional Officer James Morgan was on duty in A Wing, Tier 1 that same date. Officer Morgan maliciously and deliberately provoked Inmate Newman, taunting him about his wife's imminent death and the prison's denial of a furlough to be at her bedside. Officer Morgan then assaulted Inmate Newman by striking him with his fists. Inmate Newman attempted to defend himself.

4. Officer Morgan than gave a call over the radio for reinforcements. Officer Austern came to the scene and joined the assault on Inmate Newman. Correctional Officer Austern grabbed Inmate Newman and repeatedly banged Inmate Newman's head against the steel bars of the cell nearest the assault while Correctional Officer Morgan held Inmate Newman by the legs. Inmate Newman was rendered unconscious by the blows, but the assault continued.

5. As a result of this assault, Inmate Newman was severely and permanently injured.

6. Defendant Joann Gill is the director of the Maximum Security Facility and at the time of the above-mentioned incident was directly responsible for the training of officers under her supervision. As director, she is responsible for the actions of her employees.

WHEREFORE, plaintiff requests that he be awarded

1. Compensatory damages in the amount of $800,000 costs for pain and suffering in the amount of $3 million and $10 million for punitive damages.

2. Any and all such further relief that the court deems proper.

        Respectfully submitted,

        J.D. Long
        Attorney for Plaintiff
        1727 S. Main Street
        Baltimore, Maryland 19378
        724-4521

STATE COURT OF THE STATE OF MARYLAND
CIVIL DIVISION

John Newman
  Plaintiff

v.   CA NO. 42-78

Correctional Officer David Austern, et al.

ANSWER

Defendants Austern, Morgan and Gill come before this court and respectfully represent the following in regard to plaintiff's complaint in Civil Action 42-78.

    1. Paragraph #1 is admitted.

    2. Paragraph #2 is admitted.

    3. The first two sentences in paragraph #3 are admitted, but the following three sentences are denied.

    4. The first sentence of paragraph #4 is admitted by Defendants Morgan and Austern. Defendant Gill states she has no knowledge of that first sentence of paragraph #4. The remaining sentences of paragraph #4 are denied.

    5. As to paragraph #5, defendants deny that any injury sustained by the plaintiff was the fault of anyone but the plaintiff himself and state that they have no knowledge of the severity and/or permanence of the injury.

    6. Defendants admit paragraph #6, but deny that Defendant Gill is responsible for all actions of her employees.

COUNTERCLAIM

    1. Paragraph 1 and 2 and the first two sentences of paragraph 3 of Plaintiff's complaint are incorporated herein. Inmate Newman was returning to his cell escorted by Correctional Officer Morgan (Defendant) after Newman had received an adverse decision on his furlough request. He turned on Officer Morgan and attacked him. Officer Morgan attempted to restrain the inmate but the inmate was too agitated to be restrained by Morgan alone. After calling the command center for assistance, Officer Morgan continued his attempt to free himself from the inmate's hold. Officer Austern arrived shortly thereafter and the two officers succeeded in temporarily subduing the inmate. The inmate then broke out of the officer's hold, striking Officer Morgan and causing him injury. The inmate then lost his balance, fell and struck his head against the steel bars of the nearby cell.

    WHEREFORE, Defendant Morgan, Austern and Gill respectfully request

    1. That Plaintiff's claim for relief be denied in full;

    2. That Defendant Austern be awarded $10,000 in damages for pain and suffering and compensatory damages for the injury he sustained;

    3. That the court award any and such other relief as it deems fitting.

Respectfully submitted,

G.T. Swann
111 Second Avenue
Baltimore, Maryland 19727
281-7232

if served with a summons and/or complaint naming the correctional officers as defendants in a civil action arising out of an incident connected with their employment. The answer filed by the defendant's attorney will deny or admit each of the plaintiff's statements. (See sample answer on following pages.)

Where do correctional officers find attorneys to defend them when a complaint has been filed? In most cases (see the chart on pages 131, 132) the state or local government will provide legal representation at no cost to the employee. Usually, the state Attorney General's office or the county or city attorney will conduct the defense. It is possible, although extremely rare, that a conflict of interest could arise between the various defendants in such a suit so that one office could not represent, for example, both the Department of Corrections and the employee. In the event of such a conflict, the officer should investigate the state's policy regarding the payment of attorney's fees for state or county employees.

Discovery

Much of a civil case takes place before trial. Almost all of these activities concern themselves with discovery—the process whereby the parties to the suit find out what the other side's case is all about. You should keep in mind that in civil cases, unlike criminal cases, discovery is wide open.

RESULTS OF 1975 SURVEY: HOW FIFTY STATES AND CANADA PROVIDE LIABILITY COVERAGE TO THEIR OFFICER AND EMPLOYEES*

State	Legal Assistance	Indemni- fication	Comments
Alabama	Yes	No	
Alaska	Yes	Yes	No limit
Arizona	Yes	No	
Arkansas	Yes	No	
California	Yes	Yes	Punitive damages not covered
Colorado	Yes	Yes	Covers tort and §1983
Connecticut	Yes	Yes	Immunity law
Delaware	Yes	No	Bills in drafting stage
Florida	Yes	Yes	
Georgia	Yes	No	
Hawaii	Yes	No	Provided by collective bargaining agreement
Idaho	Yes	Yes	
Illinois	Yes		
Indiana	Yes	No	
Iowa	Yes	Yes	Bill passed in 1975
Kansas	Yes	No	
Kentucky	Yes	No	
Louisiana	Yes	Yes	Indemnification limited to §1983 actions
Maine	Yes	Yes	Ad hoc determination
Maryland	Yes	No	But may apply to Board of Public Works for help
Massachusetts	Yes	Yes	Limited to $10,000
Michigan	Yes	Yes	Not required to indemnify
Minnesota	Yes	No	Limited to tort actions
Mississippi	Yes	No	

*Conducted by Correctional Law Project, American Correctional Association.

State	Legal Assistance	Indemni-fication	Comments
Missouri	Yes	Yes	Limited to $100,000
Montana	Yes	Yes	
Nebraska	Yes	Yes	Ad hoc determination
Nevada	Yes	Yes	
New Hampshire	Yes	Yes	Broad protection given
New Jersey	Yes	Yes	No punitive damages
New Mexico	Yes	Yes	
New York	Yes	Yes	
North Carolina	Yes	Yes	Limited to $30,000
North Dakota	Yes	Yes	Bonding fund
Ohio	Yes	No	
Oklahoma	Yes	No	Limited to civil and civil rights actions
Oregon	Yes	Yes	
Pennsylvania	Yes	Yes	Legal help usually not provided in criminal cases; No limit
Rhode Island	Yes	Yes	Decided on case by case basis
South Carolina	Yes	Yes	Limited to $350,000
South Dakota	Yes	No	Provided up to $3,000 for legal assistance
Tennessee	Yes	No	
Texas	Yes	Yes	Bill enacted in 1975
Utah	Yes	Yes	
Vermont	Yes	Yes	Indemnification limited to $100,000 and discretionary
Virginia	Yes	Yes	
Washington	Yes	Yes	
West Virginia	Yes	No	
Wisconsin	Yes	Yes	Indemnification limited to $100,000
Wyoming	Yes	Yes	Limited to $250,000
Canada	Yes	Yes	

Within reason, a party can find out almost everything there is to learn about the other party's case. In all jurisdictions the discovery rules are designed so that many cases will be settled out of court—the more the plaintiff and defendant learn about the strengths and weaknesses of each other's case, the more likely they will be to settle the case.

The three most common types of discovery devices employed in civil cases are: 1) *interrogatories*, 2) requests for production of documents, and 3) *depositions*.

Interrogatories are written questions that can usually be asked only of parties to civil actions (plaintiffs or defendants, not witnesses), and must be answered by the party under oath. In the hypothetical case of *Newman v. Austern, et al.*, the attorney for Newman might send the state's attorney representing the officers a set of these written questions, which the officers would be required to answer in writing under oath. The state's attorney will work with the officers and submit the answers to the opposing side. The state's attorney might likewise submit written questions that the inmate would be required to answer in writing under oath.

Requests for production of documents require the party served with the request to deliver to the other side all reports, examinations, memoranda, etc., concerning the case. Remember that all reports you prepare are probably obtainable by the other side (through discovery) if the matter described in the report is the subject of civil *litigation*. For example, the inmate's attorney would probably request the production of the institution's medical records on the inmate, any reports written, any photographs taken, etc.

A deposition is an oral question-and-answer session involving either a party or a witness. It is conducted by the attorney calling the deposition. The questions and answers are recorded word for word by a court reporter and the answers are given under oath. The person being deposed should concentrate on being as clear and accurate as possible in answering questions. If the answers at the deposition are different from any answers given at the later trial, the attorney can cross-examine the witnesses or party as to why the answers are different. Both witnesses and parties are entitled to have counsel assist them at any deposition.

If Officer Austern were deposed in the hypothetical case, he, his attorney and the inmate's attorney would meet, probably at the office of the inmate's attorney. After being sworn in by the court reporter, the inmate's attorney would question him about his actions, training, prior history in the corrections field and his specific actions during the alleged assault.

The Trial

If a civil suit is not settled, there is a trial. In a criminal case, the burden is on the prosecution to prove the defendant guilty beyond a reasonable doubt. In a civil suit, the plaintiff also has the burden of proof, but the burden is less severe than in a criminal case. The plaintiff in a civil suit must prove his or her case by what is called the *"preponderance of the evidence,"* meaning that most of the evidence must support his side of the case. The reason for the greater burden in a criminal case is based on the historical legal requirement of greater certainty (provided by government evidence) when a person's freedom is at stake.

*Instructions for Correctional Personnel
When Testifying at Trial*[15]

Reprinted below is a set of instructions for correctional personnel when testifying at trial. Remember these are general instructions and sometimes may not fit the particular situation you find yourself in. Discuss these matters with your attorney before trial.

1.   Dress appropriately. Remember that you are testifying in a court of law and clothes should be suitable for the dignity of the occasion. Flashy or unusual clothing should not be worn. Men should avoid leisure suits. Women should wear everyday office apparel. Law enforcement officers should ask whether they should wear a uniform. When entering the courtroom, check with the attorney calling you or with the bailiff, to see if any special order has been made concerning witnesses, e.g., special waiting room.

2.   Do not engage in any discussion with jurors or prospective jurors. If you cannot avoid a casual, chance contact with a juror, take particular care not to discuss the case or anything connected with it and terminate the encounter as soon as you reasonably can. Furthermore, do not discuss the case with anyone while at the courthouse, especially when your conversation might be overheard by jurors, the oppos-

ing party or his attorney, or indeed any other person. If you are in doubt whether you should discuss the case with someone who questions you, first consult with the attorney calling you. On the other hand, it is expected that you will have talked previously with a variety of persons about what you have seen or heard, e.g., family members, friends, lawyers, etc.

3. You will be questioned first by the attorney for the party calling you. Next, you will be cross-examined by the attorney for the opposing party. Then you will again be questioned by the first attorney. The judge may permit further questioning by both sides and occasionally question you himself or herself.

4. Speak loudly enough to be heard by anyone in the courtroom. If there is a jury, aim your voice at the most distant juror. Sit up in the witness chair and do not cover your mouth with your hand or engage in other nervous movements. These distract the jurors and the judge, and detract from the effectiveness of your testimony. Don't shake your head in response to a question. Answer yes or no as appropriate.

5. Tell the truth simply and directly. Do your best to keep calm. A conscious effort to avoid the appearance of undue anxiety and tension will often help you. Be polite and courteous at all times, regardless of how much you may be provoked by the questions which may be asked of you. Remember that simply by answering, you do not "adopt" the tone of the question. For example:

> *Question:* Do you mean to sit there and tell me you discussed this case with the defendant's attorney before telling your story to the jury?
>
> *Answer:* Yes.

6. Listen to the questions asked of you. Wait for the questioner to end before answering. Make sure that you understand what is asked. If you don't understand the question, say so. Pause briefly before answering and think about the question. This is especially important if a considerable length of time has passed since the events about which you are to testify. In such a case, if you answer too quickly, it may suggest that your answers have been memorized or perhaps are even made up.

7. Answer only the question asked. Keep your answers short. Do not give a long, narrative statement unless specifically called for. Don't volunteer information. Try to answer "yes" or "no" to questions on cross-examination, but don't be afraid to ask the judge if you may explain any answer, particularly if the answer you have given may be misleading because of the way the question was asked.

8. Testify from memory. Don't attempt to memorize earlier statements. You may consult notes you made at the time or shortly after the event. These will normally become available to opposing counsel. If you made a mistake in an earlier statement, change it. It is not *perjury* for you to change an earlier statement which was not intentionally inaccurate or mistaken (whether it was made under oath or not).

> *Question:* Then you admit that you are changing your sworn statement?
>
> *Answer:* Yes

9. You do not have to know the answer to every question asked of you. If you do not know the answer, simply say that you do not know. If you cannot recall simply state that you do not remember. Above all, don't guess or engage in speculation.

10. Expect to be asked about earlier statements you may have made, whether recorded by a court reporter (such as a deposition), handwritten or even oral. If, during cross-examination, an attorney reads to you from earlier testimony or an earlier statement, listen carefully to what is read before answering the questions.

11. During cross-examination, do not look at your attorney or the attorney for the side calling you. Maintain eye contact with the attorney questioning you and with the judge or the jurors.

12. If you are asked questions about what the plaintiff or someone else may have said, do not be afraid to state the actual language they used, even if it includes profanity or obscenities.

13. Above all, be sincere and candid. Even if you have to admit mistakes, it is quite probable that your testimony will be accepted if you are responsive, courteous, and sincere. It is only human to make mistakes and the judge or jury will appreciate and understand your honesty in admitting them. In no event should you display hostility toward the opposing attorney, nor should you attempt to "get smart." You will only undermine your testimony if you do.

14. Upon conclusion of your testimony, you will be excused. It is preferable that you leave the courtroom and not remain in the spectators' section because you may give the impression you have an improper interest in the outcome of the case. If there are special reasons why you wish to stay in the courtroom, consult with the attorney who called you.

Payment of Damages and Costs

After the trial, the factfinder (either jury or judge) decides the verdict and the judge announces the judgment for either the defendant or plaintiff. At this time the defendant, for example, might be found liable for an injury to the plaintiff and the judge announces a judgment for the plaintiff in the amount of a certain sum of money.

In the hypothetical case of *Newman v. Austern, et al.*, the judge could order Officer Austern to pay $50,000 to the injured inmate. Where will Officer Austern get this money? Will the state pay or *indemnify* the officer? (Note the chart on pages 131, 132 which lists the indemnification policies of the various states as of 1975.)

As you will see, most states provide financial aid or indemnification for officers found to be liable for their acts. However, most jurisdictions will not pay punitive damages against officers. Punitive damages, as the name implies, are intended as punishment. They are damages awarded not because an officer was negligent, or forgetful, or even incompetent, but rather because the officer deliberately and maliciously did something or failed to do something that resulted in injury to the plaintiff.

Inmates may also request, in addition to other forms of *relief*, that the state pay for their attorney's fees. This decision is left to the discretion of the court. In the absence of a statute, courts normally do not grant the winning party attorney's fees unless the losing party is guilty of *bad faith*.

Under the Civil Rights Attorney's Fees Award Act of 1976, the court is specifically authorized to award reasonable attorney's fees to the winning party (other than the United States) as part of costs in Section 1983 suits.[16] This has occurred in a number of recent cases.

Hutto v. Finney, discussed before, demonstrates how a court may award attorney's fees:

> *After a series of cases involving hearings, appeals, and several remedial orders to correct the unconstitutional conditions of the Arkansas penal system, the District Court in Arkansas ordered the defendants—the Commissioner of Corrections and the Arkansas Board of Corrections—to pay $20,000 in counsel fees to the inmates' attorney out of Department of Corrections funds. The court based its order on a finding of bad faith because several improvements it had ordered in prison conditions had not been made. The Court of Appeals ordered an additional $2,500 in attorney's fees for the appeal to be paid by the defendants under the Civil Rights Attorney's Fees Award Act of 1976, and did not make a finding of bad faith as to the appeal.*
>
> *The Supreme Court upheld both awards, finding that they were within the discretion of the court and that the award for bad faith served the same purpose as a fine for civil contempt, which might incline the Corrections Department to act so that further litigation would be unnecessary.*[17]

It is also possible for the court to order an inmate who loses a case to pay the state's attorney fees. Obviously, this is unlikely to occur except in a few cases where inmates with money file suit.

Treatment of Inmate Plaintiffs or Witnesses

Correctional officers and officials should be careful not to show any hostile feelings or take any retaliatory actions against inmates involved in the cases. To deny them privileges or threaten them verbally or physically would constitute interfering with the court process and might result in the officers or officials being charged with contempt of court or a separate criminal offense. In addition, if a judge involved in a case is told that such actions are taking place, this may contribute to a decision against the institution and its employees.

Problem 46

Inmate Jones and Correctional Officer Smith have a confrontation in the institution over a discipline charge. A fight takes place. Jones is hurt and files suit against Smith. Two weeks later Smith sees Jones and Jones yells, "I'll see you in court." What should Smith do in this situation?

References

1. 42 U.S.C.A. §1983.

2. Monell v. Department of Social Services of the City of New York, 436 U.S. 658, 98 S.Ct. 2018 (1978).

3. Aldredge v. Turlington,   F.Supp.   (N.Fla. 1978).

4. Monell v. Department of Social Services of the City of New York, Supra.

5. Procunier v. Navarette, 434 U.S. 555, 98 S.Ct. 855 (1978).

6. Mack v. Johnson, 430 F.Supp. 1139 (E.D. Pa. 1977).

7. 435 U.S. 247, 98 S.Ct. 1042 (1978).

8. 416 U.S. 396, 94 S.Ct. 1800 (1974).

9. Carey v. Piphus, Supra.

10. Owen v. City of Independence, Missouri,   U.S.   , 100 S.Ct. 1398 (1980).

11. Carey v. Piphus, Supra.

12. ABA and ACA Correctional Law Project, "Legal Responsibility and Authority of Correctional Officers," 1976.

13. Adapted from materials from the District of Columbia Department of Corrections.

14. Adapted from an article written by Dempsy Johnson and published by the *American Journal of Corrections*, Nov. - Dec. 1977, with permission from the publisher.

15. Taken from "General Instructions to First-Time Witnesses." Prepared by W. ERIC COLLINS, Deputy Attorney General, San Francisco, California 92102. Copyright pending. Written reproduction without the express, prior written permission of the author is forbidden.

16. 42 U.S.C.A. §1988

17. 437 U.S. 678, 98 S.Ct. 2565 (1978).
Reinhard v. Moreland, U.S. Dist. Ct. No. 15-6-Civ. (M.D. Fla. 1977).

six
OVERVIEW
OF THE
CRIMINAL
JUSTICE
PROCESS

Correctional personnel work with persons incarcerated before trial and persons serving sentences. Knowledge of the criminal justice process through which these persons are passing will enable personnel to better perform their jobs, to understand their duties in regard to the inmate, and to assist the inmate by explaining the system.

The criminal justice process itself consists of everything that happens to a person from the time of arrest until the person is freed. That freedom may be gained almost immediately—at the police station—or after serving time in a penal institution. Freedom may also come at any stage in between or even after release from a penal institution, when a person is finally released from parole.

An *arrest* means that a person suspected of a crime is taken into custody. A person can be taken into custody in one of two ways: by an arrest *warrant* or by a warrantless arrest both of which must be based on probable cause. A person, once taken into custody and not free to leave, is considered to be under arrest, whether the officer states that or not.

ARREST

FIGURE 3   A General View of the Criminal Justice System.

This chart seeks to present a simple yet comprehensive view of the movement of cases through the criminal justice system. Procedures in individual jurisdictions may vary from the pattern shown here. The differing weights of line indicate the relative volumes of cases disposed of at various points in the system, but this is only suggestive since no nationwide data of this sort exists.

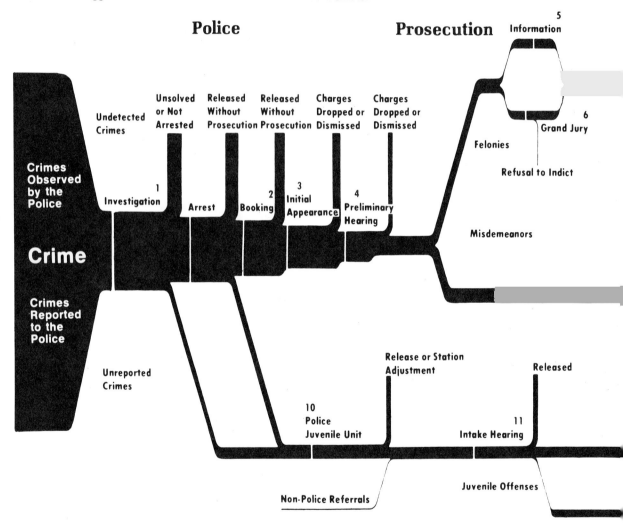

1. May continue until trial.

2. Administrative record of arrest. First step at which temporary release on bail may be available.

3. Before magistrate, commissioner, or justice of peace. Formal notice of charge, advice of rights. Bail set. Summary trials for petty offenses usually conducted here without further processing.

4. Preliminary testing of evidence against defendant. Charge may be reduced. No separate preliminary hearing for misdemeanors in some systems.

5. Charge filed by prosecutor on basis of information submitted by police or citizens. Alternative to grand jury indictment.

6. Reviews whether Government evidence sufficient to justify trial. Some States have no grand jury system; others seldom use it.

Courts   # Corrections

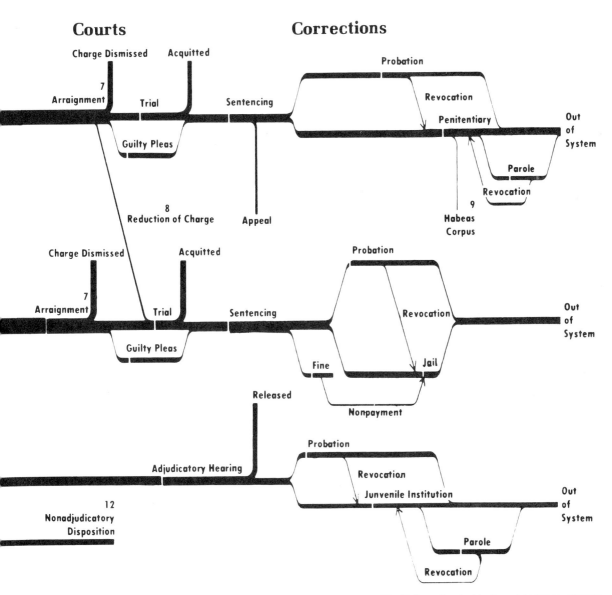

7. Appearance for plea, defendant elects trial by judge or jury (if available).

8. Charge may be reduced at any time prior to trial in return for plea of guilty or for other reasons

9. Challenge on constitutional grounds to legality of detention. May be sought at any point in process

10. Police often hold informal hearings, dismiss or adjust many cases without further processing

11. Probation officer decides desirability of further court action

12. Welfare agency, social services, counseling, medical care, etc, for cases where adjudicatory handling not needed

This is a modified version of a chart published in the President's Commission Report, *The Challenge of Crime in a Free Society*, note 11, p. 39 *supra*, at pp. 8–9. Modification from *Introduction to the Criminal Justice System*, Second Edition, by Hazel B. Kerper as revised by Jerold H. Israel, West Publishing Company, © 1979. Reprinted by permission of the publisher.

An arrest warrant is a court order that commands that the person named in it be taken into custody. A warrant is obtained by filing a complaint before a judge or magistrate. The person filing the complaint is generally a police officer but may also be a victim or a witness. The person making the complaint must set out and swear to the facts and circumstances of the alleged crime. If, on the basis of the information provided, the judge finds *probable cause* to believe that an offense has been committed and that the accused committed it, a warrant will be issued.

There are many occasions when the police don't have time to get a warrant and so may make a warrantless arrest based on probable cause. Probable cause is defined as a reasonable belief that a person has committed a crime. This reasonable belief may be based on less evidence than that necessary to prove a person guilty at trial. As an example, suppose the police receive a radio report of a bank robbery. An officer sees a man, matching the description of the bank robber, waving a gun and running away from the bank. The officer would have probable cause to stop and arrest the man.

There is no exact formula for determining probable cause. Police must use their own judgment as to what is reasonable under the circumstances of each case. In all cases probable cause requires more than mere suspicion or a hunch. There must be some facts that indicate that the person arrested has committed a crime.

Problem 47

Witnesses see two masked men flee from a holdup in an unidentified light-colored car. Later that day, in a neighboring town, police alerted to the crime see two men traveling very slowly in a light-colored car.

a. Based on what you know, do you think the police have probable cause to arrest the occupants of the car?

b. If the police stop the car for a traffic violation, can they question the men about the holdup? Can they order the men out of the car?

Problem 48

The police receive a tip that a drug pusher named Richie will be flying from New York to Washington sometime on the morning of September 8. The informer describes Richie as being a tall man with reddish hair and a beard. He also tells police that Richie has a habit of walking real fast and that he will be carrying illegal drugs in a brown leather bag.

On the morning of September 8, the police watch all passengers arriving from New York. When they see a man who fits the description—carrying a brown leather bag and walking fast—they arrest him. A search of the bag reveals a large quantity of heroin.

a. Based on what you know, do you think the police had probable cause to arrest Richie? Why or why not?

b. Should the police have obtained a warrant before arresting Richie? Why or why not?

Even without probable cause, a police officer may stop and question an individual if the officer reasonably suspects the person of being involved in some criminal activity. In such a case, the police officer may ask for some identification and for an explanation of the suspicious behavior. If asked specific questions about a crime with which he or she may be involved, the individual does not have to answer. However, a refusal to cooperate may result in further detention. In some cases it may provide sufficient additional evidence to result in a valid arrest. For example, suppose a police officer has reason to suspect someone of a crime and the person refuses to answer the police officer's questions or attempts to flee when being approached by the officer. This

conduct, when considered together with other factors, might provide the probable cause necessary to arrest. In addition, if a police officer, based on his or her experience, thinks a person is behaving suspiciously and is likely to be armed, the officer may *stop and frisk* (pat down) the suspect for weapons.

A police officer may use as much physical force as is reasonably necessary to make an arrest. If a police officer uses too much force or makes an unlawful arrest, the accused may bring a civil action for damages or possibly a criminal action for violation of civil rights. In addition, many police departments have established procedures for handling citizen complaints about police misconduct. It should be noted, however, that a police officer is never liable for false arrest simply because the person arrested did not commit the crime. Rather, it must be shown that the officer acted maliciously or had no reasonable grounds for suspicion of guilt.

The Case of the Unlucky Couple

After an evening at the movies, Lonnie Howard and his girl friend Susan decide to park in the empty lot behind Briarwood Elementary School. Several beers and two marijuana cigarettes later, they are startled by the sound of breaking glass from the rear of the school.

Unnoticed in their darkened car, Lonnie and Susan observe two men loading office equipment from the school into the back of a van. Quickly concluding that the men must be burglars, Lonnie revs up his engine and roars out of the parking lot onto Main Street.

Meanwhile, unknown to Lonnie and Susan, a silent alarm has also alerted the police to the break-in at the school. Responding to the alarm, Officer Ramos heads for the school and turns onto Main Street just in time to see Lonnie's car speeding away.

Problem 49

a. If you were Officer Ramos, what would you do in this situation? If you were Lonnie, what would you do?

b. If Officer Ramos chases after Lonnie, would he have probable cause to stop and arrest him?

c. How do you think Officer Ramos would act once he stopped Lonnie? How do you think Lonnie and Susan would act?

d.   Roleplay this situation. As Officer Ramos, decide what you would say and how you would act toward the occupants of the car. As Lonnie and Susan, decide what you would say and how you would act toward the police.

e.   What could Lonnie and Susan do if they were mistakenly arrested for the burglary? What could they do if they were abused or mistreated by Officer Ramos?

SEARCH AND SEIZURE

The Fourth Amendment to the U.S. Constitution: *The right of the people to be secure in their persons, houses, papers, and effects, against unreasonable searches and seizures, shall not be violated, and no warrants shall issue, but upon probable cause, supported by oath or affirmation, and particularly describing the place to be searched, and the persons or things to be seized.*

Americans have always valued their privacy. They expect to be left alone, to be free from unwarranted snooping or spying, and to be secure in their own homes. These expectations of privacy are important and are protected by the U.S. Constitution. The Fourth Amendment sets out the right to be free from "unreasonable searches and seizures" and establishes conditions under which search warrants may be issued.

Balanced against the individual's right to privacy is the government's need to gather information. In the case of the police, this is the need to collect evidence against criminals and to protect society against crime.

The Fourth Amendment is not an absolute right to privacy, and it does not prohibit all searches—only those which are unreasonable. In deciding if a search is reasonable, the courts look to the facts and circumstances of each case. As a general rule, courts have held that searches and seizures are usually unreasonable unless authorized by a valid warrant. Note that this is different from the arrest rule, which prefers but does not necessarily require a warrant.

Searches with a Warrant

A search warrant is a court order obtained from a judge who must be convinced that there is a real need to search a person or place. Before a judge issues a warrant, someone —usually a police officer—must appear in court and testify under oath concerning the facts and information that provide the probable cause or good reason to believe that a search is justified. This sworn statement of facts and circumstances is known as an *affidavit*. If a judge decides to issue a search warrant, the warrant must specifically describe the person or place to be searched and the particular things to be seized.

Once a search warrant is issued, the search must be executed within a limited period of time, such as ten days. Also, in many states a search warrant must be executed only in the daytime, unless the warrant expressly states otherwise. Finally, a search warrant does not necessarily authorize a general search of everything in the specified place. For example, if the police have a warrant to search a house for stolen televisions or other large items, it would be unreasonable for them to look in desk drawers, envelopes, or other small places where a television could not possibly be hidden.

Problem 50

a.   Examine Figure 4, an affidavit for a search warrant. Who is requesting the warrant? What are the searchers looking for? What persons or places are sought to be searched? What facts and circumstances are given to justify the search?

FIGURE 4   Affidavit for Search Warrant

Form A. O. 106 (Rev. Apr. 1973)

**Affidavit for
Search Warrant**

United States District Court
FOR THE
Eastern District of Missouri

Docket No._A_____

UNITED STATES OF AMERICA   Case No._11246____

VS.

John Doe   **AFFIDAVIT FOR
SEARCH WARRANT**

BEFORE Michael J. Thiel, Federal Courthouse, St. Louis, Missouri
   Name of Judge¹ or Federal Magistrate   Address of Judge¹ or Federal Magistrate

The undersigned being duly sworn deposes and says:

That he has reason to believe that (on the person of) Occupants, and
(on the premises known as) 935 Bay Street, St. Louis,
Missouri, described as a two story, residential dwelling, white in
color and of wood frame construction.....

                in the   Eastern   District of Missouri

there is now being concealed certain property, namely
                                        here describe property

Counterfeit bank notes, money orders, and securities, and
plates, stones, and other paraphernalia used in counterfeiting
and forgery,

which are
            here give alleged grounds for search and seizure²
   in violation of 18 U.S. Code ¶471-474

    And that the facts tending to establish the foregoing grounds for issuance of a Search Warrant
are as follows:' (1) Pursuant to my employment with the Federal Bureau of Investigation, I
received information from a reliable informant that a group of persons were conducting
an illegal counterfeiting operation out of a house at 935 Bay Street, St. Louis, Missouri.
(2) Acting on this information agents of the FBI placed the house at 935 Bay Street under
around the clock surveillance. During the course of this surveilance officers observed
a number of facts tending to establsh the existence of an illegal counterfeiting operation.
These include: observation of torn & defective counterfeit notes discarded in the trash
in the alley behind the house at 935 Bay Street, and pick-up & delivery of parcels at
irregular hours of the night by persons known to the FBI as having records for distribution
of counterfeit money.

                    Barry I. Cunningham Special Agent
                        Signature of Affiant.
                    Federal Bureau of Investigation
                        Official Title, if any.

Sworn to before me, and subscribed in my presence, December 3rd , 19 78

                    Michael J. Thiel
                        Judge¹ or Federal Magistrate.

b.   Examine Figure 5, a search warrant. Who authorized the search? When may the search be conducted? Considering the affidavit, do you think the judge had sufficient grounds to authorize the warrant? Is there anything missing from the warrant?

c.   As a general rule, why do you think the Fourth Amendment requires police to obtain a warrant before conducting a search? Why do you think there is a general requirement that searches be conducted during daylight hours?

d.   Under what conditions do you think police should be allowed to search without a warrant?

Searches without a Warrant

While the police are generally required to get a search warrant, the courts have recognized that there are also a number of situations when searches may be legally conducted without a warrant.

■ *Search Incident to a Lawful Arrest.* This is the most common exception to the warrant requirement, and it allows the police to search a lawfully arrested person and the area immediately around the person for hidden weapons or for evidence that might be destroyed.

■ *Stop and Frisk.* A police officer who reasonably thinks a person is behaving suspiciously and is likely to be armed may stop and frisk the suspect for weapons. This exception to the warrant requirement was created to protect the safety of officers and bystanders who might be injured by a person carrying a concealed weapon.

■ *Consent.* When a person voluntarily agrees, the police may conduct a search without a warrant and without probable cause. Normally a person may only grant permission to search his or her own belongings or property. There are some situations, however, in which one person may legally allow the police to conduct a search of another person's property (e.g., parent-child, teacher-student).

■ *Jail and Prison Searches.* Correctional personnel are authorized to conduct cell and body searches of pretrial and convicted prisoners without a warrant. See Chapter 3 for more discussion.

■ *Plain View.* If an object connected with a crime is in plain view and can be seen by an officer from a place where he or

FIGURE 5   Search Warrant

Form A. O. 93 (Rev. Nov. 1972)   Search Warrant

𝔘𝔫𝔦𝔱𝔢𝔡 𝔖𝔱𝔞𝔱𝔢𝔰 𝔇𝔦𝔰𝔱𝔯𝔦𝔠𝔱 𝔒𝔬𝔲𝔯𝔱
FOR THE

Eastern District of Missouri

UNITED STATES OF AMERICA	Docket No. A
vs.	Case No. 11246
John Doe	**SEARCH WARRANT**

To Any sheriff, constable, marshall, police officer, or investigative
  officer of the United States of America.
  Affidavit(s) having been made before me by
  Special Agent, Barry I. Cunningham

that he has reason to believe that { on the person of / on the premises known as }

  on the occupants of, and
  on the premises known as 935 Bay Street, St. Louis, Missouri
      described as a two story, residential dwelling, white in
      color and of wood frame construction .....

in the Eastern   District of Missouri

there is now being concealed certain property, namely
      Counterfeit bank notes, money orders, and securities, and
      Plates, stones, **and other paraphernalia** used in counterfeiting and
          forgery

and as I am satisfied that **there is probable cause to believe** that the property so described is being
concealed on the person or premises above described and that the foregoing grounds for application for
issuance of the search warrant exist.

  You are hereby commanded to search within a period of ___10_____ (not to exceed 10
days) the person or place named for the property specified, serving this warrant and making the
search { ~~in the daytime (6:00 a.m. to 10:00 p.m.)~~ / at anytime in the day or night[1] } and if the property be found there to seize it,
leaving a copy of this warrant and a receipt for the property taken, and prepare a written inventory of
the property seized and promptly return this warrant and bring the property before me as required
by law.

Dated this 3rd   day of December   , 19 78   _Michael J. Thiel_____ ,
                                                                      Judge or Federal Magistrate.

[1]Special circumstances must be alleged for a nighttime warrant.

she has a right to be, it can be seized without a warrant. For example, if a police officer issuing a routine traffic ticket observes a gun on the seat of the car, the officer may seize the gun without a warrant.

■ *Hot Pursuit.* Police in hot pursuit of a suspect are not required to get a search warrant before entering a building that they have seen the suspect enter. It is also lawful to seize evidence found during a search conducted while in hot pursuit of a felon.

■ *Vehicle Searches.* A police officer who has reasonable cause to believe that a vehicle contains *contraband* may conduct a search of the vehicle without a warrant. This does not mean that the police have a right to stop and search any vehicle on the streets. The right to stop and search must be based on probable cause.

■ *Emergency Situations.* In certain emergencies, the police are not required to get a search warrant. These situations include searching a building after a telephoned bomb threat, entering a house after smelling smoke or hearing screams, and other situations where the police don't have time to get a warrant.

■ *Border and Airport Searches.* Customs agents are authorized to search without warrants and without probable cause. They may examine the baggage, vehicle, purse, wallet, or similar belongings of persons entering the country. Body searches or searches conducted away from the border are allowed only on reasonable suspicion. In view of the danger of airplane hijacking, courts have also held it reasonable for airlines to search all carryon luggage and to search all passengers by means of a metal detector.

Problem 51

Examine each of the situations below. Decide whether the search and seizure is lawful or unlawful and explain your reasons.

a. Jill's former boyfriend breaks into her apartment and looks through her desk for love letters. Instead he finds drugs, which he turns over to the police.

b. After Joe spends the night at a hotel, the police ask the maids to turn over the contents of the waste basket and they find notes planning a murder.

c. A student informs the principal that Bob, another student, is selling drugs on school grounds. The principal opens Bob's locker with a master key, finds drugs, and calls the police.

d. The police see Dell—a known drug pusher—standing at a bus stop on a downtown street. They stop and search him and find drugs in his pocket.

e. Susan is arrested for reckless driving. After stopping her, the police search her purse and find a pistol.

f. Larry is observed shoplifting items in a store. Police chase Larry into his apartment building and arrest him outside the door of his apartment. A search of the apartment reveals a large quantity of stolen merchandise.

g. The police receive a tip from a reliable informant that Rudy has counterfeit money in his office. Acting on this information, they get a search warrant and find the money just where the informant told them it would be.

h. Sandy is suspected of receiving stolen goods. The police go to her apartment and ask Claire, her roommate, if they can search the apartment. Claire says it's OK, and the police find stolen items in Sandy's dresser.

While the language of the Fourth Amendment is relatively simple, search and seizure law is quite complex. Courts tend to look at the law on a case-by-case basis, and there are many exceptions to the basic concepts. Once an individual is arrested, it is up to the courts to decide whether any evidence found in a search was legally obtained. If the courts find that the search in question was unreasonable, any evidence found in the search, as well as any evidence to which the police were led because of the search, cannot be used at the trial against the defendant. This principle, called the *exclusionary rule*, does not mean that a defendant cannot be tried or convicted, but it does mean that the particular evidence that was seized in an unlawful search cannot be used at trial. The inability to use such evidence at trial may make it very difficult or, in some cases, impossible to convict the person who was searched. (For a further discussion of the exclusionary rule, see the section "Pretrial Motions and the Exclusionary Rule.")

The Case of Fingers McGee

Officers Smith and Jones receive a radio report of a robbery at the Dixie Liquor Store. The report indicates only that the suspect is male, about six feet tall, and wearing old clothes. Some five minutes earlier Fingers McGee saw the owner of the Dixie Liquor Store chasing a man carrying a sack and what appeared to be a knife down the street. McGee "thinks" the man looks like Bill Johnson, a drug addict who lives in a house a few blocks away. Officers Smith and Jones encounter McGee on a street corner.

Problem 52

a. Roleplay this encounter. As the officers, decide what questions to ask McGee. As McGee, decide what to tell the officers.

b. Assuming McGee tells the police what he knows, what should the police do then?

c. Should the police get a search warrant before going to Johnson's house? If they go to Johnson's house without a warrant, do they have probable cause to arrest him? Why or why not?

d. If the police decide to enter Johnson's house, what should they do? Should they knock and announce themselves or should they break in unannounced?

e. If the police enter the house, decide whether Johnson can be arrested, where the police can search, and what, if anything, can be seized.

INTERROGATIONS AND CONFESSIONS

After an arrest has been made, it is standard police practice to question or interrogate the accused. These interrogations have often resulted in confessions or admissions, which were later used as evidence at trial.

Balanced against the police's need to question suspects are the constitutional rights of persons accused of a crime. The Fifth Amendment to the U.S. Constitution provides citizens with a *privilege against self-incrimination*. This means that a suspect has a right to remain silent and cannot be forced to testify against himself or herself. Under the Sixth Amendment a person accused of a crime has the right to the assistance of an attorney.

For many years the Supreme Court held that a confession was not admissible as evidence if it was not voluntary and trustworthy. This meant that the use of physical force, torture, threats, or other techniques that could force an innocent person to confess was prohibited. Later, in the case of *Escobedo v. Illinois,* the Supreme Court said that even a voluntary confession was inadmissible as evidence if it was obtained after denying the defendant's request to talk with an attorney. While some defendants might ask for an attorney, other people might not be aware of their right to remain silent or of their right to have a lawyer present during questioning.[1] In 1966, the Supreme Court was presented with such a situation in the case of *Miranda v. Arizona.*[2]

The Case of Miranda v. Arizona

Ernesto Miranda was accused of kidnapping and raping an eighteen-year-old girl near Phoenix, Arizona. The girl claimed she was on her way home from work when a man grabbed her, threw her into the back seat of a car, and raped her. Ten days later Miranda was arrested, placed in a lineup, and identified by the girl as her attacker. The police then took Miranda into an interrogation room and questioned him for two hours. At the end of the two hours, the officers emerged with a written and signed confession. This confession was used as evidence at trial, and Miranda was found guilty.

Miranda later appealed his case to the U.S. Supreme Court, arguing that he had not been warned of his right to remain silent and that he had been deprived of his right to counsel. Miranda did not suggest that his confession was false or brought about by coercion, but rather that he would not have confessed if he had been advised of his right to remain silent or of his right to an attorney.

Problem 53

a. Do you think Miranda's confession should have been used as evidence against him at trial? Why or why not?

b. Do you think police should be required to tell suspects their rights before questioning them?

c. Do you think anyone would confess after being warned of their rights?

After considering all the arguments, the Supreme Court ruled that Miranda's confession could not be used at trial because it was obtained without informing Miranda of his constitutional rights. As a result of this case, police are now required to inform persons accused of a crime of the following Miranda rights *before questioning begins.*

MIRANDA WARNINGS

That they have the right to remain silent. That anything they say can be used against them in court.

That they have the right to a lawyer and to have one present while they are being questioned.

That if they cannot afford a lawyer, one will be appointed for them before any questioning begins.

Suspects sometimes complain that they were not read their Miranda rights and that the entire case should therefore be dropped and charges dismissed. Failure to give Miranda warnings, however, does not affect the validity of an arrest. The police only have to give Miranda warnings if they want to use statements from the accused. In fact, in his second trial Miranda was convicted on other evidence.

The *Miranda* case has been very controversial. It illustrates the delicate balance between the protection guaranteed the accused and the protection provided society from crime. This balance is constantly changing, and the effect of the *Miranda* case has been somewhat altered by more recent cases, such as *Harris v. New York.*[3]

The Case of Harris v. New York

Fred Harris was arrested and charged with selling drugs to an undercover officer. At the time of his arrest, Harris made several statements indicating that he was indeed selling heroin. These statements, however, were made before he was warned of his right to remain silent.

During his trial, Harris took the stand and denied selling drugs to the officer. At this point the prosecutor introduced Harris's earlier statements to contradict his testimony at trial. The defense attorney objected, but the judge allowed the use of the earlier statements, and Harris was convicted.

Harris appealed his case to the U.S. Supreme Court, arguing that according to the Miranda rule no confession or statements of a defendant made prior to being warned of his rights could be used at trial.

Problem 54

a. If you were the judge at Harris's trial, would you have allowed his earlier statements to be used as evidence? If so, how do you justify this in view of the Supreme Court's ruling in the *Miranda* case?

b. Which statements do you consider more reliable, those made at trial or those made immediately after arrest?

c. *Harris v. New York* was decided by the U.S. Supreme Court in October, 1971. Paraphrased below are the opinions of two of the justices on the Court. Which of these opinions do you agree with and why?

Opinion #1 *Any* evidence obtained before giving the Miranda warnings should not be used at trial. It would be wrong for the courts to aid lawbreaking police officers. Allowing the use of illegally obtained statements to impeach or contradict testimony at trial would discourage defendants from taking the stand in their own defense.

Opinion #2 Defendants cannot be forced to testify, but if they do, they give up their right against self-incrimination and can be cross-examined like any other witness. Since Harris took the stand and told a story different from the one he had given the police, the prosecutor was entitled to introduce the earlier statement for the sole purpose of cross-examining the defendant and impeaching his testimony.

PROCEEDINGS BEFORE TRIAL

Before a case ever reaches the courtroom, several preliminary proceedings take place. Some of these proceedings are standard for every case, while others may result in the charges being dropped or in a plea of guilty by the defendant.

Booking and Initial Appearance

After an arrest the accused is normally taken to a police station for booking—the formal process of making a police record of the arrest. Following this, the accused will usually be fingerprinted and photographed. In certain circumstances the police are allowed to take fingernail clippings, handwriting specimens, or blood samples.

Within a limited period of time following the arrest and booking, the accused must appear before a judicial officer. At this initial appearance the judge or magistrate will explain the defendant's rights and advise him or her of the exact nature of the charges. The defendant will also be appointed an attorney or given the opportunity to obtain one. In a misdemeanor case, the defendant will be asked to enter a plea of guilty or not guilty. The judge may also set *bail* at this time. In a felony case the initial appearance is known as the *presentment*. As in a misdemeanor case the defendant will be informed of the charges and advised of his or her rights, but a plea is not entered until a later stage in the criminal process, known as the felony *arraignment*.

The most important thing decided at this initial appearance is whether the defendant will be released from custody, and, if so, under what conditions.

Bail and Pretrial Release.

An arrested person can usually be released for the period of time before trial under a bail system. The purpose of bail is to assure the court that the defendant will return to court and, in many states, to assure the safety of other persons or the community as a whole.

The right to bail has been recognized under federal and state law in all but the most serious cases, such as murder. Some states even grant the right to bail in very serious cases. Laws in the federal system and most states do provide for detention without bail in certain situations, for example, where the defendant was arrested while on parole or probation for a prior conviction.

A bondsetter, usually a judge or magistrate, sets the bail for persons eligible for bail after considering a variety of factors. These include the nature and circumstances of the offense charged, the weight of the evidence against the person, family ties, employment, financial resources, character and mental condition, past conduct, length of residence in the community, record of convictions, and any record of appearance or failure to appear in court.

A bondsetter has two main options in determining what bail to set:

■ personal recognizance or unconditional release, where the accused is freed on a promise to return to court at a specified time and date; and

■ conditional release, where particular conditions are placed on the accused.

Common forms of conditions include release to the custody of a third party whereby a person or organization agrees to supervise the accused. Restrictions may also be placed on travel, where the accused lives and contact the accused has with others. A money bond may be required of the accused who must deposit a percentage of the bond (10% is frequently used) in the court's registry in order to be released. If a person released on bond fails to return, the court keeps the money and is entitled to collect the other percentage (e.g., 90%).

The accused may be required to pay a surety bond. A bonding company, in exchange for collateral and a fee from the accused, promises the court that the accused will appear. For example, a defendant with a $2,000 surety bond might be released after putting up $2,000 in collateral (something worth more than $2,000) with the bonding company and paying $160 (8%) fee to the company. If a person released on a surety bond fails to return, the court has the right to require the bonding company to pay the full bond to the court.

When a surety bond is set, the accused generally has the option of paying the full bond into the court to secure release. In the example of the $2,000 surety bond, the accused would have the option of depositing the full $2,000 in cash with the court.

The Eighth Amendment to the U.S. Constitution states, "excessive bail may not be required." However, many persons are detained in jail before trial because they do not have money for bail. Many persons consider this to be unfair and unconstitutional. In recent years, more programs have been established to release defendants without a money bond.

Many state laws require that the least restrictive bail be imposed that would accomplish the purposes of bail, i.e., appearance and safety. Only when it is determined that the least restrictive bail (unconditional release) will not sufficiently ensure appearance and safety, may a more restrictive bail be imposed.

Problem 55

BAIL HEARING

Below are five persons who have been arrested and charged with a variety of crimes. In each case decide whether the person should be released and, if so, under what conditions. Choose from one of the following options and discuss your decision: (1) money bond—set an amount; (2) personal recognizance—no money required; (3) conditional release—set the conditions; and (4) pretrial detention.

Case 1

Name: Jerry Davis   Age: 26
Charge: Possession of Narcotics
Residence: 619 30th Street, lives alone, no family or references
Employment: Unemployed
Education: Eleventh grade
Criminal Record: As a juvenile had five arrests, mostly misdemeanors. As an adult had two arrests for petty larceny and a conviction for possession of dangerous drugs (probation was successfully completed).
Comment: Defendant arrested while leaving a pharmacy carrying a large quantity of morphine. Urine test indicates defendant presently using narcotics.

Case 2

Name: Gloria Hardy   Age:23
Charge: Prostitution
Residence: 130 Riverside Drive, Apt. 10
Employment: Royal Massage Parlor; reportedly earns $1,500
    per week
Education: Completed high school
Criminal Record: Five arrests for prostitution, two convic-
    tions; currently on probation.
Comment: Vice detective alleges defendant involved in pros-
    titution catering to wealthy clients.

Case 3

Name: Stanley A. Wexler   Age: 42
Charge: Possession and Sale of Narcotics
Residence: 3814 Sunset Drive, lives with wife and two chil-
    dren
Employment: Self-employed owner of a drugstore chain, net
    worth $250,000
Education: Completed college, advanced degrees in Pharma-
    cy and Business Administration
Criminal Record: None
Comment: Arrested at his store by undercover police after at-
    tempting to sell a large quantity of unregistered morphine.
    Alleged to be a bigtime dealer. No indication of drug
    usage.

Case 4

Name: Michael D. McKenna   Age: 19
Charge: Armed Robbery
Residence: 412 Pine Street, lives with parents
Employment: Waiter, Vanguard Restaurant; earns $100 per
    week
Education: Tenth grade
Criminal Record: Eight juvenile arrests, runaway, possession
    of marijuana, illegal possession of firearms, and four bur-
    glaries; convicted of firearms charge and two burglaries;
    spent two years in juvenile facility.
Comment: Arrested after being identified as assailant in a
    street holdup. Alleged leader of a street gang. Police con-
    sider dangerous. No indication of drug usage.

Case 5

Name: Walter Lollar   Age: 34
Charge: Possession of Stolen Mail and Forgery
Residence: 5361 Texas Street, lives with common-law wife
    and two children by a prior marriage.

> Employment: Works thirty hours per week at a service station; earns minimum wage
> Education: Quit school after eighth grade; no vocational skills
> Criminal Record: Nine arrests—mostly drunk and disorderly and vagrancy. Two convictions: (1) driving while intoxicated (fined and lost license); (2) forgery (completed two years probation).
> Comment: Arrested attempting to cash a stolen social security check. Probation officer indicates defendant has a drinking problem.
>
> What's your opinion of the bail system? Should it be easier or harder to get out of jail prior to trial? Discuss your reasons.

Defendants who are not able to make bond or who are locked up without bond are called pretrial detainees (rights discussed in Chapter 3). Even though these individuals are locked up, they are still presumed innocent of a crime. Therefore, they must be accorded rights in addition to the rights of persons who are convicted of a crime (see discussion in Chapter 3).

Since the typical jail houses several categories of people, jail administrators have the duty to make classification decisions as persons are committed to the jail. State statutes generally require separation of males from females, adults from juveniles, convicted persons from pretrial detainees, and sex offenders, drug addicts, security risks and the mentally ill from the general jail population.

Correctional officers may find themselves liable for injuries caused by an inmate who should have been segregated if the officers had seen behavior that possibly indicated a need for segregation (e.g., mental disease) and did nothing about it.

Preliminary Hearing

A *preliminary hearing* serves as a screening device to determine if there is enough evidence to require the defendant to stand trial. The prosecutor is required to establish the commission of a crime and the probable guilt of the defendant.

In most states the defendant has the right to be represented by an attorney, to cross-examine prosecution witnesses, and to call witnesses in his or her favor. If the judge finds no probable cause, the defendant will be released. However, dismissal of a case at the preliminary hearing does not always mean the case is over because the prosecution may still submit the case to a grand jury.

Grand Jury

A grand jury is a group of between sixteen and twenty-three persons charged with responsibility for determining whether there is sufficient cause to believe that a person has committed a crime and should be made to stand trial. The Fifth Amendment to the U.S. Constitution requires that before anyone can be tried for a serious crime in federal court, there must be a grand jury indictment.

To secure an indictment a prosecutor will present evidence designed to establish that a crime has been committed and that there is probable cause to believe the defendant committed it. Neither the defendant nor his attorney has a right to be present, and the prosecutor is not required to present all the evidence or call all the witnesses, as long as the grand jury is satisfied with the merits of proceeding to trial.

Although grand jury indictments are only required in federal court, many states also use a grand jury indictment process. Other states bring defendants to trial following a preliminary hearing or based on a criminal information—a formal accusation detailing the nature and circumstances of the charge—filed with the court by the prosecutor.

Felony Arraignment and Pleas

After an indictment is issued (or, if not an indictment, after the prosecutor files an information) the defendant will be required to appear in court and enter an initial plea. If the defendant pleads guilty, the judge will set a date for sentencing. If the defendant pleads not guilty, the judge will set a date for trial and ask the defendant if he or she wants a jury trial or a trial before a judge alone.

Nolo Contendere is a plea by the defendant that does not admit guilt but also does not contest the charges. It is equivalent to pleading guilty, and the only advantage of this plea is that it cannot be used as evidence in a later civil trial for damages based on the same set of facts.

Pretrial Motions and the Exclusionary Rule

One of the most important preliminary proceedings is the pretrial motion. After the indictment or information is filed, a defendant may file a number of formal requests or motions seeking to have the case dismissed, or to obtain some advantage or assistance in preparing the case. Among the more common pretrial motions are the following: *motion for discovery of evidence,* which is a request by the defendant to examine, before trial, certain evidence in the possession of the prosecutor; *motion for a continuance,* which seeks more time to prepare the case; and *motion for change of venue,* which is a request to change the location of the trial to avoid community hostility, for the convenience of witnesses, or for other reasons.

Perhaps the most important and controversial of these motions is the *motion to suppress evidence,* which alleges that certain evidence the government plans to use at trial was obtained illegally and should be thrown out. Most commonly, the defense attorney tries to exclude evidence obtained as a result of a police search or a confession obtained as a result of police interrogation. Motions to suppress evidence have been used in federal courts since 1914, but it was not until 1961, in the now famous case of *Mapp v. Ohio,* that the Supreme Court required their use in state court. The Court decided that any evidence obtained by the police in an unreasonable search (as defined by the courts) must be excluded from use at trial.[4]

Since the *Mapp* decision, courts have been flooded with motions to suppress evidence, and the decision on the motion has become one of great importance. As a practical matter, if the judge rules that the evidence was unlawfully obtained, the case is often dismissed because the state has insufficient evidence to present. If the judge rules against the motion and says the evidence can be used, the defendant often pleads guilty.

The Case of Brewer v. Williams

On an afternoon in 1968 a ten-year-old girl disappeared from the YMCA in Des Moines, Iowa. Soon after the girl's disappearance, Robert Williams, a resident of the YMCA, was seen in the lobby carrying a large bundle. A witness later told police that he saw two legs sticking out of the bundle. Before anyone could stop him, Williams drove off. His car was found the next day in Davenport, Iowa some 160 miles away. A warrant was issued for his arrest and Williams later turned himself in. Williams was warned of his right to remain silent and was allowed to talk to his attorney, who advised him not to say anything to the police. In return, the police agreed not to question him until he returned to Des Moines to meet with his lawyer.

On the ride back to Des Moines Williams expressed no desire to talk about the case but did carry on a discussion with the officers. One of the detectives, knowing Williams was a religious man, stated that they should stop and locate the girl's body "because her parents were entitled to give her a Christian burial." After apparently thinking this over, Williams made several incriminating statements and then directed the police to the girl's body.

Williams was later convicted of murder but appealed the decision, claiming that the evidence obtained during the trip was in violation of his constitutional right to assistance of counsel. The Iowa Supreme Court ruled that the evidence was admissable in court because Williams volunteered it. Arguing that this decision was in violation of the U.S. Constitution, he took the case to the federal courts. The U.S. District Court disagreed with the Iowa Supreme Court. The district court said that the evidence should have been excluded because the police had used a subtle form of interrogation in violation of their agreement not to question him and because they had failed to prove that Williams knowingly and intentionally waived his right against self-incrimination.[5]

Problem 56

a. What's the purpose of excluding illegally obtained evidence? What are some advantages and disadvantages of the exclusionary rule? What's your opinion of the rule?

b. How does the exclusionary rule apply to the case of *Brewer v. Williams*? If you were the judge, would you allow the incriminating statements made by Williams and the fact that these statements led police to the body of the murdered girl to be used as evidence? Why or why not?

c. Do you think the police violated William's constitutional right to assistance of counsel? Do you think Williams waived those rights by talking to the police?

d. How would you feel about excluding the evidence if you were Williams? If you were his defense attorney? If you were the parents of the murdered girl? If you were the police?

e. The case of *Brewer v. Williams* was finally appealed to the U.S. Supreme Court. How do you think the Court ruled on this matter?

The rationale behind the exclusionary rule is that the police should not be allowed to benefit from the violation of a constitutional right and that excluding evidence at trial will deter police misconduct. On the other hand, some people argue that the exclusionary rule allows criminals to go free (i.e., guilt though acknowledged may not be proved), destroys respect for the courts, and punishes society rather than police.

Plea Bargaining

Contrary to popular belief, the great majority of criminal cases never go to trial. Rather, most defendants who are convicted plead guilty before trial. In many minor cases, such as traffic violations, the procedure for pleading guilty is simply to sign a form waiving the right to appear and to mail the court a check for the amount of the ticket or fine. In major cases guilty pleas result from a process of negotiation between the accused, the defense attorney, and the prosecutor. This process, known as plea bargaining, involves granting certain concessions to the defendant in exchange for a plea of guilty. Typically, the prosecution will either allow the defendant to plead guilty to a less serious charge or recommend a lighter sentence on the original charge.

Plea bargaining allows the government to avoid the time and expense of a public trial, and the defendant often receives a lighter sentence than if the case had resulted in a conviction at trial. When accepting a guilty plea, the judge is responsible for deciding if the plea was made freely, voluntarily, and with knowledge of all the facts. Thus, once a defendant pleads guilty, it is very hard to withdraw it.

Plea bargaining is very controversial. Some critics charge that plea bargaining allows dangerous criminals to get off with light sentences. Others, more concerned with the plight of the defendant, argue that the government should be forced to prove guilt beyond a reasonable doubt at trial and further charge that the system is unfair to the accused, particularly if the prosecution has a weak case. Some states have banned plea bargaining altogether. Why would states do this?

Problem 57

a. Should plea bargaining be allowed? Do you think plea bargaining offers greater advantages to the prosecutor or the defendant? Explain your answer.

b. Marty, who is twenty-two years old, is arrested and charged with burglarizing a warehouse. He has a criminal record, including a previous conviction for shoplifting and two arrests for auto theft. The prosecution has evidence placing him at the scene of the crime. The defense attorney tells him the prosecution will reduce the charge to petty larceny in exchange for a guilty plea. If you were Marty, would you plead guilty to the lesser charge? Why or why not?

c. Suppose Marty pleads guilty after being promised probation by the prosecutor, but instead he receives a long prison term. Is there anything he can do about this?

d. Do you think anyone accused of a crime would plead guilty if they were really innocent? Explain your answer.

The Sixth Amendment to the U.S. Constitution: *In all criminal prosecutions, the accused shall enjoy the right to a speedy and public trial, by an impartial jury of the State and district wherein the crime shall have been committed, which*

THE TRIAL

district shall have been previously ascertained by law, and to be informed of the nature and cause of the accusation; to be confronted with the witnesses against him; to have compulsory process for obtaining Witnesses in his favor, and to have the Assistance of Counsel for his defense.

Due process of law means little to the average citizen unless and until he or she is arrested and charged with a crime. This is because many of the most basic rights set out in the U.S. Constitution apply to persons accused of a crime. Due process is perhaps best defined as the constitutional duty imposed on government, i.e., the courts and law enforcement officials, to see that the basic rights of an accused person are protected by using proper procedures before taking away the defendant's property or liberty interests. These basic rights include the rights to have a jury trial, to be prosecuted in public and without undue delay, to be informed of their rights and of the charges against them, to confront and cross-examine witnesses, to refuse to testify against themselves, and to be represented by an attorney. These rights are the essence of due process of law and, taken together, they make up the overall right to a fair trial.

Right to Trial by Jury

The right to a jury trial is guaranteed by the Sixth Amendment to the U.S. Constitution and is applicable in both federal and state courts. However, a jury is not required in every case and, in fact, juries are not used very much. As we have already seen, most criminal cases are resolved by guilty pleas before ever reaching trial. Jury trials are not required for certain minor offenses—generally those punishable by less than six months in prison. Defendants can *waive* (give up) their right to a jury trial; in some states, waivers may occur in the majority of cases.

Jury panels are selected from voter registration or tax lists and are supposed to be generally representative of the community. Federal law requires that juries consist of twelve persons who must reach a unanimous verdict before finding a person guilty. State courts are not required to use twelve jurors nor are they required to reach a unanimous verdict. However, the U.S. Supreme Court has held that juries in state courts must have at least six jurors.

Problem 58

a. Why is the right to a jury trial guaranteed by the Bill of Rights? Why would someone choose not to have a jury trial?

b. Do you think jury verdicts should be unanimous? Why or why not?

Right to a Speedy and Public Trial

The Sixth Amendment to the U.S. Constitution provides a right to a speedy trial in all criminal cases. The Constitution does not define "speedy" exactly, and courts have often had trouble deciding what this term meant. To remedy this problem, the federal government and some states have set specific time limits within which a case must be brought to trial.

There are essentially two types of speedy trial problems:

1. *Delay in presenting a criminal charge to a grand jury or in filing of the information.* The Supreme Court has held that the defendant must prove substantial prejudice, coupled with intentional delay by the government for the purpose of gaining unfair advantage, before a dismissal will be granted. Some courts have held that in narcotics cases the specific advantage gained need not be proven because the government has an advantage if a substantial length of time has passed between the narcotics transaction and the filing of criminal charges. It must be understood, however, that in all jurisdictions, a long delay in bringing charges usually does not by itself constitute substantial prejudice.

2. *Delay in bringing the accused to trial.* To determine whether delay occurring between the filing of an indictment or information and trial violates the defendant's right to a speedy trial, the courts apply the test set out by the Supreme Court in the landmark case of *Barker v. Wingo.* This test requires the courts to look at four factors: the length of the delay, the reason for the delay, the defendant's claim of speedy trial rights during the delay, and the prejudice (if any) to the defendant. Based on these, the court must decide if the case should be dismissed.[6]

Congress has passed a Speedy Trial Act which, in addition to the Sixth Amendment rights under *Barker v. Wingo,* requires the federal government to prosecute all criminal cases within a particular length of time, regardless of whether the defendant is in jail or free on bond. This act requires dismissal of the case if the delay is greater than these limits. Some states have also passed such speedy trial acts. In addition, some federal circuit courts have imposed speedy trial time limits (as a constitutional right) on the state courts within their jurisdiction. Defendants often waive the speedy trial requirements because of unavailability or illness of an important witness, or because of the need for more time to prepare the case.

The Constitution also sets out a right to a public trial. In most cases the general public is freely admitted, although judges may limit the number of spectators and, in certain cases, may exclude the public completely, such as in juvenile cases and cases involving crimes against small children. In 1979 the Supreme Court held that if the prosecution and defense agreed, the judge could bar the public from pretrial proceedings.[7] However, in 1980 the same court made clear, in Richmond Newspapers, Inc. v. Virginia (444 U.S. 896, 100 S.Ct. 2814) that absent extraordinary circumstances, the press and public cannot be excluded from public trials.

Problem 59

a.   Why is the right to a speedy trial important? How soon after arrest should a person be brought to trial? What are the reasons for and against bringing a defendant to trial in a short time after arrest?

b.   Do you think it would be a good idea to televise criminal trials? Why or why not?

Right to Confront Witnesses

The Sixth Amendment provides persons accused of a crime with the right to confront (face-to-face) the witnesses against them and to ask them questions by way of cross-examination. Although a defendant has the right to be present in the courtroom during all stages of the trial, the U.S. Supreme Court has said that this right may be restricted if the defendant becomes disorderly or disruptive. In such instances judges have the power to remove the defendant from the courtroom, to cite him for *contempt of court*, or, in extreme circumstances, to have the defendant bound and gagged.

Freedom from Self-Incrimination

Freedom from self-incrimination means that the defendant cannot be forced to testify against him or herself. This right comes from the Fifth Amendment and can be exercised in all criminal cases. In addition, the prosecutor is forbidden to make any statement drawing the jury's attention to the defendant's failure to testify.

While a defendant has a right not to testify, this right can be waived. Moreover, a defendant who takes the witness stand in his or her own criminal trial must answer all questions.

Related to the right against self-incrimination is the concept of *immunity*. Immunity laws force a witness to answer all questions, even those which are incriminating. However, no evidence obtained directly or indirectly from the compelled testimony can be used against the person in a later criminal prosecution. Prosecutors often use these laws to force persons to testify against codefendants or others involved in the crime.

Problem 60

a. If you were a defense attorney, what would be the advantages and disadvantages of placing a criminal defendant on the stand?

b. If you were a member of the jury in a criminal trial, what would you think if the defendant failed to testify? Would you be affected by the judge's instruction not to draw any conclusion from the defendant's failure to testify?

c. If a defendant is forced to stand in a lineup, give a handwriting sample, or take an alcohol breath test, does this violate the privilege against self-incrimination?

Right to an Attorney

The Sixth Amendment provides that "in all criminal prosecutions, the accused shall enjoy the right to have the assistance of counsel for his defense." Until 1938 this meant that, except in capital cases, a defendant only had the right to an attorney if he or she could afford one. However, in that year the Supreme Court required the federal courts to appoint attorneys for indigent defendants in all federal felony cases. Twenty-five years later, in the case of *Gideon v. Wainright*, the Supreme Court extended the right to appointed counsel to *all* felony defendants, whether in state or federal court.[8] In 1972 the Supreme Court further extended this ruling by requiring that no imprisonment may occur, even in misdemeanor cases, unless the accused is represented by an attorney.[9]

As a result of these decisions, criminal defendants who cannot afford an attorney are appointed one free of charge by the government. These attorneys may be either public defenders or private attorneys.

For persons in jail before trial, their right to counsel includes not only the appointment or retaining of counsel, but also their right to reasonable access to counsel. Jails have an obligation to provide reasonable visiting hours for attorneys and areas for the attorney and client to speak with reasonable privacy. Cases are still being filed and argued on what constitutes reasonable access. Is the rule of permitting an inmate ten phone calls per day to her or his attorney reasonable access? The Supreme Court has not ruled specifically on the times, places, and procedures required. Individual courts continue to decide on a case-by-case basis whether the overall procedures of particular jails provide reasonable access to attorneys. Another issue regarding right to counsel in jail involves government informants. The U.S. Supreme court has ruled that the right to counsel is violated by a paid informant who deliberately elicits incriminating statements from a jail cellmate.[10]

Problem 61

a. Do you think court-appointed attorneys will be as good as those who are privately paid? Why or why not?

b. Assume a defendant wanted to handle his or her own defense. Would this be allowed? Do you think this is a good idea?

c. Assume a lawyer knows that his or her client is guilty. Would it be right for the lawyer to try to convince the jury that the person is innocent? Why or why not?

General Sentencing Rules

SENTENCING

If a person is convicted of or pleads guilty to a crime, he or she will be sentenced by the judge (or a jury in some states) who heard the case. Most states require a period of time between judgment of guilt and sentence.

In most felony cases, a pre-sentence investigation is made or, in some states, a pre-sentence conference is held. The investigation is usually made by a probation officer who interviews the defendant and a variety of other persons in an attempt to present the court with accurate and complete information about the defendant's entire living situation.

The defendant is entitled to counsel at sentencing unless counsel is waived. When it is time for sentencing, the defendant is usually entitled to speak to the court before sentence is given.

A judge can sentence a defendant to almost any term in prison that the statute under which the defendant has been convicted allows, or the judge may sentence the defendant to spend no time in prison (suspend sentence or grant probation). In short, the judge has the broad power, or discretion, to sentence the defendant in the way the judge feels will best suit the needs of both the defendant and society. This discretion accounts for differences in sentences defendants receive.

People often ask: "Why sentence a person to jail or a reformatory? What good does it do?" There are no easy answers to these questions, but over the years people have suggested that there are four basic reasons why society, through sentencing, sends people to an institution for a period of time:

1. *Rehabilitation*—this means that the prisoners will be reformed by the experience in an institution. In other words, if by committing a crime they have wronged society, this "wrong" (we call it a "crime") will be explained to them and programs will be offered whereby they can become successful members of society upon release.

2. *Retribution*—this means punishment for punishment's sake. You are probably familiar with the scene in old movies where a mob of people want to lynch the cattle rustler or the horse thief. That was the response of society to a crime. Today, society still asks that persons who have committed a crime be punished for what they have done.

3. *Deterrence*—The theory of deterrence is that if people know they are going to be punished when they commit a crime, fewer crimes will be committed. A second theory of deterrence is that a person who has been punished will not commit a second crime because of the unpleasant nature of the first punishment.

4. *Protection*—There are some people who are so dangerous that they must be removed from society in order to protect the citizens of the community. This type of person is the hardened criminal who knows no way of life other than crime and who is a danger to the citizens of the community because of his or her conduct and attitude.

When sentencing a convicted defendant, the judge weighs the above theories in his or her own mind. But since judges are human and no two think exactly alike, they often reach different conclusions as to the correct sentence. There is a national trend to impose strict guidelines on sentencing decisions. This is discussed later in the chapter.

Types of Sentences

The established limits within which judges exercise their discretion in sentencing are set down by statutes. Listed below are examples of sentence guidelines that are followed in almost all jurisdictions:

Mandatory Minimum Statutes   These laws limit the judge's discretion by declaring that a defendant convicted of a certain crime (or convicted of a certain crime more than once) must be sentenced to imprisonment for at least an established amount of time. For example, if a state law provides that a person convicted twice of a violent crime while armed must receive a mandatory minimum sentence of not less than five years, the defendant cannot be sentenced by the judge to probation, suspended sentence or anything less than five years.

Multiple Offender (Recidivist) Statutes   A "*recidivist*" is a person who has been convicted of a crime a number of times. Multiple offender statutes allow judges to impose a greater sentence upon those who commit the same crime (or in some jurisdictions, any crime) more than once. Some jurisdictions allow sentences up to 1-1/2 times the maximum sentence for committing the crime a second time. Some statutes triple the penalty the third time the crime is committed. Under federal law, the maximum penalty for carnal knowledge (rape) of a female is 15 years. However, with a second conviction for the same offense, the defendant can receive a 30-year maximum.

Special Sentencing Statutes   Many state and federal laws provide for special types of sentencing. These are sometimes geared to convicted persons with drug, alcohol or psychological problems.

In addition, all states have laws geared to the sentencing of juveniles. Some states have laws requiring institutional treatment for youths. These laws may set a maximum length of time but no minimum.

Suspended Sentence   Under this type of sentence, no jail time is served. The sentence will begin to run if the defendant commits another offense or if his or her conduct warrants incarceration (for example, breaking a condition of probation). There can be suspension of "imposition" of the sentence (where there may be a verdict or plea but no announced sentence) or suspension of "execution" (where a sentence is pronounced but there is no incarceration). Some states permit the court to order a jail term as a condition of probation.

Probation   This is usually given to a defendant in connection with suspension of a sentence. Instead of being sentenced to prison, the convicted defendant is placed "on probation." Being "on probation" means that one must comply with the conditions of probation established by the court.

A defendant on probation must always remember that the probation is in place of going to prison—the sentence has been suspended—and that if probation is violated, many jurisdictions allow the imposition of the entire suspended sentence. Probation will be discussed further on p. 184 of this chapter.

Restitution   Restitution means "making it up" to the victim of the crime so that he or she can recover whatever was lost. This is not often used by the courts in place of imprisonment, but it is sometimes imposed as a condition of probation. There is a growing trend across the country to use this condition of probation.

Fines   The Supreme Court has decided two important cases dealing with fines imposed on indigents. In *Williams v. Illinois*, the Court held that an indigent defendant imprisoned for failure to pay a fine could not serve more than the maximum time required by statute.[11] In *Tate v. Short*, the court held that where no prison penalty existed an indigent could not be jailed because of inability to pay the fine.[12]

Concurrent - Consecutive Sentences

A person who is convicted of (or who pleads to) more than one charge or crime at the same time can be given either concurrent or consecutive sentences. If the defendant is sentenced concurrently, he or she serves both sentences at the same time. For instance, if the defendant is sentenced to two terms of one to three years but serves the sentence concurrently, he or she serves one to three years and is eligible for parole in one.

If a convicted defendant is sentenced consecutively, he or she must serve the sentences one after another. For example, if the defendant is sentenced to two one to three-year sentences consecutively, he or she has been sentenced to a term of two to six years and is eligible for parole after two years. If the court does not specifically state whether the sentences will be consecutive or concurrent, the general rule is that they will be concurrent. A court may not impose consecutive sentences for two crimes that have the same elements of proof and arise out of the same incident.

Credit for Time Served in Jail

Many times a defendant has already served time in jail when the court imposes a sentence. This is either because the defendant has not made bond or because he or she has been in jail awaiting parole or probation revocation. In some states, the law requires that the time already served be credited toward the sentence. The federal statutes and some state statutes credit the defendant with time spent in jail for charges that result in the sentence. Other states leave this to the judge's discretion.

The states also differ on whether time spent successfully on probation will be credited to the defendant if probation is revoked. In some, the sentence runs while the defendant is on probation, and in others, no credit is allowed.

Capital Punishment

The most severe and controversial form of sentencing is the death penalty. The death penalty has a long history in American law. During the colonial years capital punishment was imposed for a number of different crimes, although in later years it was generally reserved for murder, rape, and kidnapping. Crimes for which capital punishment is imposed are called *capital offenses*. Since the 1930's the use of the death penalty has gradually declined. For example, in 1935 there were 199 executions in the United States, in 1960 there were 56, and by 1967 there was only 1. Finally, in the 1972 case of *Furman v. Georgia*, the U.S. Supreme Court ruled that the death penalty, as then administered, was in violation of the Constitution.

The Court did not rule out the use of the death penalty as a punishment but rather held that capital punishment was being arbitrarily applied and left too much discretion to the judge or jury in each case.[13] After the *Furman* case, many states changed their laws to comply with the Supreme Court decision. In 1976 the Court held that the death penalty was not necessarily "cruel and unusual punishment" in violation of the U.S. Constitution.[14]

More than thirty-five states now have laws that authorize the use of the death penalty in certain cases. In line with the Supreme Court ruling on this issue, most of these laws forbid the state from automatically imposing the death penalty in murder cases. Rather, they require that the judge and jury consider any factors that might raise or lower the seriousness of the offense. These are known as *aggravating and mitigating factors*.

Opponents of capital punishment argue that it is morally wrong to take the life of anyone convicted of a crime. They also contend that the death penalty does not deter crime. In support of this contention, they cite studies which show that most murders result from fear, passion, mental disorder, or anger of the moment. Thus, they say the death penalty is no more of a deterrent than the possibility of a long prison term. Opponents also point to the possibility of executing an innocent person. Unlike lesser sentences, the death penalty cannot be reversed if new evidence is found.

Those favoring the use of capital punishment point to opinion polls, which indicate that most Americans favor the death penalty and say that it is morally justifiable to take the life of a convicted murderer. They also argue that it does serve as a deterrent to crime and that it will save the government the cost of keeping convicted murderers in prison for long periods of time.

Problem 62

a. Do you favor or oppose use of the death penalty? Explain your answer. If you favor it, to what crimes should it apply?

b. If you oppose the death penalty, what do you think is the strongest argument in favor of it? If you favor the death penalty, what do you think is the strongest argument against it?

Recent Developments in Sentencing

As noted above, most sentencing in this country is imposed under the theory that inmates will be either rehabilitated or deterred, or that society will be protected or receive retribution. However, there is a growing opinion that correctional facilities do not rehabilitate or deter people, that society has to be protected from only a very few people, and that retribution, except in crimes of violence and then not every crime, is unimportant. In addition, under most sentencing statutes judges have had almost unlimited discretion to impose either a particular term of years or no incarceration at all. This practice has led to sentences that do not necessarily reflect the crime for which the person has been convicted, but rather reflect the judge before whom the conviction was obtained.

These factors and others have led a number of states to abolish indeterminate sentences and discretion on the part of the judges. (Congress is presently considering similar legislation for federal courts.) These state legislatures have imposed "determinate sentences" whereby the term of years that can be imposed (if any) is specifically stated, and judges have very little discretion. Although certain factors to guide the judge in determining the sentence are included in the statutes (i.e., the age of the convicted person, the type of crime, the criminal record of the felon, whether the victim was injured, etc.), a lesser or greater sentence than recommended by the statute cannot be imposed unless the judge notes specific findings of fact as to why the greater or lesser sentence is appropriate. This legislation also provides for meaningful appellate review.

Some of these new laws also abolish the concept of granting parole and parole supervision following serving a sentence. However, the concept of reducing time served in prison for good behavior, sometimes called earning "good time", has usually been continued.

"Post-conviction relief" is any action in a court which either reverses or modifies the defendant's conviction.

POST-CONVICTION RELIEF

Appeals

An appeal is a direct attack on the conviction. Although the U.S. Supreme Court has never declared that an appeal of a conviction is required by the Constitution, all states and the federal system do provide some system of appellate review from a criminal conviction.

Appeals are expensive—probably more expensive than trials themselves. However, in recent years, a number of appellate cases have determined that the rights of needy defendants include the right to a review of their convictions.

For example, one Supreme Court case held that a convicted indigent was entitled to a free transcript on appeal.[15] Federal appellate courts are required to appoint counsel for indigents appealing their cases.[16]

Appellate rules of procedure differ widely from state to state. Because of the many procedures involved, an appeal can move very slowly.

Not every issue can be appealed. The next sections describe some limitations on appeals.

Uncontested Issues   During the course of a trial some matters are stipulated (agreed to by the defendant, defense attorney and the prosecutor), such as the names of witnesses, days of the week when particular events happened, the fact that a particular person is a duly sworn police officer, etc. Issues that were agreed upon at trial are not arguable on appeal, and the court will not let the defendant present the matter in the appellate *brief*.

Also, during a trial the attorneys object to questions or answers or evidence offered by the other side. Ordinarily, the failure of a defendant to object to a matter introduced at trial will mean that the defendant cannot argue on appeal that the matter should not have been introduced in evidence. In other words, the failure of the defense attorney to object will mean that the issue is not available to the defendant on appeal.

Reversible and Harmless Error   Mistakes occur at every trial. An appellate court reviews the record to determine whether the particular mistake injured or prejudiced the party who is appealing the decision in the case. If the mistake did affect the outcome, it is called "reversible error" since the appellate court will change (reverse) the judgment of the trial court.

If it did not prejudice the complaining party, the mistake is called "harmless error." For example, the admission of an illegally obtained confession is "harmless" (although it is a serious error) if the appeals court is certain that, based on all the evidence, the defendant would have been convicted even without the confession.

If the error is not objected to by counsel at trial and is not set forth in the appellate brief, the general rule is that the court may not consider the error. There are exceptions, however, that permit an appellate court to consider errors not raised on appeal. Such errors include "fundamental" and "plain" errors. Fundamental error occurs when a very important right of the party, usually a right given by the Constitution, is denied. Plain error is a mistake on the record that is very clear to the court. For instance, if the trial court did not have the authority (jurisdiction) to hear the case, this would be apparent (plain) to the appellate court and would be raised by the court itself.

Motion for a New Trial

Following a verdict of guilty, there is a period of some days or weeks before sentencing. Many courts will not hear a motion for a new trial until after sentencing. In some jurisdictions, appeals and motions for a new trial are filed "after entry of judgment," which means after sentence is imposed. However, all jurisdictions impose very strict time limits within which such a motion can be filed.

Usually, a motion for a new trial must be based on one or more of the following: (1) a verdict contrary to the weight of the evidence; (2) misconduct that affected the jury; (3) prosecutorial bad faith; (4) incorrect evidentiary ruling by the court; (5) incorrect instructions to the jury; and (6) newly discovered evidence.

"Bad faith" by the prosecutor means that he or she deliberately violated a rule of the court that he or she was aware of at the time. The motion is made to the judge who presided over the trial. A denial of the motion is appealable.

Some examples of bad faith include failure of the prosecutor to turn over to the defense attorney evidence favorable to the defendant, an attempt by the prosecutor to intimidate or threaten the defendant's witnesses, and the offering of testimony known to be untrue by the prosecutor.

By far the most frequent motion for a new trial is based on newly discovered evidence. This motion may appear to be an easy one to make because there is usually some favorable evidence to the defendant that was not introduced at trial. However, not any evidence can be used.

First, the defendant must show the court that the evidence in question was not discovered until after the trial was completed and the verdict was entered. Second, the defendant must show that the evidence in question *could not have been discovered or was unknown* before the verdict. In other words, the defendant must convince the court that the evidence in question was hidden in some way so that neither the defendant nor his or her attorney could have known about it. Third, the evidence in question may not be evidence that would be used only to impeach a government witness. In other words, the evidence may not be the kind that is helpful to the defendant's attorney only in discrediting a government witness. Fourth, even if the above three conditions are met, the defendant must show the court that the evidence in question is likely to change the verdict if a new trial is granted. This last requirement is very difficult, because it is really a requirement that the evidence in question be very important and, in fact, crucial. Obviously, any evidence that important would probably have been known to the defendant before the trial ever began.

The denial of a motion for a new trial can be appealed to the next highest court.

Most state courts have time limits within which a motion for a new trial must be filed. If the evidence is discovered after the time limit has expired, habeas corpus is the only means by which the new evidence may be shown to a court.

Habeas Corpus—Attacking the Underlying Conviction

Habeas corpus is discussed in more detail in Chapter 5. It is a form of post-conviction relief because it is most often employed to challenge the underlying conviction after the ordinary appeal process is completed or time for appeal has run out.

State Habeas Corpus   State habeas corpus statutes can generally be used to challenge confinement based on an illegal conviction as well as to challenge illegal conditions. The procedures are the same as described in Chapter 5: the inmate files the "application" or "motion" for habeas corpus and the writ is issued by the judge alone. This is the most common kind of "attack" on the conviction. However, there are often many restrictions on these actions, depending on the state statute. For example, usually an inmate must have exhausted all other state remedies, including an appeal of the case, before the writ of habeas corpus will be recognized. A state prisoner is not entitled to raise the same issues again and again in the writs.

Federal Habeas Corpus   Federal habeas corpus under 28 U.S.C. §2241 (c) (3) is available to state prisoners attacking their convictions in state courts only after they have exhausted all other state remedies. A violation of federal law or a constitutional right must be alleged.

The motion must be filed in the place where the inmate is confined, regardless of whether he or she was convicted there. For example, an inmate attacking her conviction under federal habeas corpus in Texas must file her motion in the District Court where the prison is located.

Again, there is a limit on the number of habeas corpus motions that can be filed. The present Supreme Court has begun to limit the use of federal habeas corpus by state prisoners. This may be in part because the court believes many motions that are filed have no merit, and in part because the number of motions filed has greatly increased.

In a major recent decision, *Stone v. Powell*, the Supreme Court severely limited the grounds on which a state prisoner may be granted federal habeas corpus relief. The court held that habeas corpus may not be granted on the ground that evidence obtained in an unconstitutional search and seizure was introduced at trial, where the state had already provided an opportunity for full and fair litigation of the Fourth Amendment claim.[17] Some legal scholars believe that other grounds for constitutional challenge will also be ruled as improper for a habeas corpus action in the near future.

Federal prisoners file a 28 U.S.C. §2255 motion. If this motion is attacking the conviction, it is filed in the court where the sentence was imposed. It should be noted that *Stone v. Powell*, involved state prisoners, but it is likely that courts will also see it as restricting a federal prisoner's right to attack a conviction based on an alleged illegal search.

Motion to Correct or Reduce Sentence

Most sentences are limited to a maximum term by law. But some courts mistakenly exceed the maximum term prescribed by law. Under such circumstances, a motion to correct sentence is filed.

Unlike other motions described in this chapter, a motion to correct or reduce a sentence is *not* a motion attacking the underlying conviction.

Sometimes a *motion to reduce sentence* is a motion for leniency: it asks the court to reconsider the sentence that has been imposed and to look more favorably on the defendant. Some states have review panels with the power to reduce or increase the sentence imposed by the court. Application to the review panel is made by the inmate within a specified time.

Revocation of Probation

When a person on probation violates a condition of probation or commits a new crime, the probation may be revoked. Violations other than arrest for a new offense are called "technical violations." In some states, probationers arrested for a new offense may be held in jail without bond for a specified number of days.

Most states and the federal government require by statute that there be a revocation hearing after notice to the probationer. The probation officer makes a recommendation at this hearing. If probation is revoked, the original sentence under the statute may be imposed, perhaps with no credit given for time served on probation, depending on the state statute.

The U.S. Supreme Court in the case of *Gagnon v. Scarpelli* held the following procedures necessary for a probation revocation hearing:

1. At a preliminary as well as final revocation hearing, the probationer must be given: notice of the charges, an opportunity to appear and present evidence, a partial right to confront and cross-examine witnesses, a right to a truly independent factfinder, and a right to a written finding of facts.

2. An indigent probationer who may have difficulty presenting his or her version of the disputed facts or presenting complicated evidence must have appointed counsel.

3. Where appointed counsel is denied, the probationer is entitled to have reasons for the refusal in writing.[18]

Parole

Introduction   Parole is release from prison for the remainder of the inmate's sentence. During this period, the inmate, called a parolee, will be under the supervision of a parole officer and be required to obey certain conditions. The purpose and theory of parole is to "reform" or "rehabilitate" the parolee and to protect society by supervising him or her before he or she is given total freedom in the community.

The parole process has five possible stages: (1) the inmate becomes eligible for parole consideration; (2) the parole release decision is made, usually after a hearing; (3) if parole is granted, a release date is set in the future and the inmate remains incarcerated until that date; (4) supervised release on parole; and (5) revocation of parole if a condition of parole is violated.

There is no constitutional right to parole, in fact before 1877, there was no parole. Parole is created by federal and state statutes and each state and federal legislature has the power to abolish or to change the terms of the parole laws. In some places, parole has now been abolished.

Problem 63

The law revision commission in your state or jurisdiction is considering the elimination of parole. Inmates, correctional personnel from the local state correctional institution, members of the local parole board and citizens from the community are given an opportunity to comment on the proposed change. What recommendation do you think each group would make? List the arguments each group would make to support their recommendation.

Eligibility for Parole Consideration What the federal or state parole statute says will determine when an inmate becomes eligible for parole consideration. Most require that a certain minimum portion of the sentence be served. For instance, an inmate may be required to serve one third or the minimum term of the total sentence before parole will be considered. For serious crimes, some states require that two-thirds of the sentence be served.

In most states, this eligibility date may be advanced because "good time" is earned. Good time is credit awarded because of good behavior to reduce the release date.

If an inmate is not released after being considered on the parole eligibility date, the inmate must be released on the mandatory release date. This date is computed by subtracting good time earned from the maximum time to be served on the sentence. For instance, if an inmate serves a 3 to 9 year sentence in a state that sets the parole eligibility date at one third the sentence, the first parole eligibility date is at 3 years. If the inmate earns 10 days of good time per month, the eligibility date is moved up 10 days for each month in prison, provided good time is not taken away for disciplinary infractions. If the inmate is denied parole each time he or she was eligible, he or she would have to be released in 9 years minus the good time earned.

Parole Decision   Inmates have no absolute right to parole at the time they become eligible for consideration for parole. A paroling authority, usually a state or county parole board for nonfederal inmates and the U.S. Parole Commission for federal inmates, makes the decision to release or to continue confinement.

How do parole authorities make their decision? There are two basic types of parole release statutes: one which requires the parole board to grant parole unless certain specified factors are present;[19] and one which permits parole if the parole authority finds a reasonable probability the prisoners can be released successfully. Most states have the second type of statute which gives much more discretion to the parole authority.

The Supreme Court recently rejected inmates' claim that any state-created parole system gives rise to a constitutionally protected right of due process in the parole decision process. The Court found that due process was required only under the first type of parole statute described above, because the state provides an "expectancy of release." When inmates have a state-given expectancy of release, they must be given an opportunity to be heard (not necessarily a formal hearing) and, upon denial of parole, a statement of the reasons, in general terms, informing them in what respects they "fall short of qualifying for parole."

The second type of parole statute does not give inmates any right to parole, since it merely holds out a hope that parole might be granted.[20] The Supreme Court said each statute must be examined on a case-by-case basis. Several states have also determined that their statutes do not create any parole "expectancy" or right.[21] However, even under this type of parole statute, the decision cannot be made so arbitrarily or capriciously as to be beyond the discretion of the parole authority.[22]

Problem 64

Determine whether the parole release statutes below require due process protections and state your reasons.

Statute 1: Discretionary release on parole shall not be granted merely as a reward for good conduct or efficient performance of duties while confined but after considering if there is a reasonable probability that, if such inmate is released, he will live and remain at liberty without violating the law, and that his release is not incompatible with the welfare of society and will not so depreciate the seriousness of his crime as to undermine respect for law.

Statute 2: Whenever the Board of Parole considers the release of a committed offender who is eligible for release on parole, it shall order his release unless it is of the opinion that his release should be deferred because:

a. There is a substantial risk that he will not conform to the conditions of parole;

b. His release would depreciate the seriousness of his crime or promote disrespect for law;

c. His release would have a substantially adverse effect on institutional discipline; or

d. His continued correctional treatment, medical care, or vocational or other training in the facility will substantially enhance his capacity to lead a law-abiding life when released at a later date.

Parole Rescission What happens in the situation where an inmate has been granted parole but is not actually released —can the parole authority change its order of parole without giving the inmate a hearing?

The Supreme Court has not ruled on this issue and the lower courts have approached the problem in three different ways: (1) that this is similar to parole revocation and requires the due process afforded at parole revocation hearings;[23] (2) that this is an extension or modification of the initial parole release hearing, therefore no written notice or hearing is required;[24] and (3) that this is similar to a disciplinary penalty of loss of good time and requires a *Wolff v. McDonnell* due process hearing.[25]

Conditions of Parole Once paroled, most parolees are assigned parole officers whose duties are to help them readjust to society, help with jobs, arrange for counseling, etc. These officers are also responsible for making sure their parolees follow certain conditions. As with probation, these conditions must be reasonable. Common conditions are to require parolees to report regularly to a parole officer; to refrain from associating with known criminals; to abstain from liquor or to use it in moderation; to remain in the community and to keep the employment to which they were released; to keep their whereabouts and activities known; not to possess firearms nor to drive an automobile without permission; and generally not to change their status in any way without prior notification and approval of the parole officer.

Problem 65

a.   Upon release from prison, Earl McNight started working at a nightclub which employed other ex-convicts. The Parole Board decided this was a violation of his parole condition prohibiting contact with ex-convicts and revoked his parole. Do you think the Board's decision was proper?

b.   While on parole, Phillip and Daniel Berrigan, two priests who were leaders in the Vietnam anti-war movement, had been granted permission by the Parole Board to leave their district for speechmaking. However, the Parole Board would not grant permission for them to travel to North Vietnam to visit with religious leaders. Do you think their decision was proper?

Revocation of Parole   Once parole has been granted, it may be revoked for a violation of any condition or for commission of a new crime. Some of the reasons given for the power to revoke parole are that: (1) parole is a matter of grace, given by the executive; (2) the parolee has agreed by contract with the authorities to abide by certain conditions and must not violate them; and (3) the parolee is still officially in custody, even though allowed to remain in the community.

Issuing a Warrant   Parole authorities can issue a warrant if parolees commit a new offense or violate one of the conditions of parole. Under federal law, a warrant must be issued "as soon as practicable" after discovery of the alleged violation and the warrant must provide written notice of the conditions violated, the parolees' rights, and possible action that may be taken.

Preliminary Hearing   Under the U.S. Supreme Court case of *Morrissey v. Brewer*, parolees are entitled to a preliminary hearing to determine whether there is probable cause to believe that they have committed a parole violation. At this hearing, parolees are allowed to speak on their own behalf and to bring letters from people who can provide relevant information concerning the parolees' behavior. The parolees must receive notice of the hearing and the violation and also have a right to a more complete revocation hearing later.[26]

Problem 66

Ben, a parolee, had his apartment searched without a warrant and narcotics were found. This illegally-seized evidence was introduced at a revocation hearing, although it could not be placed in evidence at trial because of the exclusionary rule.

a. Should it be permitted in evidence at the revocation hearing? Why or why not?

b. Does a parolee have a right to privacy and a right to the protection of the Fourth Amendment?

Revocation Hearing   Under the *Morrissey* decision, before parole is revoked, parolees are entitled to minimum due process, including:

1. written notice of the charges;

2. disclosure to the parolees of evidence against them;

3. an opportunity to be heard in person and to present witnesses and evidence;

4. the right of confrontation and cross-examination of witnesses;

5. a "neutral and detached" hearing body, such as the parole board; and

6. a written statement of the reasons why parole was revoked.

Later, in the probation revocation case of *Gagnon v. Scarpelli*, the Supreme Court said that the need for appointment of counsel for indigents should be left to the discretion of the state revoking authority. However, the Court decided that there is a "presumptive" right to counsel where the individuals deny the violations and where, even though they do not contest the existence of the violations, they have some complicated reasons why they should not be locked up.[27] This rule applies to parole revocation situations.

In most states, the parolee whose parole is revoked will not receive any credit toward the sentence for time spent on parole. This means that parolees who are on parole for four years and have their parole revoked could be made to serve the rest of their sentence as if they had never been on parole. Some states grant credit for time spent successfully on parole, while a very few states grant credit for time on parole plus good time credits accumulated while on parole.

Problem 67

Martha has been on parole for one year. She was released from prison after serving a minimum 2 years for second degree burglary. She has several prior convictions for minor offenses including disorderly conduct and simple assault. Most of her trouble with the law has resulted from her drinking, because she is an alcoholic.

While on parole, she has attended Alcoholics Anonymous and has been living with her mother and working as a seamstress in her community. She moved in with her boyfriend and did not report in for three weeks to her parole officer. Her parole officer issues a warrant, alleged she violated two of her parole conditions: (1) to keep her parole officer informed of her whereabouts; and (2) to maintain regular contact with her parole officer.

a. Should her parole be revoked?

b. Would your answer be different is she were also seen drinking in a bar and a parole condition was to refrain from drinking?

c. Would it be different if she had been arrested for petit larceny but claims she is innocent? What if she is tried and acquitted, can her parole still be revoked?

References

1. 378 U.S. 478, 84 S.Ct. 1758 (1964).
2. 384 U.S. 436, 86 S.Ct. 1602 (1966).
3. 401 U.S. 222, 91 S.Ct. 643 (1971).
4. 367 U.S. 643, 81 S.Ct. 1684 (1961).
5. 430 U.S. 387, 97 S.Ct. 1232 (1977).
6. 407 U.S. 514, 92 S.Ct. 2182 (1972).
7. Gannett Co. v. DePasquale, 443 U.S. 368, 99 S.Ct. 2898 (1979).

8. 372 U.S. 335, 83 S.Ct. 792 (1963).

9. Argersinger v. Hamlin, 407 U.S. 25, 92 S.Ct. 2006 (1972).

10. U.S. v. Henry,   U.S.   ,100 S.Ct. 2183 (1980).

11. 399 U.S. 235, 90 S.Ct. 2018 (1970).

12. 401 U.S. 395, 91 S.Ct. 668 (1971).

13. 408 U.S. 238, 92 S.Ct. 2726 (1972).

14. Gregg v. Georgia, 428 U.S. 153, 96 S.Ct. 2909 (1976).

15. Griffin v. People of the State of Illinois, 351 U.S. 12, 76 S.Ct. 585 (1956).

16. Ellis v. U.S., 356 U.S. 674, 78 S.Ct. 974 (1958).

17. Stone v. Powell, 428 U.S. 465, 96 S.Ct. 3037 (1976) and Wolff v. Rice, 428 U.S. 465, 96 S.Ct. 3037 (1976).

18. 411 U.S. 778, 93 S.Ct. 1756 (1973).

19. The Model Penal Code recommends this type of statute.

20. Greenholtz v. Inmates of the Nebraska Penal and Correctional Complex, 442 U.S. 1, 99 S.Ct. 2100 (1979).

21. No legitimate expectation of parole: Boothe v. Hammock, 605 F.2d 661 (2nd Cir.1979); Austin v. Armstrong. 473 F.Supp. 1114 (D.Nev.1979); Shirley v. Chestnut, 603 F.2d 805 (10th Cir.1979); Robinson v. Mabry, 476 F.Supp. 1022 (D.Ark.1979); Campbell v. Montana State Bd. of Pardons, 470 F.Supp. 1301 (D.Mont.1979), Due process applies: Young v. Duckworth, 394 N.E.2d 123 (Ind.1979). See also Matter of Sinka, 92 Wash.2d 555, 599 P.2d 1275(1979).

22. Brown v. Lundgren, 528 F.2d 1050 (5th Cir. 1976).

23. Williams v. U.S. Board of Parole, 383 F.Supp. 402 (D.Conn.1974).

24. Sexton v. Wise, 494 F.2d 1176 (5th Cir. 1974); Koptik v. Chappell, 321 F.2d 388 (D.C.Cir.1963).

25. Jackson v. Wise, 390 F.Supp. 19 (D.C.Cal.1975).

26. 408 U.S. 471, 92 S.Ct. 2593 (1972).

27. Gagnon v. Scarpelli, Supra.

appendix A GLOSSARY OF LEGAL TERMS

Abridge infringe upon; take away from; restrict.

Adversary Proceeding a hearing at which opposing sides present their point of view.

Affirm to agree with the decision of a lower court.

Agency a government administrative division that is responsible for enforcing laws and promulgating rules for regulating a particular subject area, i.e., corrections.

Allegation statement of fact from one side's point of view that will be proven true or false at a hearing or trial.

Allege to claim an unproven fact to be true.

Amendment a change or addition to a bill or law.

Appeal a procedure of review by which a higher court or agency examines lower court decisions for errors and either upholds the lower court's decision or reverses it.

Appellate a type of court that hears cases appealed from lower courts.

Arbitrator a person with the power to hear and settle a dispute.

Arraignment appearance of a criminal defendant before a judge in court, where the charges are read and a plea is entered. In a misdemeanor case, this may be the first appearance. In a felony, it is usually after a grand jury indictment is issued.

Assault a physical attack or

threat of attack by a person with the apparent ability to carry out the threat.

Attest swear that something is true; usually in writing.

Bad Faith acting in a manner which indicates that a person is intentionally misleading, deceiving, or is prompted by some bad motive.

Bail the security provided as assurance that a person under arrest will return to court.

Balancing Test a decision-making process used by the court to balance two opposing interests and resolve the issue.

Bar to prohibit or keep from.

Beneficiary a person who receives money or property through a trust, will, insurance policy or contract.

Binding enforceable or having the force of law.

Bond a form of money bail required by the courts to allow the accused person to be released from jail before trial.

Brief a written argument stating one's case that is filed with an appellate court.

Burglary breaking and entering a building with the intent to commit a felony.

Capital Crime a crime for which one can receive the death penalty.

Censor to keep part or all of something from being written, published or looked at.

Charge to formally accuse of a crime.

Circuits the 11 geographical divisions of the U.S. that each contain U.S. District Courts and a Court of Appeals that hears appeals from the District Courts in the circuit.

Civil Case a lawsuit brought against a person or organization asking for money damages, or for court orders requiring that action be taken or stopped.

Claim lawsuit.

Collective Bargaining a process for labor and management to meet and work out an agreement to settle labor conditions and disputes.

Conjugal Visit a visit in a correctional institution that allows an inmate and spouse to have sexual intercourse.

Constitutional Claim a claim in a lawsuit alleging violation of a constitutional right.

Contraband certain goods, the possession, import or export of which is illegal.

Contract a legally enforceable agreement between two or more persons; each party promises to do some act or make some payment.

Corporal Punishment physical punishment such as whipping or beating.

Counsel an attorney

Criminal Case a court proceeding to determine the guilt or innocence of one charged with an act that violates a penal law.

Cross-Examination the opposing side's right to question a witness during a trial or hearing.

Custody to have responsibility for the care and keeping of a person or thing.

Damages money asked for and awarded by a court in a civil case to a person for injuries or losses suffered through the fault of another.

Declaratory Relief   a court judgment that states the rights of the parties regarding some legal matter; no action is ordered, nor are damages awarded.

Defendant   a person who is alleged to have committed some wrong; a party in either a civil or criminal suit.

Deposition   a form of discovery where a witness's sworn statement or testimony is taken out of court, usually with the lawyers for both sides present and a court reporter to record everything said; the manuscript of the proceeding is also a deposition.

Discovery   the pre-trial process of obtaining information from the other side in a lawsuit (depositions and interrogatories are two types of discovery).

Due Process of Law   a phrase in the Fifth and the Fourteenth Amendments meaning that persons have a right to be treated fairly before the government takes away their liberty or property.

Enact   to put into effect as a law.

Enjoin   to order a person or organization by court decree to stop doing something; injunctive relief.

Equal Protection   phrase in the Fourteenth Amendment meaning that persons in similar situations have a right to be treated equally under the law; not discriminated against.

Felon   person who has been convicted of a felony.

Felony   a crime punishable by a prison sentence of a year or more.

Findings   a court's rulings or decisions on questions of law or fact, i.e., the court "found" that . . .

Grand Jury   a group of 12 to 23 people who hear preliminary evidence and decide whether a person should be formally charged with a crime.

Grounds   basis or foundation for an action; legal basis for filing a lawsuit.

Habeas Corpus   Latin phrase meaning "You have the body." A legal procedure (writ) available to anyone to challenge an illegal custody or confinement.

Hold   to decide or rule.

Homicide   act of killing a person.

Immunity   protection from prosecution or liability.

Incarcerate   to confine in a jail or prison.

Incriminate   to make a person look guilty or to show involvement in a criminal offense.

Indemnification   a security given by one person or institution to reimburse another for loss or damage.

Indictment   a formal charge by a grand jury, accusing defendant of a crime.

Information   a formal accusation of a crime made by a public official such as a prosecuting attorney (like indictment, but not made by grand jury).

Injunction a court's order directing a person not to do something, or to perform some act.

Injunctive Relief relief from some particular act granted by a court order; to *enjoin*.

Injuries wrongs, damages or hurts to a person's body, property, rights or reputation.

Instrument a tool, weapon, or document.

Instrumentalities tools or other items involved in carrying out some act.

Interrogatories a set of written questions directed to the opposing side in a lawsuit.

Invalid not enforceable or legally binding.

Jail an institution that holds accused persons prior to trial (pre-trial detainees) and sometimes short-term convicted inmates.

Judgment a court's final decision in a case.

Jurisdiction the geographical or subject area in which a court, judge or official has authority to act.

Jurisprudence the study of law and the philosophy of law.

Larceny stealing.

Lawsuit proceeding in which one person or organization sues another for money damages and/or asks for a court order; a civil action or civil case.

Legislature an official group of people who make and pass laws.

Liability a legally enforceable obligation or responsibility for something, as for a debt or harm to another.

Litigation a lawsuit.

Lobby to influence a legislator's vote on a bill, or to persuade a legislator to write a bill.

Malpractice a lack of competence or care (negligence) on the part of professionals (i.e., doctors and lawyers) so as to cause injuries to their patients or clients.

Mandamus a proceeding brought to compel a person to do some act; a court order that some action be taken.

Mediator a person who helps two or more parties settle a dispute (like an arbitrator in arbitration hearings).

Misdemeanor a crime punishable by less than a year in prison.

Mock simulated; an imitation or make-believe act such as a mock hearing.

Motion a request to a judge or decision maker to make some ruling or take some action on a matter involved in a lawsuit.

Negligence the failure to take reasonable care in doing something or in not doing something for someone to whom a duty is owed, thereby causing harm or injury to that person.

Nolo Contendere Latin phrase meaning "I will not contest it;" a type of plea to a criminal charge, in which the defendant does not directly admit guilt but also does not contest or deny the charge, and therefore accepts whatever punishment is ordered.

Parole supervised release from prison before the full sentence is served.

Penitentiary a prison.

Perjury lying under oath.

Petit Larceny theft of an item worth less than a certain sum; the amount varies from state to state.

Plaintiff a person who files a lawsuit against another.

Precedent an appellate court's decision on a question of law that guides future decisions of lower courts on similar questions of law.

Presentment a hearing where persons arrested for misdemeanors appear before a judge to be read their rights and to make their pleas.

Pretrial Detainees persons charged with a crime who are being held in jail until trial.

Prison an institution for the incarceration of felons.

Probation a form of sentence by which a person convicted of a crime is allowed to remain in the community instead of serving a jail or prison sentence.

Pro se to appear in court and represent oneself without a lawyer.

Prosecute to proceed against an individual, in a criminal case; i.e., the state prosecutes.

Proximate Cause the legal cause of an accident or injury.

Quell to subdue, quiet.

Recidivist a repeat offender; a person who has been convicted of a crime more than once.

Relief court ordered compensation or assistance given to the party that wins a civil lawsuit; this includes money damages or court orders and may be referred to as declaratory relief or injunctive relief.

Remand to send back, as when a court sends (remands) a case back to a lower court for some further determination.

Remedy a correction of some wrong; a compensation for an injury or harm.

Reverse to set aside (void) a lower court's decision and make a new one.

Rule a court's decison on a matter.

Scope of Authority subject areas of responsibility and control.

Sovereign Immunity a government's freedom from being held liable for money damages in civil actions.

Statute law made by legislatures.

Suit lawsuit.

Summons a court paper notifying a person that he or she is being sued and requiring his/her presence in court at a certain time and place.

Third Party Custody a form of bail in which a person is put under the care or supervision of another person not involved in the criminal charges.

Tort   a civil wrong involving a breach of some obligation that results in injury to a person.

Undue   too much; excessive; improper.

Use Immunity   protection given by the government to a person in return for testifying; it prevents the government from using any statements made during that testimony, or any evidence discovered because of the testimony, as evidence in a later criminal prosecution of that witness.

Verdict   a decision by a judge or jury in a case.

Void   not enforceable or valid; not legally binding.

Warrant   a paper issued by a judge or magistrate authorizing some action such as an arrest or a search of some premises.

Writ   a court order requiring that a certain act be done, or that a certain act not be done.

appendix B
SPECIFIC AMENDMENTS TO THE CONSTITUTION

Amendment 1

Congress shall make no law respecting an establishment of religion, or prohibiting the free exercise thereof; or abridging the freedom of speech, or of the press; or the right of the people peaceably to assemble, and to petition the Government for a redress of grievances.

Amendment 4

The right of the people to be secure in their persons, houses, papers, and effects, against unreasonable searches and seizures, shall not be violated, and no Warrants shall issue, but upon probable cause, supported by Oath or affirmation, and particularly describing the place to be searched, and the persons or things to be seized.

Amendment 5

No person shall be held to answer for a capital, or otherwise infamous crime, unless on a presentment or indictment of a Grand Jury, except in cases arising in the land or naval forces, or in the

Militia, when in actual service in time of War or public danger; nor shall any person be subject for the same offense to be twice put in jeopardy of life or limb; nor shall be compelled in any criminal case to be a witness against himself, nor be deprived of life, liberty, or property, without due process of law; nor shall private property be taken for public use, without just compensation.

Amendment 6

In all criminal prosecutions, the accused shall enjoy the right to a speedy and public trial, by an impartial jury of the State and district wherein the crime shall have been committed, which district shall have been previously ascertained by law, and to be informed of the nature and cause of the accusation; to be confronted with the witnesses against him; to have compulsory process for obtaining witnesses in his favor, and have the Assistance of Counsel for his defense.

Amendment 8

Excessive bail shall not be required, nor excessive fines imposed, nor cruel and unusual punishments inflicted.

Amendment 9

The enumeration in the Constitution, of certain rights, shall not be construed to deny or disparage others retained by the people.

Amendment 10

The powers not delegated to the United States by the Constitution, nor prohibited by it to the States, are reserved to the States respectively, or to the people.

Amendment 11

The Judicial power of the United States shall not be construed to extend to any suit in law or equity, commenced or prosecuted against one of the United States by Citizens of another State, or by Citizens or Subjects of any Foreign State.

Amendment 13

SECTION 1. Neither slavery nor involuntary servitude, except as a punishment for crime whereof the party shall have been duly convicted, shall exist within the United States, or any place subject to their jurisdiction.

Amendment 14

SECTION 1. All persons born or naturalized in the United States are subject to the jurisdiction thereof, are citizens of the United States and of the State wherein they reside. No state shall make or enforce any law which shall abridge the privileges or immunities of citizens of the United States; or shall any State deprive any person of life, liberty, or property, without due process of law; nor deny to any person within its jurisdiction the equal protection of the laws.

appendix C ANSWERS TO PROBLEMS

Answer to Problem 1

This introductory exercise is designed to illustrate:

a. the pervasiveness of law;

b. that the law concerns both civil and criminal matters; and

c. the positive nature of law (i.e. most laws are protective, not punitive.)

There is an infinite set of possible answers to this problem. The following are listed for purposes of illustration.

Activity	Laws	Type of Law
1. Sorting mail	Cost of postage	Federal
	Rules on opening and reading mail	U.S. Constitution and agency rules
	Rules on obscenity	Court-made laws and agency rules

2. Taking count	Time count taken	Agency Rules
	Escaped inmates	State law; agency rules
3. Feeding residents	Quality of food	Constitution; federal and state law; health codes
	Food additives	Federal agency
	Nutrition content	Federal agency; court-made law
	Religious diets	Constitutional and court-made law
	Health diets	Constitutional law and court-made law

Answer to Problem 2

a. Your opinion will form your answer to this question. The arguments for convicting them of murder include: they violated the law to which they are subject, and no legal defenses apply; people who take the life of another are guilty of murder; any mitigating circumstances will be considered at sentencing but are not relevant to the issue of guilt. The arguments against convicting them include: the law did not apply to them, since they were their own society; the law of survival is a higher law; the sailors had the defense of mental insanity; while a contract to commit a crime is illegal, their agreement formed the law of their own society.

b. This question just points out that a middle ground to answering this problem would be to prosecute and convict, but then sentence the person to a light sentence (probation) because of the mitigating circumstances.

c. Some would say that this boat was like a correctional institution where people are isolated and are forced to make their own rules to survive. In an institution, however, one often has two sets of rules: unwritten ones developed by the inmates, and rules — both written and unwritten — developed by the administration and correctional personnel. Some might feel that the question of whether society's laws, such as constitutional rights, should be enforced in a prison is similar to the question of whether society's law prohibiting homicide should be enforced in the shipwrecked sailor case.

As mentioned in Chapter 1, this is an actual case, *Regina v. Dudley and Stephens*, (1884) where the people involved were tried and sentenced to death in England. The Queen, however, later reduced the sentence to six months' imprisonment.

Answer to Problem 3

a. In 1965 the District Court ruled that corporal punishment was permissible but officials were required to develop written rules to explain what offenses could be punished by whipping and how much punishment was permitted. The District Court in 1967 again upheld corporal punishment. In 1968 the U.S. Court of Appeals, 8th Circuit, reversed this decision.

b. In 1965 the District Court ruled that corporal punishment was permissible, basing its decision on two Supreme Court decisions from other states. These decisions permitted use of the strap and said most courts that had decided the issue agreed it was not cruel and unusual punishment.

The decision was binding only on the parties in the 1965 case. In 1968 the U.S. Court of Appeals reversed the District Court decision and ruled that corporal punishment was not permissible in prisons.

c. The District Court in the 1967 case based its decision on the 1965 case and on the historical viewpoint that corporal punishment and use of the strap, standing alone, did not constitute cruel and unusual punishment. The court could have ruled differently.

d. This court set a new precedent based on changed views, and rejected the arguments used to back up the prior cases. The Court of Appeals is a higher court than the District Court and is not required to follow the lower court's decisions. Nor are decisions from courts of other states binding in this court, because federal courts are considered higher than state courts in resolving constitutional issues and because state courts are a separate system apart from the federal court system.

e. No. The case only decided the issue of corporal punishment and did not deal with the other circumstances involving use of force. As can be seen in Chapter 2, correctional personnel do have the right to use force under certain circumstances, although when and how much depends on local laws and rules.

f. A prison might try to do this but because many courts have cited the 1968 case favorably, it is likely that the U.S. Supreme Court would in the end rule against the prison. It is also possible that an inmate who received corporal punishment would win a suit for damages against both the institution and the correctional personnel who took part.

Answer to Problem 4

a. The suit is a civil one. In a criminal suit, the government (federal, state, county, or city) starts the action against a person or organization and claims that a particular criminal law has been violated. In a civil suit, a person, organization or the government brings an action seeking either money damages or a court order. For example, in this case it might order the city either to make repairs or close down the facility.

b. This suit can be brought in either state or federal court. In order for the federal court to have jurisdiction of the case, there must be a "federal issue". In this case, that issue would be that the conditions of the facility violated the Constitution's ban on cruel and unusual punishment. As a practical matter, the federal court might be more inclined toward granting relief to the inmates than the state court. In the past, federal judges have seemed to rule more frequently in the inmates' favor in suits by inmates, though some state courts are beginning to take a more active role in this area.

c.   1. The Eighth Amendment's ban on cruel and unusual punishment and the due process clause of the U.S. Constitution.

2. State constitution's ban on cruel and unusual punishment and due process clause.

3. State and local laws and/or regulations on fire safety, jail regulations, building and health codes.

4. Professional correctional standards, which are not law, may also be used to judge the legality of particular conditions.

d. Yes, attorneys for both sides will argue how court-made law from their own and other states should be considered by the judge in deciding the case in their favor. In this case, other cases involving jail conditions will be cited by both sides.

e. The court could find the plaintiffs entitled to no relief and dismiss the case.
The court could find the plaintiffs entitled to relief and do any or all of the following:

1. award money damages;

2. enjoin the jail officials from operating the jail in this manner;

3. appoint an expert (master) to oversee the running of the jail;

4. release all inmates from the jail or transfer them to other institutions and order the building closed;

5. set up a timetable of scheduled changes, holding the officials in contempt if they fail to meet the schedule; and

6. make defendants pay for plaintiffs' attorney's fees.

f. 1. If the court orders changes to be made, it is up to the legislature to appropriate this money. The legislature cannot be specifically ordered by the court to set aside monies for the jail because of the separation of powers doctrine but a number of courts have created pressure that led to legislative appropriations. The agency that runs the jail will be responsible for implementing any court order in the case.

2. The court may keep jurisdiction over the case to see that its orders are being followed and that conditions improve. Officials may be held in contempt by the court if changes are not made.

Answer to Problem 5

a. This question calls for your opinion. As standards have been developed by a number of different groups, this process has been criticized for not taking into account views other than those of the group that has written them. (For example, some correctional administrators have criticized the American Bar Association for developing its standards based mainly on the views of lawyers and giving little consideration to the experience of those who work full-time in corrections.) The reader should decide whether each of the groups listed in Problem 5 has a right to have input into new standards and if each will add something to such a process.

b. This is also a question calling for an opinion. One advantage of mandatory standards is the resulting national uniformity that might make it clear to correctional personnel, lawyers, inmates and judges what should take place in institutions, and might result in more equal treatment of both correctional administrators and inmates nationwide. Disadvantages include the belief among many that law enforcement is best decided on a state or local level and that under our system of federal-state government this has been expressly left to the states. Many believe the federal government has exceeded its power in local affairs and that this is bad in corrections and in other areas. Others object because they feel mandatory national standards do not allow for the real differences and needs of local communities, e.g., rural versus urban settings.

c. You may answer this question with your opinion. An advantage of using standards is that correctional personnel and others may have spent considerable time trying to develop "reasonable" standards for an institution to follow and that this will prevent judges from making unrealistic demands on correctional personnel. Disadvantages may be that the standards will not be appropriate for the institution involved in the case, and that local correctional personnel may not have been involved in drawing up the standards or may not have known of them before the case.

Answer to Problem 6

a. Though Officer Lewis may have violated his institution's rules by being abusive and therefore could be subject to discipline, Inmate Frank has committed a criminal assault as well as broken institutional rules. Officer Lewis under Standard II-A-1b above seems to have properly defended himself against physical assault.

b. Physical force may be used here to enforce institutional regulation II-A-1e. However, this is subject to the requirement that the minimum force necessary be used. A push that is hard enough to cause the inmate to smash into the wall is clearly excessive and could subject the officer to a civil lawsuit.

c. While Marshall may use force to enforce institutional rules, the use of force to punish an inmate for breaking the rules is forbidden.

d. Use of chemical agents is permitted to prevent an act that could result in death or severe bodily harm to the person himself or to others, or to prevent serious damage to property. However, it should only be used if it is the minimum force necessary; that does not appear to be the case here. If Green was in isolation and could have been controlled by officers in some other manner, the use of tear gas was unnecessary. These facts were taken from a Virginia case, *Greear v. Loving*, 391 F.Supp. 1269 (W.D. Va. 1975), where the court held that the use of tear gas was a proper security action, because it had taken five correctional officers to subdue the inmate. He had been on a destructive rampage and, with reason, the officers feared for his safety and for their own. In addition, he had received numerous warnings. As for leaving the inmate for 11 hours, the court found this all right since the windows were left open and the medical care provided at the next available time was sufficient. However, under Standard II-A-2 above, the use of tear gas would only be justified here if a properly trained employee used the tear gas with the permission of the warden. Under this standard, steps would also have to be taken as soon as possible to allow the inmate to wash those parts of his body exposed to the gas, and he should not have been left for 11 hours (see Standard II-A-2).

e. Physical force may be used to enforce regulations and to prevent a riot. The minimum force requirement may mean that, in this case, the inmate should have been moved to a segregation area. This is what occurred in the actual case, *Landman v. Royster*, 333 F.Supp. 261 (E.D. Va. 1971), where the court held that tear gas should not be used to subdue a man who did not pose a serious threat to others.

Answer to Problem 7

a. At this point, Burke probably may not shoot the inmate because he is not sure it is a weapon, but he must make some effort to warn the officer.

b. and (**c.**) If an officer is reasonably sure an inmate has a deadly weapon and that deadly force is necessary to stop it, deadly force may be used.

Answer to Problem 8

In most states, officers may not shoot an escaping inmate unless the inmate is a convicted felon. In some states, any escaping inmate may be fired at for purposes of stopping the escape. Local rules may also spell out specific procedures to follow, such as verbal warnings to halt or possibly firing a warning shot if this would not be dangerous under the circumstances.

Answer to Problem 9

Although correctional officials are divided on whether it is advisable to use force or negotiate with inmates when hostages are involved, modern correctional theories suggest that mediation and negotiation should be attempted before deadly force is used. However, if the emergency nature of the situation makes less violent means impossible, deadly force may be used.

Answer to Problem 10

The officer may be liable for damages for his negligent shooting. The sheriff or person responsible for weapons training or the state or local government unit may also be liable for failing to train the officer properly under the theory of vicarious liability.

Answer to Problem 11

The court in this case, *Holda v. Kane County*, Cir. C., Kane Co., Ill. (1977), held the county liable for gross negligence, finding that conditions in the jail facilitated the attack. Punitive damages of $500,000 and $175,000 in compensatory damages were awarded. It is also possible that the jailer in charge of the institution and/or the officers on duty might be liable in a situation of this kind.

Answer to Problem 12

In this case, *Cottrell, Admin. v. Hawaii*, (1975), the court did not hold the state liable since it found that Gomez' own aggressive behavior was the cause of his death. An often used theory in law is that persons should not benefit from their own wrongdoing. However, it is possible that if an institution or individual was clearly responsible for a gun coming in, liability might be found.

Answer to Problem 13

The court awarded a $1,095,000 trust fund payable from the state to compensate for the losses to the boy, his mother, and his father. *Figueroa v. Hawaii*, 604 P.2d 1198 (1979).

Answer to Problem 14 (Roleplay)

There is no definite answer for how to classify Beam. To a certain extent it may depend on how he acts at the hearing and his answers to questions posed by the committee. The overall goal of the roleplay is to emphasize the duty institutions have to protect their inmates, and to show how many factors must be considered in classification decisions. It also should be noted that officials or the institution may be held liable if such factors are not considered.

Factors the committee should consider at the hearing and in their decision include:

1. his crime may subject him to abuse from other inmates;

2. his experience in machine shop work and the restriction against working if in maximum security;

3. the danger from the other inmates if he is placed in medium;

4. the danger of suicide if he is placed in minimum security as well as special needs because of his epilepsy.

Answer to Problem 15

In this hypothetical case, there was a direct violation of the jail's rule by a correctional officer. This negligence is directly connected to the escape and the injury would likely be considered a "probable and foreseeable consequence" of the act. If there is no state immunity law, the officer might be held liable in this situation. Knowledge by the officials of the officer's frequent acts of negligence, and their failure to take any action, might also result in holding them personally liable.

Answer to Problem 16

In this case, *Smith v. Miller*, 241 Iowa 625, 40 N.W. 2d 597 (1950), the state court cited this as a factor for the jury to consider in deciding whether the sheriff should be held liable for the injuries to the inmates. Obviously, whoever was responsible for the placement of the key and correctional officer might be held liable. It would have to be proven that a "reasonable" correctional officer would not have placed an officer so far away and that the injury could have been prevented if the officer were closer.

Answer to Problem 17

The facts given are those of *Bryan v. Jones*, 530 F.2d 1210 (5th Cir. 1976), where it was decided that the jury should be allowed to consider whether the sheriff was acting in good faith when he relied on the District Attorney's Office notice that the imprisonment was legal. If so, the jailer would not be liable. The right to raise this defense in a Section 1983 Civil Rights Act case presented a technical legal issue, and the court said: "In a case such as this one, where there is no discretion and relatively little time pressure, the jailer will be held to a high level of reasonableness as to his own actions. If he negligently establishes a record keeping system in which errors of this kind are likely, he will be held liable. But if the errors take place outside of his realm of responsibility, he cannot be found liable because he has acted reasonably and in good faith." Consequently, the case was remanded for a new trial, at which time the defendant sheriff was allowed to present a good faith defense to liability.

Answer to Problem 18

In this case, *DiFebo v. Keve*, 395 F.Supp. 1350 (D. Del. 1975), the federal court said that the facts did not constitute a claim under

Section 1983 (not "deliberate indifference" as required by *Estelle v. Gamble*, see Chapter 3). But the court said the facts would be sufficient to establish a negligence claim under state tort law. If a state court found that the warden or other personnel had been negligent in not replacing the glasses and that this caused further damage, the individuals responsible and/or the local government unit might be liable.

Answer to Problem 19

a. Reasons against this include:

> 1. Cost. It is doubtful any insurance company would agree to insure any injury received for any reason.

> 2. The limit on any given inmate's claim would be less than the inmate might be able to recover from a court case.

> 3. Officers no longer fearing personal liability will have less reason to respect the rights of inmates.

> 4. Injury claims by one inmate often raise questions about overall conditions of prisons or jails, and courts order broader relief.

> 5. It takes the court out of contact with conditions within the correctional system.

b. This asks for your opinion. In addition to the points set out above, the same positive and negative factors pertaining to workers' compensation outside of prison apply: relief in shorter time and relief regardless of fault versus smaller recoveries. Also, because inmates have a harder time getting counsel, more cases might be remedied under workers' compensation.

c. In *Meredith v. Workers' Compensation Appeals Bd.*, 19 Cal. 3d 777, 140 Cal. Rptr. 314, 567 P.2d 746 (1977), the court found that the system did not violate the inmates' rights in this case, but future cases might be decided differently.

Answer to Problem 20

a. Diane Rawlinson succeeded in her challenge to this regulation. She had to show first that the rule had a discriminatory impact on women, which she did through statistics showing that many more women than men were under 5'2". The correctional institution then had the burden (which, in this case, it failed to carry) of showing that the height and weight requirements were necessary for performing the job of correctional officers. *Dothard v. Rawlinson*, 433 U.S. 321, 97 S.Ct. 2720 (1977).

b. This claim is proper under the law, but if the correctional institution is able to show that the test was professionally developed and was not designed to discriminate, and that it was related to the requirements of the job, it would fall within the exception to the law and be permitted.

c. The courts have not ruled on this particular issue. A court faced with the problem would have to decide which "right" was more important in this situation, privacy for inmates or no discrimination for officers. If employers may discriminate because of a bona fide occupational qualification, it appears likely that most courts would side with the inmates' right to privacy in this situation. This case points out the problems a court must deal with in trying to accomodate the conflicting rights of more than one group.

Answer to Problem 21

a. This calls for an opinion. Some reasons for and against it are written in the text.

b. Those in favor of unions would probably argue that each of these problems or complaints could be resolved better if correctional administrators, state officials, legislators and the public were able to hear the views of correctional officers. Unions might use methods such as press releases, position papers, meetings, negotiations, strikes or slowdowns, picketing and lobbying to get across their viewpoints on these issues.

c. Those against unions argue that the viewpoint of correctional personnel can be included without the expense of unions or the antagonism they might build up. Unions, they argue, may create an adversarial relationship and undermine morale and discipline. They may also argue that strikes and slowdowns can be very dangerous. Additionally, officers may be divided in their loyalties between union and nonunion members which has the potential of causing problems.

Answer to Problem 22

a.

Reasons for Limiting in Correctional Institution:	Reasons Against Limiting in Correctional Institution:
1. Deterrence	1. Rehabilitation

2. Punishment

3. Rehabilitation

4. Internal order of institution

5. Cost

6. Security

7. Administrative inconvenience

2. Constitutional rights still exist

3. Loss of freedom is a great enough punishment

Note that these may not be accepted by the court as reasons for restricting the rights of inmates and that some of the reasons given do not apply to pretrial inmates.

Answer to Problem 23

Some argue that pretrial detainees should have more rights since they are presumed innocent of any crime, and that in many cases those in jail would be on the street enjoying the full rights of ordinary citizens if they had had the money to pay bond. Others argue, however, that the vast majority are guilty and it is too difficult to provide rights in an institution. Others justify restricting rights in the interest of security or orderly functioning of the institution, which the U.S. Supreme Court has permitted. In *Bell v. Wolfish* (cited in the student text), the Supreme Court's test for pretrial inmates was whether they were being "punished". The court contrasted this with the test for convicted inmates, which is whether the punishment is "cruel and unusual".

Answer to Problem 24

a. The First Amendment protects you in your phone conversation unless you are making a threat on the President's life. You cannot be convicted of a crime for saying the President is a bum. However, time, place and manner in regard to free speech may be regulated. In all likelihood, you could stand on a park bench and state your criticisms of the President, unless you drew a large crowd that caused a disturbance, blocked traffic, etc. Blocking traffic will generally not be tolerated nor can you incite a riot; you could be arrested and convicted. In some instances, a permit may be required to speak in a public place.

b. Private writings may be kept at home with no problem. If you said the same things to a crowd on a street corner, or on television, the test is likely to be whether there was a clear and present danger that the crowd or viewing audience would be incited to use force and violence. If there were no such danger, the speech would be protected, and if you were arrested, you would not be convicted. To be convicted, you would have to make an actual "call to action" rather than a theoretical statement.

c. The wearing of armbands is symbolic speech, which the Supreme Court said in *Tinker v. Des Moines Indep. Community School Dist.*, 393 U.S. 503, 89 S.Ct. 733 (1969), was protected speech. Students could not be expelled or suspended unless the wearing of armbands resulted in a "substantial disruption" of the educational process.

d. The government may not censor the mail. If you take action or take part in a conspiracy, you may have broken the law and may be subject to criminal prosecution.

Answer to Problem 25

a. Yes, *Sostre v. McGinnis*, 442 F.2d 178 (2nd Cir. 1971), held that punishing Sostre for putting his thoughts on paper without giving him prior warning and without knowing whether he intended to distribute them violated his First Amendment rights. (This case, however, should not be cited in the roleplay but could be discussed after arguments are brought out on both sides and a decision is made.)

b. The court did not resolve this issue but it did state that in the absence of arbitrariness or discrimination, had the warden chosen to *confiscate* the writings rather than to punish Sostre, the court would probably not have overturned the warden's judgment. The warden, however, would have to show there was a clear and present danger that possession of the writings would be likely to result in circulation among other inmates, which in turn would be likely to subvert prison discipline.

c. The court said that a rule forbidding Sostre to hand out such writings to other inmates would be justified.

Answer to Problem 26

a. Although the Supreme Court has not ruled on this issue, an inmate would probably be protected by the First Amendment for verbal criticism of a jail's operation. However, time, place, and manner may be regulated, so that reasonable limits on activities that may pose a danger to prison security will be allowed. Therefore, seeking out other inmates to discuss his views, which would cause a security problem, could probably be limited if not completely stopped.

b. This answer is subject to local rules. Courts have differed on the extent of a prisoner's right to possess materials and magazines with sexual content or subjects. Some courts have held that regulations giving broad authority on this matter to prison officials are too "vague" or "overbroad". Other courts have banned magazines that are clearly obscene under the Supreme Court standard. Courts differ on whether *Playboy* or *Hustler* are obscene, though most have ruled they are not.

c. The institution's reasons for taking it away might include preventing escape plans, or prison officials might argue that it contains information on the construction of weapons or the dismantling of existing security systems. These legitimate security concerns would permit the opening, reading and censoring of incoming unofficial mail. A pretrial detainee's mail right depends on the institution's rules and local court cases. Some courts have only permitted the opening of mail to inspect for contraband and have said it cannot be read. Mail most often protected has been that from attorneys or courts. The issue of whether mail to and from family or friends may be restricted has not yet been settled by the Supreme Court.

Answer to Problem 27

a. The Supreme Court in *West Virginia State Bd. of Educ. v. Barnette*, 319 U.S. 624, 63 S.Ct. 1178 (1943) agreed with the Jehovah Witness' claim that such a requirement violated their First Amendment rights. This religion viewed saluting the flag as giving homage to something other than God — a violation of their beliefs.

b. No, you can read what you want outside prison and the courts have upheld the right to Black Muslim literature in prison as well.

c. In *Cruz v. Beto*, 405 U.S. 319, 92 S.Ct. 1079 (1972), the Supreme Court ruled that a Buddhist inmate could not be prevented from using the chapel or writing his religious supervisor. If there are enough Buddhist inmates, however, an institution might be required to pay for a Buddhist chaplain. The courts have not yet dealt with this issue.

d. In *Banks v. Havener*, 234 F.Supp. 27 (E.D. Va. 1964), an inmate was allowed to wear a religious medal even though jewelry had been banned from prisoners in other cases for security reasons. A later case held that a "no beard" rule violated the religious free-

doms of Sunni Muslims in New York because their religion advised them to wear beards. *Monroe v. Bombard*, 422 F.Supp. 211
(S.D.N.Y. 1976). However, other courts might find security problems resulting from religious jewelry or wearing beards to be more
important than the right to religious freedom.

e. Most cases disallowing services for inmates in segregation have
been upheld. However, some courts have encouraged institutions
to find alternate methods to afford religious practice for those in
solitary confinement.

Answer to Problem 28

Many believe there are a number of positive benefits gained by
permitting inmates to pratice their religion. They argue that it en-
courages self-reflection and a desire to change past behavior, that
it gives a sense of meaning to an otherwise meaningless life, and
that support from the religious community may assist the inmate
by requiring discipline and constructive use of time. On the whole,
religion may also bring about a better atmosphere within the institution.

Answer to Problem 29

Assuming the institution decides this is a religion and not merely a
cover-up for what otherwise would be impermissible activities:

a. It could be argued that paying for any chaplain may be unconstitutional because it is establishing religion, but courts have
not as yet dealt with either this issue or the issue of paying for
chaplains of certain religions.

b. Institutions do not have to provide pizza as communion because
to do so may constitute unconstitutional establishment of religion
and/or because such a practice may be costly or an administrative
burden. It could also be argued that pizza for use in religious services is an obviously unreasonable request for a religion as was
decided in the *Theriault* case cited on p. 71, when inmates requested steak and wine.

c. The institution must provide use of the chapel to all religions if
requested. However, although it may not discriminate or prohibit
practice of religions with smaller congregations, the institution is
permitted to take the size of any religious congregation into account when giving preference in terms of scheduling.

d. If the institution permits the practice of large special services
for any religion, it may not be able to justify preventing the mem-

bers of the Church of the New Faith from having a similar service. If no such services are permitted to any religious group, the warden would be justified in denying this request if such a service would be a danger to the security of the institution.

e. Unless the institution can show some threat to security, the inmates will be allowed to circulate their rules. This would be especially true if other groups are allowed to circulate their rules.

f. Though there have been no cases on this issue, it is doubtful that the constitution requires complete privacy during their religious services. Even if inmates argued that their religion required privacy, the duty of correctional officers to insure safety of the inmates would probably outweigh the religious right.

Answer to Problem 30

Attorneys for the inmates might raise the following arguments concerning the rules: (1) they increase frustrations; (2) they are detrimental to helping one's family, attitude and rehabilitation; (3) the visits are too short; (4) the visits are too remote and impersonal because they are by telephone and through a glass; and (5) if family or friends work nights, they are unable to visit. They would argue that these rules violate inmates' First Amendment rights to freedom of speech and religion.

The attorneys for the institution might argue to keep the present rule because it is: (1) too expensive to detail more officers in visiting area; (2) a danger to security to have officer there; (3) a security danger to allow contact visits; (4) a telephone can be monitored to help determine if the inmate is rehabilitated or to detect escape plans; and (5) too much visitation can set back rehabilitation.

Whether the law should be involved in this issue calls for an opinion that may depend on whether one believes visitation is a constitutional right or a privilege to be granted or withheld as correctional officials desire.

a. It is up to the judge to decide whether the rules are so restrictive that they constitute "punishment" for pretrial detainees or are cruel and unusual punishment for convicted inmates. In *Wolfish*, however, courts were instructed by the Supreme Court not to interfere with restrictions on pretrial detainees unless they amounted to punishment. If the institution can convincingly argue that there is a no punishment motive for the rule (i.e., security) and that these limits are not excessive, a court may uphold the rule.

However, if pretrial detainees can make a convincing argument that the reason for the rule is punishment and/or that the limits are excessive in relation to the purpose for the rule (security), they may be held unconstitutional.

b. The answer to this question is left up to you. Consideration might include whether such changes might lessen inmate frustration, the ability of the institution to accommodate changes, and balancing the time to fight the case with how important you think it is to keep the rules.

Answer to Problem 31

In re Reynolds, 25 Cal.App. 3d 131, 157 Cal. Rptr. 892 (1979) is the basis for this problem. In that case:

a. the court found that wearing the union button was "speech" as protected by the Constitution; and

b. where the department had not claimed past disruption caused by wearing the button, the inmates were allowed to obtain and wear buttons.

Answer to Problem 32

a. Citizens have First Amendment freedoms of speech and the press that protect these actions.

b. Freedom of the press is the First Amendment right involved. However, few cases have been decided on this issue. One case, *Kirkland v. Hardy*, (U.S. District Court for D.C., 1972) did result in a consent decree allowing the newspaper to be published if no names of correctional employees were used. It is probably a valid assumption that material circulating in the prison and naming correctional officials may properly be banned. Some courts have upheld the right of inmates to publish criticism of prison officials, advocate legitimate use of prison grievance procedures or urge inmates to contact public representatives, as long as the publications don't attempt to break down prison discipline or cause disruptions. *Guajardo v. Estelle*, 580 F.2d 748 (5th Cir. 1978).

c. Questions of freedoms of speech and the press are raised here. The *Saxbe* case and the *Houchins* case cited in the student text allow prison and jail officials to provide no greater right to individual interviews with inmates by the press than the general public has. Therefore, the paper could correspond with him, and if the inmates have a right to visit with the general public, they may also talk to the press.

Answer to Problem 33

a. In this case, *Seale v. Manson*, 326 F.Supp. 1375 (D.Conn. 1971) the court ruled for Seale and against Huggins. Arguments for hair restrictions are usually based on health reasons and the need for identification of inmates. Most cases have sided with prison officials on the issue of hair and beards where there is a reasonable written policy on the issue.

In regard to jewelry, conflicts may arise over its possession and most courts have, therefore, upheld its ban. However, if the jewelry has a message or is part of a religion, it is more likely to be allowed. Some courts have held jewelry should only be banned if it could be used as a weapon. *Rowland v. Jones*, 452 F.2d 1005 (8th Cir. 1971).

b. In the Seale case, the court upheld the right to wear a beard, stressing that he was a pretrial detainee and had not been convicted.

Answer to Problem 34

a. As discussed in Chapter 6, the police may only search a person on the street when they have probable cause or in a limited number of other situations. They may, however, always search a person who is under arrest, and this is one of the rationales for the broad power of correctional employees to search inmates.

b. Possible examples would be: (1) based on an informer's tip; (2) following a riot; (3) after an assault has taken place; (4) when inmates return from court; and (5) when evidence of drug use has been found in an area.

c. If a correctional employee has reason to believe an inmate is planning an escape, the employee may conduct a search. Recent cases have said, however, that searches may not be used for harassment, and once an hour for three straight days may be unreasonable. Due to the extensive problems regarding contraband and security in a prison, probable cause is not needed for routine searches. In *Wolfish*, the Supreme Court ruled that inmates need not be present during searches of their cells.

d. Body cavity searches are regarded by courts as greater invasions of privacy and, in the case presented here, the court ruled that unless the inmates in segregation were going to mix with the general population, there was no need for a body cavity search whenever an inmate entered or left segregation. *Hodges v. Klein*, 412 F.Supp. 896 (D. N.J. 1976). Although courts don't see strip searches as a great invasion of privacy, the trend is toward requiring that such searches be conducted with maximum courtesy, maximum respect for the person's dignity and minimum physical discomfort to the person being searched. *McCray v. State*, 456 F.2d 1 (4th Cir. 1972). As the text notes, the Supreme Court in *Wolfish* upheld, 5-4, body cavity searches on less than probable cause after visitation.

Answer to Problem 35

a. ON STREET

Meet with attorney and tell all.

Line up witnesses to establish alibi defense.

Try to find person who did it if you are innocent.

Talk to victim or other witnesses.

Suggest attorney file motion to dismiss case or motion to suppress identification.

Do research in law library to assist attorney.

Line up character witnesses and letters for sentencing if convicted.

Live with family.

Maintain job or find employment, which will more likely lead to probation if you are convicted.

b. IN JAIL

Meet with attorney and tell all.

Meet with jailhouse lawyer and receive help.

Talk to family and friends to get them to line up witnesses for alibi and to find out who did it.

Suggest attorney file motion to dismiss or suppress identification.

Do research in law library.

Write letter or ask friends to line up witnesses and letters for sentencing.

Note that all items in list (a) can be done by someone on the street (perhaps with the exception of talking to the victim or other witnesses who may not cooperate), but that the circumstances of being incarcerated restrict performing list (b).

c. A police officer could not stop you from doing any of the things in (a). Jail authorities cannot stop you from doing the things in (b) but they can limit your activities by regulating the time and place you do them. They can also restrict your ability to do such things as research in the law library by maintaining a less than adequate law book collection, or by restricting the hours of use available to you.

d. In *Williams v. Leeke*, 584 F.2d 1336 (4th Cir. 1978), the court found that this program violated the Sixth Amendment. The court's finding was that city jail prisoners are entitled to reasonable access to the courts, and that this was not provided to a person serving a substantial sentence of confinement if, without other legal assistance, his only access to a law library was so restricted as to be meaningless.

e. This case was consolidated for hearing with (d). The court found that if Williams were an ordinary prisoner and if the prison only provided a law library with limited access, it would be unconstitutional. However, where known security risks were given legal assistance along with library books brought to their cells, the right of access was satisfied.

Answer to Problem 36

a. The problems with each of these items may be as follows:

1. Where will they go? Who will pay additional costs?

2. Same as (1). Will overcrowding be created elsewhere, which will result in more cruel and unusual punishment?

3. Same as (1). Why these standards? Why not just state standards?

4. Same as (1).

5. This is not as great a problem as others.

6. This may call for a great amount of construction.

7. Cost. Is this a constitutional right or just a policy that should be made by correctional officials or the state legislature and not by a judge?

b. This calls for an opinion on exactly what our society should provide inmates in institutions.

c. The judge may be able to do this by keeping watch to see that his or her orders are carried out. Judges can, and in some cases, have held correctional officials who don't carry out orders to be in contempt of court and have even jailed some for short periods. A special master was ordered and hired in this case to oversee compliance by the department. The "Separation of Powers" principle

of our government does not usually allow a judge to force a legislature to appropriate money, though the judge may be able to create
public pressure on legislators to act. The judge may also do what
was done here and order the institution to be closed. This will
force state officials or legislators to act or, possibly, to let prisoners
go.

Answer to Problem 37

a. and **b.** These are both from the case of *Todaro v. Ward*, 431
F.Supp. 1129 (S.D.N.Y. 1977), which found these aspects of the prison medical system to violate the cruel and unusual punishment
clause of the Eighth Amendment because they constituted "deliberate indifference" to the inmates' needs.

c. In this case, the court ruled that there was not enough evidence
to place a duty on prison officials to segregate.

d. The facts clearly show grounds for both a Section 1983 lawsuit
on grounds of cruel and unusual punishment or due process, as
well as a state tort action. A state criminal action of assault against
the correctional personnel involved might also be brought.

Recent cases have made it clear that correctional personnel
have a duty to act, if possible, to prevent such attacks. If the officer
was in danger if he tried to stop it, he nevertheless should have
called for help.

e. This is the case of *Bourgeois v. United States*, 375 F.Supp. 113
(N.D. Tex. 1974), where inmates were able to prove a constitutional violation of the Eighth Amendment.

Answer to Problem 38

a. Failure to provide medical care to this inmate could result in liability for the officer as well as for the state or municipality. To
file a successful Section 1983 suit, the inmate must show the denial
was the result of "deliberate indifference." A negligence or medical malpractice suit might also be filed in state court. Officers
should follow the procedures in their institution for seeing a doctor, and officials should have doctors available on either a
short-call basis or full-time within the institution.

b. These are the facts in *Estelle v. Gamble*, cited in the student
text, where the U.S. Supreme Court found that the situation did
not give rise to a cruel and unusual punishment claim since it was
not "deliberate indifference" on the part of correctional officials.
The court went on to say that the inmate might file a medical
malpractice suit in the state courts.

Answer to Problem 39

In *Kershaw v. Davis*, U.S. Dist. Ct. (N.D. Pa. 1977), the court found a constitutional violation for failing to provide women with work release programs. The court stated that this female had a valid claim for wages she would have earned if allowed to participate in the program.

Answer to Problem 40

a. The probable answer would be that you would protest such a firing. You would investigate the institution's or agency's rules regarding firing and possibly see an attorney. You should demand a hearing where you would get to tell your side of the story and present evidence to refute the charges against you.

b. An employee in this situation would generally claim that his or her right to due process had been violated and that the following should be provided before dismissal:

1. written notice of charges against the employee;

2. a hearing with the right to hear the evidence against him or her, to cross-examine witnesses, etc.;

3. an attorney and representation at the hearing; and

4. a transcript of the hearing, a written decision and the right to appeal.

Answer to Problem 41

a. Where the action taken by the institution may be in *retaliation* for the employee's exercise of his right to form and participate in a permitted union, the courts have held that he is entitled to a hearing.

b. Firing may be a proper remedy in this case, but the doctor is probably entitled to a hearing. In one case, the court ruled that a corrections employee was denied his right to due process in a similar situation. He was denied a property interest in his job, because he had a reasonable expectation of continuing in his job as the result of a state statute allowing discharge only for just cause. *Faulkner v. North Carolina Dept. of Corrections*, 428 F.Supp. 100 (W.D. N.C. 1977).

c. In *Seales v. Malcolm*, 61A.D. 2d 920, 403 N.Y.S. 2d 5 (1978) the court reduced the officer's punishment from dismissal to a suspension because it found that dismissal was too great a punishment for the employee's act.

Answer to Problem 42

If the roleplay is followed as described in the student text, the following legal points are illustrated:

1. When the report is read the inmate is properly being given notice of the charges against him, but *Wolff v. McDonnell* required that inmates receive written notice at least 24 hours before the hearing to give them an opportunity to prepare a defense. Therefore, the request for a postponement should have been granted.

2. The denial of legal counsel was proper under *Wolff* because Gray is literate and the issues are not so complex that a lawyer or someone substituting for a lawyer is necessary or required.

3. The board could legitimately decide not to allow cross-examination of Officer Jones if it believed this to be better for security and necessary to avoid disruption within the institution.

4. The board's unwillingness to allow Gray to call Miller or hear testimony from Miller might be seen by some courts as a denial of due process. However, the U.S. Supreme Court has usually left this to the discretion of correctional officials.

5. The board can refuse to allow the 10 witnesses on grounds that they would not be necessary, and it probably could refuse to allow calling even one of them because it is not claimed that anyone saw the incident.

6. Gray can be asked to leave the room because the U.S. Supreme Court has said that correctional officials may decide that this is necessary for security in the institution. In addition, Reynolds might not be willing to testify in Gray's presence out of fear of reprisal.

NOTE: All of the above answers are based on what the U.S. Supreme Court has said is the minimum due process required. However, other courts and many state and local correctional agencies have gone further and provided the right to call witnesses, to cross-examine and to be represented by a person of the inmate's choice. The answers above may be different in some areas when one refers to the local rules or court decisions.

Answer to Problem 43

The District Court held that a *Wolff* type hearing before transfer was required except in the rare case of an emergency. The hearing was to permit the inmate to prepare a defense against the transfer. *Meachum* and *Montanye* were distinguished by the court which found that this transfer to H-House was not a mere relocation of prisoners. *Meachum* and *Montanye* involved disciplinary transfers from the general population of one prison to the general population of another where the conditions were less favorable. The transfer in this case, for serious misconduct, was to a punitive setting resembling solitary and providing very different "treatment." *Hardwick v. Ault*, 447 F.Supp. 116 (M.D. Ga. 1978).

Answer to Problem 44

a. Most cases are filed in federal court because federal judges have traditionally been viewed as more willing than state judges to find that the Constitution provides greater protection to inmates. Since state judges are often elected, they are seen as more closely tied to the government of that state, and are viewed as less willing to take action to enforce the rights of inmates and more willing to go along with the local government.

b. While state and federal courts have the same range of remedies available (e.g., injunctions, damages), certain defenses available to correctional personnel in negligence suits in state courts are not available in federal courts (i.e., "sovereign immunity"). Moreover, attorneys may be more easily obtained in federal court by inmates since attorney's fees may be awarded in federal court without a showing of the institution's bad faith.

Answer to Problem 45

a. This was not an actual case, but courts would probably hold that correctional officials should have found a way to get him access to the law library even though he was in solitary confinement.

b. No, because the right of access to a law library or a suitable alternative was clearly established in the 1976 case of *Bounds v. Smith*, and the prison officers "reasonably should have known" about the law.

c. The fact that Williams won his release after access to the library might make him eligible for damages on the theory that he spent an extra year in prison because of the violation.

Answer to Problem 46

A correctional officer should act as a professional at all times when in contact with inmates. Although it may be difficult, the officer should ignore such a remark.

Answer to Problem 47

a. The police do not have probable cause to arrest the occupants of the car. There are hundreds of "light-colored" cars in any community and "mere suspicion" is not enough to justify an arrest. However, the police may stop the car and investigate the occupants (i.e., ask them for identification and their purpose). Evidence uncovered in such an investigation might provide the probable cause needed to arrest, for example, if the police saw a gun on the seat of the car.

b. They can question the men about their identity and present activities. In the course of this questioning, the police may discover evidence or more information to provide probable cause for arrest.

Answer to Problem 48

a. This arrest is based on probable cause. The facts are loosely based on those of *Draper v. United States*, 358 U.S. 307 (1959). There, the Court held that probable cause for arrest can come from an informant's tip so long as the informant gives enough information to the police to conclude that a crime is or was being committed, and the informant is known to be credible (believable) or the information is reliable. In this case, when the police saw that the time of arrival and appearance of the person exactly fit the description, they had sufficient information to conclude a crime was being committed. The informant was credible because he had furnished accurate information in the past. There are other ways an informant may show his credibility or the reliability of his information, including that the informant was a crime victim, eyewitness, innocent bystander, or one of the criminals committing the crime.

b. The police should not have tried to obtain a warrant because they did not have enough evidence to obtain one until they saw the man fitting the description, thus corroborating the tip. Unless they arrested Richie then, they would have lost him and the evidence.

Answer to Problem 49

a. Officer Ramos would probably pursue Lonnie's speeding car, while radioing for assistance. Lonnie's behavior, fleeing the scene, may be understandable under the circumstances, but it provides the officer with reason to stop him.

b. The officer certainly may stop the car and investigate further. If the officer had reason to fear that the occupants were armed and presently dangerous, he might have them step out of the car so he could do a pat down search for weapons. He may not conduct a search of the occupants (except for the pat down search above) or the car, unless Lonnie and Susan consent to the search.

They could be arrested for possession of marihuana if the officer sees any drugs in plain view or if drugs are discovered after Lonnie and Susan consent to a search.

c. Students can offer their opinions on how each party would act.

d. The roleplay is designed to build empathy for police and citizens in such a situation as well as develop skills to be used in police-citizen contacts.

e. A citizen can bring a civil suit for false arrest or for violation of civil rights. To win a false arrest suit, a citizen must show that the arrest was illegal. For instance, an arrest without probable cause or a warrantless arrest for a misdemeanor not committed in the officers' presence is generally illegal. To win a civil rights case under Section 1983, the police must be shown to have violated the constitutional rights of the arrested persons. Here, the police acted legally, even though they made a mistake. Remember, too, that citizens are not allowed to resist an arrest, even though the police have made a mistake.

Answer to Problem 50

a. Barry I. Cunningham, an F.B.I. Special Agent is requesting the warrant. The searchers are looking for "counterfeit bank notes, money orders, securities, and plates, stones, and other paraphenalia used in counterfeiting and forgery." They are seeking to search the occupants of, and premises at 935 Bay St., St. Louis. They base their request on information received from a credible informant and F.B.I. observation of counterfeiting activity resulting from around-the-clock surveillance.

b. The search was authorized by Federal Magistrate, Michael J. Thiel. The search must be conducted within 10 days of the issuance of the warrant, i.e., by December 13, 1978. It may be conducted at anytime in the day or night. It appears that the judge had sufficient grounds for issuing the warrant. However, the law usually requires that special reasons be given for permitting the search at night, as opposed to between 6 a.m. and 10 p.m. and no special reasons are listed here.

c. The Fourth Amendment requires that a warrant be issued before a search in order to place the judgment of a neutral party (the judge or magistrate) between the police and the citizen. This requires the police to state specific reasons to justify a search and lessens the chances that the search will be an unreasonable invasion of a citizen's privacy. Searches are generally required in daylight hours as this will avoid the trauma of the "midnight knock" while seldom stifling legitimate police investigation. In addition, it may be more dangerous for police to execute warrants at night.

d. Students can give their opinions as to situations in which warrantless searches should be permitted. The discussion could point out emergency situations where there would be no time to get a warrant, consent situations where the party permits the search, and plain view situations where the police inadvertently see the items. The legally recognized warrantless searches are discussed in the student text.

Answer to Problem 51

a. Jill's boyfriend's breaking into the apartment and taking the drugs is unlawful trespass. However, there is no action by the government in this search and, therefore, the Fourth Amendment does not apply. The police can use the evidence. The situation would be different if the police had told Jill's boyfriend to look for the drugs. In that case, he would have been an agent of the police and, unless he had a warrant based on probable cause or the situation fell within an exception to the warrant requirement, the search would have been unlawful. After a motion to suppress, the evidence would have been suppressed.

b. The search is lawful. Joe has no expectation of privacy in items he throws into a hotel waste basket.

c. The search by the principal is lawful. The school owns the lockers and school administrators can take reasonable steps to protect the safety and welfare of the students. However, in some states, the court's decisions or school rules require the principal to have either probable cause or a reasonable suspicion before searching. Some schools also require that the student be present when the locker is being searched.

d. This search is unlawful. Unless they have probable cause to arrest him, they simply cannot come up to him and search.

e. This search is lawful. As long as the police make a legal arrest, they can make a complete search of her and the area within her immediate control. They would not be able to search a locked trunk or glove compartment since this area is not within her immediate control.

f. This search is unlawful. They did not have probable cause to search the apartment. As long as he was outside his apartment door, the area inside his apartment was beyond his immediate control and therefore beyond the permissible scope of the search.

g. This search is lawful. Police can use such tips as long as the informant is shown to be credible and the information is sufficient to conclude that a crime is or was being committed.

h. This search is unlawful. Claire could consent to the search of common areas of the apartment (e.g., the living room or kitchen). However, Sandy would probably retain an expectation of privacy in her bedroom. Even if the bedroom were shared, she keeps a privacy interest in the dresser, so long as she has exclusive control of that dresser drawer.

Answer to Problem 52

a. The officers should try to get *specific* information (description of the person's clothing, whether or not the person really was Johnson, exactly where Johnson lives, etc.) as well as determining how Fingers got his information.

b. If the police learn where they can find Johnson, they would proceed to his residence while radioing for a back-up unit.

c. The police may proceed without a warrant to Johnson's house to *investigate* the crime. However, on the facts given, they do not have probable cause to arrest him. The informant's tip was that he thinks the man looks like Bill Johnson.

d. Since the police do not have probable cause to arrest Johnson, they should knock and announce their purpose and authority. If Johnson consents to their entry, the police may come in. If Johnson does not invite them in, the police have no right to enter the premises. Until the police get further information to link Bill Johnson to this crime, they do not have sufficient evidence to obtain an arrest or search warrant.

e. If Johnson should invite them into the house, the police can seize any contraband or evidence in plain view. If Johnson acts in a way which leads the police to believe he is armed and presently dangerous, the police may frisk him for weapons. If contraband or evidence is seen which would give the police probable cause to arrest him, they may search him and the area within his immediate control.

Answer to Problem 53

a. Students should offer their own opinions as to whether the confession should have been admitted. Those favoring suppression of the evidence might argue that required warnings assure a defendant a right to counsel at a critical stage of the prosecution, preserve a defendant's freedom from self-incrimination, and prevent police from coercing defendants into confessing. Those favoring admission of the confession might argue that the right to counsel and freedom from self-incrimination are trial rights, not rights of arrested persons, and that if police read these warnings, defendants will not confess to crimes. The Court in the *Miranda* case did suppress the confession.

b. This question seeks student opinion.

c. Police and prosecutors were very worried that the Court's decision would result in a dramatic reduction in confessions. Several studies done in the first few years after the Miranda decision found that relatively few defendants requested attorneys, that conviction rates were unchanged, and that approximately the same number of defendants made confessions during pre-Miranda and post-Miranda years. There was also some evidence that police did not give every part of the warning (e.g., the right to counsel part), or gave the warnings in ways which discouraged any initiative on the part of defendants. Seeburgh and Wetbiek, *Miranda in Pittsburgh — A Statistical Study*, 29 U. Pitt. L. Rev. 1 (1967) and Medabie, Leitz and Alexander, *Custodial Police Interrogation in Our Nation's Capital: The Attempt to Implement Miranda*, 66 Mich. L. Rev. 1347 (1968).

Answer to Problem 54

a. Students can give their opinions as to how they would rule on this matter.

b. Some would argue that the statements made at the time of his arrest are more likely to be true than those made at trial, because he would have more time to make up a story.

c. Opinion #2 is the majority position of the Supreme Court in *Harris v. New York*, 401 U.S. 22 (1971). In a case like this, the judge would instruct the jury (if it is a jury trial) that the confession is to be considered only in determining the defendant's credibility. Of course defense attorneys don't want a jury to hear anything about a confession. As a tactical matter, in cases where a confession has been obtained in violation of *Miranda*, the defendant will seldom take the stand.

Answer to Problem 55

There is no right or wrong answer to this problem. The lack of agreement on what the bail should be points out the wide discrepancies involved in bail setting.

Answer to Problem 56

a. The purposes of excluding illegally obtained evidence are to deter police from illegal conduct, to keep the state from benefiting from unlawful behavior and to preserve the integrity of the court system by removing tainted evidence from criminal trials. The advantages are the same as the purposes.

The disadvantages are that the rule may not be an accurate method of finding the truth, that police and the state may be punished for innocent, good faith mistakes and that, in fact, the integrity of the judicial system is harmed by suppressing evidence which is incriminating and reliable, though in violation of a technical rule.

b. If a judge determines at the pretrial suppression hearing that the police violated Williams' rights, then his incriminating statements and the direct results of the statement (i.e., the discovery of the body) would be suppressed.

c. Students can give opinions, supported by reasons, on these questions.

d. These questions provide the various perspectives which different parties in the criminal justice system have on the exclusionary rule.

e. In *Brewer v. Williams*, 430 U.S. 387 (1977), the Supreme Court used Sixth Amendment right to counsel grounds to affirm the federal court's holding that the evidence had been wrongfully admitted. The Court held that Williams had, in fact, been interrogated while in custody of the police.

Answer to Problem 57

a. Some recent studies on plea bargaining conclude that it does not benefit the defendant. It was found that defendants, for the most part, did not receive lighter sentences when they pleaded guilty. It was also found that without plea bargaining there would be more dismissals and that the cost to the criminal justice system would be higher. A study in California estimated that a jury trial had an average cost of $3000, while a guilty plea costs about $215 to the system. The advantages of plea bargaining to the functioning of the court are that it saves considerable court time and money and speeds up the overall court process. Many say that without it the entire system would break down. In some cases, it also may bring about a fairer outcome for the defendant.

The disadvantages may be that some people who could not be convicted plead guilty because of poor advice from their attorneys or fear of what might happen at trial. It also may result in lesser sentences for some defendants who deserve more punishment. Additionally, it undermines respect for the courts and results in the view that the criminal justice system operates on a wheeler-dealer mentality.

b. Students should consider Marty's dilemma. If he has a criminal record and the prosecution can place him at the scene of the crime, should he "cop a plea" even if, in fact, he did not commit the crime but is fearful he will be convicted if tried?

c. In some states, Marty has the right to appeal because the actual sentence is part of the plea bargain. In most states, though, the sentence is not part of the plea and defense counsel can only tell a client what the judge is likely to do, based on the judge's prior practice and reputation. If the defense counsel *promised* probation in such a state, the defendant has grounds to withdraw the guilty plea based on inadequate assistance of counsel. However, if the prosecutor promised "to recommend probation" and the judge rejected the recommendation, Marty would not win a challenge to his sentence.

d. This is certainly a possibility, especially for persons with prior criminal records. Students should be asked for their opinions on this issue.

Answer to Problem 58

a. The right to a jury trial is supposed to guarantee a judgment by one's peers as well as to provide for community participation in the criminal justice system. These ideas are considered basic to our notions of fairness and justice.

A person might choose not to have a jury in cases where the legal issues are very complex and better understood by a judge or where the sympathy of the community would be against the defendant or in favor of the government's witness. The decision might also be affected by the particular judge assigned to the case.

b. Students can give their opinions. Some contend that allowing less than unanimous verdicts actually has the effect of watering down the standard of proof beyond a reasonable doubt. The Supreme Court has held that a jury need not be composed of 12 persons in state courts. So long as the jury is large enough to promote group deliberation and provide a possibility for obtaining a community cross-section, then smaller juries are permitted. However, a jury of fewer than six persons in a non-petty offense violates the right to trial by jury. *Ballew v. Georgia,* 435 U.S. 223 (1978). The Supreme Court in *Johnson v. Louisiana,* 406 U.S. 56 (1972) has permitted a 9 to 3 verdict in a non-capital, state criminal case, but has held that, where a six person jury is used in a non-petty case, conviction must be unanimous. *Burch v. Louisiana,* 47 U.S.L.W. 4393 (1979).

Answer to Problem 59

a. A speedy trial is important because it permits both sides to locate and call to the stand witnesses whose memories have not been unduly dimmed by the passing of time. In addition, in pre-trial detention cases, a speedy trial minimizes a defendant's loss of liberty and reduces the obvious conflict between the notion of innocent until proven guilty and imprisoning people before their trial.

b. Some places, e.g., Florida, have begun to televise criminal trials. The presence of cameras may make it more difficult for the judge, attorneys, defendants and witnesses to perform their tasks. However, public education and information about the criminal justice system is desirable.

Answer to Problem 60

a. A defendant who is articulate, presentable and free of a criminal record can be extremely convincing on his or her own behalf.

b. Jurors generally want to hear from a defendant at a criminal trial and are probably affected negatively when they do not hear the defendant tell his or her side of the case. Judges generally instruct juries not to make any inference from the failure of the defendant to take the stand, but this may actually aggravate the situation. If the prosecution makes remarks which suggest that the jury should infer guilt from the defendant's failure to testify, the defendant's right against self-incrimination has been violated.

c. As discussed earlier, the Supreme Court has held that the right against self-incrimination only protects the defendant from testimonial communications at the trial. Persons in a line-up can be asked to repeat some words or phrases which an observer heard to help in the identification process. This does not violate the right against self-incrimination.

Defendants cannot, however, be forced to take lie detector tests. Also most courts still do not permit lie detector results to be used as evidence because of the lack of scientific validation.

Answer to Problem 61

a. Most correctional personnel who work in jails hear strong criticisms of court-appointed counsel from pretrial detainees. Unfortunately, most citizens have no way to judge the quality of counsel because most have no knowlege of the legal system. High-priced private attorneys may, in some cases, be no better than some court-appointed counsel. Defendants generally are suspicious of the quality and loyalty of attorneys who are appointed for them by the same government which is prosecuting and judging them. Also, suspicion rises when the defendant can exercise no choice over which attorney is appointed.

b. In *Faretta v. California*, 422 U.S. 806 (1975), the Supreme Court held that a defendant has a constitutional right to defend him or herself if he or she has voluntarily and intelligently waived the right to counsel. A defendant who proceeds *pro se* would be required to follow all the normal procedural rules. It is almost always an extremely bad idea to defend oneself in a criminal case without a lawyer. Even lawyers are warned against this: "A lawyer who represents himself has a fool for a client."

c. Some argue that it should make no difference whether a lawyer feels the client is morally guilty, because legal guilt is determined through the adversary process; that criminal defense counsel are bound by the Canons of Ethics to defend their clients zealously and within the bounds of the law; and that the right to effective assistance of counsel would lose its meaning if lawyers assumed the role of judge and jury. Others argue that lawyers cannot do their best for someone they feel is guilty and that they should not represent someone whose case they do not personally support.

Answer to Problem 62

a. This problem is designed to explore arguments for and against the death penalty. It is worth pointing out to corrections students that several states permit the death penalty to be imposed when the victim of the homicide is a correctional employee. To be constitutional, the U.S. Supreme Court has said the death penalty cannot be automatic but the sentencing process must allow for consideration of aggravating and mitigating circumstances.

b. Requiring students to identify the most convincing arguments against their position may help them clarify their own positions.

Answer to Problem 63

Inmates, correctional personnel, parole board members, and/or citizens may identify any or all (or other), of the following reasons for eliminating parole:

Parole programs accomplish no useful purpose. Inmates participate in a variety of programs in prison to manipulate the system and do not gain any benefits from the programs. These programs are a waste of time and money.

Inmates have no notice of what will get them parole or what will result in parole denial. The anxiety involved in not knowing should not be imposed on inmates.

Inmates should be given a flat sentence to serve and this time should not be reduced for any reason.

Inmates, correctional personnel, parole board members, and/or citizens may identify any or all (or other) of the following reasons to keep a parole system:

Correctional personnel have a means of controlling inmates' behavior if there is a reward to hold out for good behavior.

Parole leads to participation by inmates in beneficial programs within the prison which can make a difference to the inmate when returned to society.

Inmates coming out on the street should be supervised and helped before being totally freed.

The possibility of an early release for good behavior in the institution makes for a more harmonious institution.

Answer to Problem 64

Statute 1 (N.Y. Executive Law Section 259-i(2)(c), McKinney Supp. (1978)) does not give rise to due process protections since it gives broad discretion to parole authorities and merely provides the hope that parole may be granted. *Boothe v. Hammock*, 605 F.2d 661 (2nd Cir. 1979).

Statute 2 (Neb. Rev. Stat. Section 88-1,114 (1)) is the statute considered by the Supreme Court in *Greenholtz v. Inmates of the Nebraska Penal and Correctional Complex*, 99 S.Ct. 2100 (1979). The Court found this statute created an interest protected by due process since it requires the Board to release *unless* one of the four factors is present.

Answer to Problem 65

a. The Court in *Arciniega v. Freeman*, 404 U.S. 4, 92 S.Ct. 22 (1971), said that the parole condition restricting association with ex-convicts was not intended to apply to incidental contacts between ex-convicts in the course of work on a legitimate job for a common employer. To assume this, would render a parolee vulnerable to imprisonment whenever an employer was willing to hire more than one ex-convict.

b. The Court in *Berrigan v. Sigler*, 162 U.S. App. D.C. 378, 499 F.2d 514 (D.C. Cir. 1974) recognized the First and Fifth Amendment rights involved (the right to travel) but upheld the Parole Board's refusal to grant permission. The Court considered the duty of the Parole Board to supervise and rehabilitate the parolees. It also mentioned as relevant the factor of the illegality of the travel to a restricted area, as designated by the Secretary of State.

Answer of Problem 66

a. Courts have consistently held that a parolee cannot complain of Fourth Amendment violations because of the privilege and custodial nature of parole and because the application of the Fourth Amendment would tend to obstruct the parole system in accomplishing its remedial purposes. Cases permitting the admission of illegally seized items at revocation hearings include: *In re Martinez*, 1 C.3d 641, 83 Cal. Rptr. 382, 463 P.2d 734 (1970); *U.S. ex rel Sperling v. Fitzpatrick*, 426 F.2d 1161 (2nd Cir. 1970) *United States v. Schipani*, 315 F.Supp. 253 (1970) aff'd 435 F.2d 26, cert. denied, 401 U.S. 983, 91 S.Ct. 119.

b. Parolees have a right to privacy and 4th Amendment protections, although they may be more limited than the rights of ordinary citizens. The court have not set the permissible limits on these rights. Today, in many states, parolees are required as a condition of parole to consent to parole officer searches of their homes or persons at any time.

Answer to Problem 67

a. Martha has clearly violated her parole conditions. The Board might not revoke her parole if she had a legitimate reason for her move and her failure to contact her parole officer. The parole officer's recommendation would be important and the law would allow the Board to revoke her if it desired to do so.

b. The Board might be more inclined to revoke her parole for this additional violation. However, a parole condition to keep an alcoholic from drinking may constitute an unreasonable and, therefore, invalid parole condition, as in *Sweeney v. United States*, 353 F.2d 10(7th Cir. 1965).

c. Martha's parole may be revoked for the petit larceny arrest, provided her due process rights were afforded. Martha's parole can still be revoked even if she is acquitted on the criminal charges. The evidence to convince the parole board that she committed the crime, although not enough to prove her guilty beyond a reasonable doubt, may be sufficient to revoke her parole. Also, since the exclusionary rule does not apply to parole revocation hearings, illegally seized evidence or confessions may be used to convince the parole board of her violation.

appendix D

Listed below are the various associations and organizations which have criminal justice standards:

ABA Standards, Tentative Draft of Standards Relating to the Legal Status of Prisoners: Ken Farelli, ABA, 1800 M Street, N.W. Washington, D.C. 20036. Price $5.00

NAC Standards, National Advisory Commission on Criminal Justice Standards and Goals, *Report on Corrections,* 1973: Superintendent of Documents, U.S. Gov't Printing Office, Washington, D.C. 20402. Price $6.95 Stock No. 027-000-00175-1

ACA Standards, Commission on Accreditation for Corrections, *Manual of Standards for Adult Correctional Institutions,* 1977, and *Manual of Standards for Adult Local Detention Facilities,* 1977: ACA Commission on Accreditation for Corrections, 6110 Executive Blvd., Suite 750, Rockville, MD 20852

ACA Correctional Law Project, *Model Correctional Rules and Regulations;* 1977: ACA, 4321 Hartwick Road, Suite L-208, College Park, MD 20740

ALI Standards, American Law Institute, *Modern Penal Code -* Part III, "Treatment and Corrections" 1962. ALI, 4025 Chestnut St., Philadelphia, PA 19104. Price $8.50 plus $0.51 for postage and handling

DOJ, U.S. Department of Justice, *Draft Federal Standards for Corrections.*

UN Standards, *The Standard Minimum Rules for the Treatment of Prisoners — In Light of Recent Developments in the Correctional Field,* United Nations, 2101 L St., N.W. Suite 209, Washington, DC. 20036 Free (limited copies).

Nebraska Jail Standards: Terry Ferguson, Kutak, Rock and Hughie, 1650 Farnum, The Omaha Bldg., Omaha, NE 60102. Free

National Council on Crime and Delinquency, *A Model Act for the Protection of Rights of Prisoners,* 2215 M St., N.W., Washington, D.C. 20032

National Sheriff's Association *Standards for Inmates' Legal Rights* 1974: The National Sheriffs' Assoc., 1250 Conn. Avenue, N.W., Washington, D.C. 20036. Price: $1.25 per pamphlet

AMA Standards, American Medical Association Jail Project, *Jail (or Prison) Minimum Standards of Care,* AMA Jail Project, 528 North Dearborn, Chicago, Ill. 60610 Free.

Della Penna, *Health Care for Correctional Institutions,* Nat'l Criminal Justice Reference Service, Box 6000, Rockville, MD 20850. One copy free.

APHA Standards, *American Public Health Association; Standards for Health Services in Correctional Institutions,* 1976: APHA, 1015 18th St., N.W., Washington, D.C. 20036. Price $5.00

Department of HEW, *Food Service Sanitation Manual,* Superintendent of Documents, U.S. Gov't Printing Office, Washington, D.C. 20402. Price $2.30

Federal Bureau of Prisons, *Institutional Sanitation* 1965: Superintendent of Industries, U.S. Penitentiary, Marion, IL. 62959. Price $6.00

appendix E
AMA'S MODELS
FOR HEALTH CARE
DELIVERY IN JAILS

Introduction*

In order to improve the medical and health care and health services of inmates, it is necessary to identify the component parts of a delivery system and analyze the ways in which these parts interact. The major parts can be defined as the *answers* to the questions:

I.   What services are provided?
II. How are services obtained?
III. Who are the service providers?
IV. Where are the services delivered?

To develop the most effective cost-efficient service delivery system, the *answers* take into account the health and medical needs of the inmates, the size of the jail population, and the resources of the community.

I. Indigent inmates and those without a personal physician are being taken care of by contractual arrangement with a local community hospital. The care is rendered in the physician's private offices or the local health agencies (hospital, laboratories, etc.). The

* Reprinted from AELE Jail Administration Law Bulletin, with permission. Sample issues may be obtained from AELE, 960 State National Bank Plaza, Evanston, IL. 60201

"turn keys" through exposure to and training from the physicians are able to "screen" all incoming prisoners and provide a medical "triage" on all requests to see a doctor. (Triage means the sorting out and classifying of illnesses to determine priority of need and proper place of treatment.) These efforts have made the medical care efficient. No dental care is provided except for emergencies, which have been extremely rare.

Coordination of activities is provided by the sheriff who has been trained in emergency medical techniques by professionals working for the local county health department. This health department's environmental unit "visits" the jail to provide expertise in sanitation, hygiene, food, and makes periodic inspections of the environmental conditions.

II. Jail B contracts with a local physician to act as the medical officer. His duties include arranging for the provision of *all* medical care rendered within and without the institution and all dental care as needed. Basic primary care is delivered at the institution while all other care is usually delivered at a local hospital where the jail medical officer is on staff. Dental care is usually delivered in a local dentist's office. The medical officer may hire allied health personnel or supervise those hired by the sheriff. These persons assist the physician with receiving screening, triage, treatments for minor or chronic medical problems, patient health, education, etc. In addition, the medical officer is responsible for periodic sanitary inspection of the jail and consults with the sheriff regarding environmental improvements.

III. Jail C has contracted with a group practice, or public or private clinic to provide 24 hour, 7 day a week, emergency and acute medical services. The contract includes receiving screening, health data collection and physical examination of every newly-admitted inmate within 24 hours of arrival at the jail. The contract also provides that in-hospital or special services will be arranged by the contracted group or clinic when these services are needed.

IV. Jail D has an institutional contract with its local hospital-based comprehensive health center for the provision of services at the jail, including dental care. A multi-disciplinary group of health workers provides the diagnostic, treatment, rehabilitative and patient education programs for the inmates. When special services and/or in-hospital care is needed, those services are provided at the comprehensive health center.

V. Small neighboring jails E, F and G are cooperating with each other to provide medical care and health services to their inmates.

These jails have rented space at a nearby hospital and contracted with some members of the medical staff for comprehensive health services to be delivered at the hospital on a fee-for-service or pre-payment basis. In addition, the contracted physicians provide training to the jail staff in emergency medical techniques and consult regarding general menu-planning, special diets and environmental conditions.

VI. Jail N, a large jail, has built its own complete hospital within the jail and provides ambulatory and in-patient care to all of its inmates. This care includes acute, chronic and rehabilitative services. The facility is staffed with all levels of health personnel; (i.e., physicians, dentists, nurses, military corpsmen, physician's assistants, psychologists, social workers, etc. who are employed by the jail.)

VII. Jail X, a small jail has contracted for all health services with Jail N, which is 60 miles away. Health care staff from Jail N come to Jail X and conduct sick call, do health screening and health data collection and physical exams on newly admitted inmates. All of the ambulatory clinics and in-patient services of Jail N's hospital are available to inmates of Jail X. In the case of emergencies, services are obtained from the local community hospital under a contract on a fee-for-service basis.

VIII. University Medical School and Teaching Hospital has cooperated with small, outlying jails, Q, R and S to meet the medical care needs of those jails' inmates. A mobile health unit equipped as a clinic and appropriately staffed with specially trained allied health personnel brings receiving screening, diagnostic, treatment and patient education services to the distant jails. The mobile unit also contains telemetry equipment which enables the full range of medical specialties available to the University to be linked to the direct service providers for the purpose of consultation as well as providing the link of communication between the health care personnel and the multi-disciplinary team of supervising physicians.

The necessary equipment including two-way closed circuit T.V.'s, electric stethoscopes, electronic measurements for ECG, heart rate, respiration, systolic blood pressure and other physiological data and the van itself were acquired with funds made available by a local foundation.

IX. Jail Y, a large jail, has established a kind of health maintenance organization which provides comprehensive health services to the inmates of the jail.

In order to do this, Jail Y has renovated its facility and added a clinic, complete with medical equipment and instrumentation necessary to deliver medical care. The jail has a pre-payment contract with a physician group for delivery of care within the new jail facility and at a community hospital when necessary. The jail employs a dentist, an optometrist, an audiologist, a podiatrist, a nutritionist, a psychologist, and social workers in addition to the full-time allied health personnel employed by the medical group.

Jail Y has offered membership in its health plan to several nearby jails and a state correctional farm. The farm and one jail have contracted with Jail Y for the complete package of services offered by the medical group on a prepayment basis; four other jails have contracted for these same services on a fee-for-service basis.

The combined average daily population for the facilities involved is around 2,600 inmates. Membership is being offered to several other facilities including community alcohol rehabilitation centers, a residential center for retarded adults and a number of half-way houses. It is hoped that new memberships will bring enrollment up to between 3,000 - 3,500 people.

X. A metropolitan jail in a county seat and the state prison network of seven institutions combine efforts for medical care delivery by using one wing of County General Teaching Hospital for in-patient care and the array of hospital clinics for ambulatory care. Transportation is provided by the respective institutions. Nurses at the larger facilities, and trained correctional staff in the smaller facilities, screen for sick call, with the former providing primary care under standing orders from the County General Teaching Hospital physician assigned to the correctional medicine program. Despite a maximum of 170 mile round trips from the most distant facility, the program is reported to be both more cost-effective and efficient than the previous medical care delivery systems operated separately at each institution.

XI. The county and city jails in the county seat combine efforts by using the county jail dispensary for sick call and the county general hospital for acute care, with guards provided by the county. Sick call is handled by the nurse from the county health department under standing orders from the county health department officer who provides medical care for inmates screened by the nurse. Jailers trained in emergency medical care and triage make physical inspections of new inmates at the time of admission and refer those with problems or complaints to the nurse.

INDEX